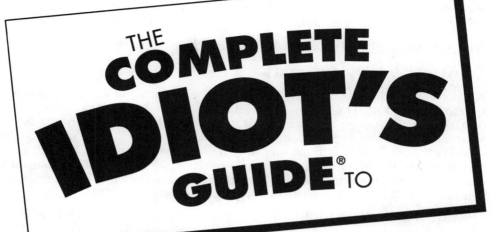

Tarot and Fortune-Telling

by Arlene Tognetti and Lisa Lenard

alpha
books

A Pearson Education Company

Numerology chapter written by Kay Lagerquist

Copyright © 1999 Amaranth

International Standard Book Number: 0-02-862737-7
Library of Congress Catalog Card Number: 98-89589

03   02   8   7

Interpretation of the printing code: the rightmost number of the first series of numbers is the year of the book's printing; the rightmost number of the second series of numbers is the number of the book's printing. For example, a printing code of 99-1 shows that the first printing occurred in 1999.

Printed in the United States of America

Note: This publication contains the opinions and ideas of its author. It is intended to provide helpful and informative material on the subject matter covered. It is sold with the understanding that the author and publisher are not engaged in rendering professional services in the book. If the reader requires personal assistance or advice, a competent professional should be consulted.

The authors and publisher specifically disclaim any responsibility for any liability, loss or risk, personal or otherwise, which is incurred as a consequence, directly or indirectly, of the use and application of any of the contents of this book.

Alpha Development Team

Publisher
Kathy Nebenhaus

Editorial Director
Gary M. Krebs

Managing Editor
Bob Shuman

Marketing Brand Manager
Felice Primeau

Development Editors
Phil Kitchel
Amy Zavatto

Production Team

Book Producer
Lee Ann Chearney/Amaranth

Development Editor
Carol Hupping

Production Editor
Robyn Burnett

Copy Editor
Lynn Northrup

Cover Designer
Mike Freeland

Photo Editor
Richard H. Fox

Illustrator
Jody P. Schaeffer

Designer
Dan Armstrong

Indexer
Tim Tate

Layout/Proofreading
Angela Calvert
Mary Hunt
Cheryl Moore
Julie Trippetti

Contents at a Glance

Contents

13 Wands: The Fruits of Your Labors, the Tools of Your Trade ... 165

14 Cups: Life, Creativity, Emotions ... 185

Part 6: More Ways to Tell the Future   323

22 "Look into My Crystal Ball..."   325

23 Tarot and Your Psychic Powers   337

Appendices

Foreword

The old adage "a picture is worth a thousand words" very aptly describes the power of the Tarot cards, for they have the power to invoke images beyond our wildest dreams. As we all know, pictures describe life in a way words alone can never express.

The Complete Idiot's Guide to Tarot and Fortune-Telling will show you, whether you're an idiot or a genius, how the images of fortune-telling cards can express your past, present, and future destiny. And you don't have to be a great Eastern Yogi to read the future. In fact, the great Western Yogi, Yogi Berra, expressed it this way: "You can observe a lot by watching." And this is the premise behind the Tarot and fortune revelation—observation!

The images of the Tarot cards date back to antiquity, some sources say to over several thousand years ago. The collection of symbols and archetypal images found in the cards are like a history of human consciousness in visual form—a picture show of the complete human drama.

When you begin to work with the cards you'll find that you are responsive to certain images but not to others. This is quite normal. Pictures, after all, are subjective and the truth that they reveal to each of us is a very personal truth. Two people can watch a film and come away with entirely different feelings about it. They both saw the same images, but picked up different messages from them. Reactions to the Tarot cards are equally as personal because our unconscious mind selects the "movies" in the cards that we are about to see. And these "movies" are really our previews of the coming attractions in our life!

Work with the images in the cards, as explained in these pages, and you will come to master the pictures to such an extent that they will instantly speak to you and invoke strong responses, just like your favorite movies do. And once you have developed a personal history with the cards, you can use this book to introduce yourself to other forms of divination (fortune-telling) such as working with crystal balls, the I Ching, psychic readings, dreamwork, and astrology.

The Complete Idiot's Guide to Tarot and Fortune-Telling will teach you to use your mind as a high-definition video camera capable of recording the subtlest of images. It will show you how to heighten your imagination—the image machine engine of human potential. Not if, but when, you become steeped in the knowledge this book has to offer, you will truly be able to see the past, present, and future with the power of vivid imagery.

The phrase: "Know thyself" is one of the oldest of adages. The sages of ancient India believed that if you are able to know your own truth, then you are worthy to know the truths of others. The ancient language of these sages is Sanskrit, and the Sanskrit word for knowledge is *Vidya*. It is the ancient root of our modern word *video*. The sages say "to see is to know," so one who sees vividly becomes a seer.

Fortune-telling is merely the ability of being able to see vividly for the benefit of oneself and others. The future is right around the corner, and with *The Complete Idiot's Guide to Tarot and Fortune-Telling* it will be within your sight.

—Dennis Flaherty

Dennis Flaherty is a practicing astrologer and Tarot reader with over 25 years of experience. He has served four times as the President of the Washington State Astrological Association, is certified in both Western and Vedic astrology, and has won many awards within the New Age community. He writes regularly for publications such as the Mountain Astrologer *and lectures at seminars and conferences. He is the founder and director of the respected NW Institute of Vedic Sciences in Seattle where he teaches, consults, and tutors on astrology and the Tarot.*

Introduction

Sometimes what you're looking for may be not so much a glimpse of the future as a glimpse of your own true self. We think that the better we know ourselves, the more likely we are to have the confidence and self-esteem to work through our life decisions fully and with the care essential to produce splendid outcomes.

The Tarot can be a wonderful tool to help you get in touch with yourself. Instead of waiting passively for life to happen *to* you—reacting to events and emotions without fully understanding or appreciating what's going on around you—you can use the Tarot to enhance your active participation in the events and emotions of your life.

Nothing but a pack of cards, you say? Think again. The Tarot can lead you on a marvelous journey of self-discovery. And you hold the key!

How to Use This Book

Having a Tarot deck to work with as you read this book will certainly enhance your Tarot journey, but it's not a requirement. In addition to the Universal Waite Deck that we use here, there are literally hundreds of Tarot decks to choose from, and you may choose to know a little bit more about the subject before you decide which deck is right for you.

This book is divided into six parts:

Part 1, "All About Tarot and Fortune-Telling," introduces you to the Tarot and its history. You'll look at the ancient and more modern symbolism that make up the Tarot and learn how to use that symbolism to hold a mirror up to yourself.

Part 2, "Getting to Know the Cards," gives you a closer look at the cards. You'll explore some of the Tarot decks available, and then do a few exercises to help you train yourself to become a better Tarot observer. Lastly, you'll start the Tarot journal you'll be keeping as you become a master of the art.

Part 3, "The Major Arcana: A Fool for the World," is where you'll start meeting each card on an individual basis. Here you'll take an archetypal journey through the Major Arcana and learn each card's upright and reversed meanings, from the Fool (Key 0) to the World (Key 21).

Part 4, "The Minor Arcana: Wands, Cups, Swords, Pentacles," continues the journey through the cards of the Minor Arcana. You'll meet each Minor Arcana suit: Wands, Cups, Swords, and Pentacles, and find out why each suit has its own particular energy. You'll learn about both the Royal Court and everyday cards for each suit, and discover that free will is an important part of the Tarot and its lessons.

Part 5, "Tarot Readings Any Fool Can Do," is where you'll find a variety of Tarot spreads to get you started doing your own work with the Tarot. After you read about each spread you will go step by step through an actual sample spread and learn how we interpreted the cards. There's room after each spread for you to try one of your own, too!

Part 6, "More Ways to Tell the Future," introduces you to some other metaphysical tools, from crystal balls to interpreting your dreams. You'll discover the connections between Tarot and astrology and Tarot and numerology, and find out why mahjongg's more than just a game your mother plays.

Extras

In addition to helping you understand and learn about the Tarot, we've provided additional information to make your journey even more enlightening and enjoyable. This includes sidebars like these:

In the Cards

This is the place you'll find fascinating extra tidbits of information that you may not have known about the Tarot.

Spinning the Wheel of Fortune

Everyone could use an extra tip here and there, and you'll find them in these boxes.

Card Catalog

These boxes introduce you to the language of the Tarot so you understand the terminology as well as the cards.

Fools Rush In

These boxes warn you against throwing caution to the winds and help you avoid making Tarot mistakes.

Acknowledgments

Lisa thanks Arlene, Arlene, Arlene, and Arlene, the Wonder Woman of the Tarot, without whom this book would not be possible. Fast, witty, clever, and—despite Temperance's projections—patient, she made this book a joy and a breeze. Thanks, too, to Bob, Joanie, Kait, and Maile, for being the patient subjects of a beginner's attempts at readings, and, as always, to the dogs and cats, for keeping the cold feet warm.

Arlene wishes to thank Lisa for being fast, quick, sharp, humorous, and keeping me to task. Lisa has been a great inspiration when I needed the knowledge and skills of a real writer pro. Our voice became one in this book. Also, I'd like to thank one of my greatest mentors, Dorothy B. Hughes (who passed on in 1987), a famous astrologer and metaphysical teacher. She called me, and I quote, "ugly accurate" when it came to my Tarot reading skill. I thank her for her deep belief in me. And to my friends, students, and family, who understood they could not get ahold of me any time they wanted because I was on-line writing with Lisa, a *big* thank you for being patient! And last but not least, thanks to Daniel Bernstein and Brad Reppen for training and educating me about the computer world and cyberspace!

And we both thank Lee Ann Chearney at Amaranth, book producer par excellence, for all the magic she makes behind the scenes. You wouldn't be reading this book without Lee Ann!

Much gratitude as well goes to Kay Lagerquist, for her way with numbers. Also thanks to Bobbie Bensaid at U.S. Games Systems, Inc., and to Karen Otis at the Museum of Fine Arts, Boston.

Thanks also to the great team at Alpha Books for their wonderful synergy and enthusiasm. Thanks to publisher Kathy Nebenhaus, editorial director Gary Krebs, managing editor Bob Shuman, assistant editor Maureen Horn, developmental editor Carol Hupping, production editor Robyn Burnett, and copy editor Lynn Northrup.

Special Thanks to the Technical Reviewer

The Complete Idiot's Guide to Tarot and Fortune-Telling was reviewed by an expert who double-checked the accuracy of what you'll learn here, to help us ensure that this book gives you everything you need to know about Tarot and fortune-telling. Special thanks are extended to David Pond.

David Pond holds a master of science degree in Experimental Metaphysics from Central Washington University. He is co-author of *The Metaphysical Handbook,* which covers Tarot, Astrology, *I Ching,* Numerology, and Palmistry. He has published chapters in two of Llewellyn's New World Astrology series, and many articles in *The Mountain Astrologer* and *The International Astrologer* magazines. David has been a professional Tarot reader and Astrologer for over twenty years.

Trademarks

All terms mentioned in this book that are known to be or are suspected of being trademarks or service marks have been appropriately capitalized. Alpha Books and Pearson Education, Inc., cannot attest to the accuracy of this information. Use of a term in this book should not be regarded as affecting the validity of any trademark or service mark.

Part 1
All About Tarot and Fortune-Telling

So you think a Tarot deck's nothing but a pack of cards? Think again. The pictures on the 78 Tarot cards are worth more than a thousand words—they paint a picture of you. Tarot symbolism encompasses everything from ancient cave paintings to Jungian archetypes, and in the process creates a unique metaphor for the story of you and where you're going.

Chapter 1

What Is Tarot?

In This Chapter

➤ Your future in a pack of cards?

➤ The reader and the Querent

➤ How Tarot works

➤ Are you a Fool?

Admit it, you're curious. Who isn't? Everyone wants to know about the future!

Hindsight may give you 20/20 vision for understanding what's happened in the past, but what (or who) helps you figure out what's coming up? When you think of fortune-tellers, do you picture Whoopi Goldberg in the movie *Ghost* channeling spirits with a crystal ball? How about the Wizard of Oz (The mighty Oz sees all, knows all!) dispensing magical powers to eager applicants who've proven themselves worthy? Is it even *possible* to "predict" or "tell" someone what his or her future will be? Remember a little thing called Free Will? We do. (We know there are some skeptics among us...)

So, right now you're curious about the Tarot. What, exactly, *do* Tarot cards have to say about the future—most particularly, about *yours*? Let's take a closer look at the cards.

Just a Pack of Cards?

We've seen you lingering in the New Age section of your local bookstore eyeing the Tarot decks. Maybe you've heard about the Tarot from friends or co-workers who've gotten readings. Their enthusiasm has you wondering. Flipping through the deck, the medieval-looking drawings on the cards seem so exotic; what could these mystical

Card Catalog

The *Tarot* is an ancient method of fortune-telling, which uses the 78 cards of the *Tarot deck* to create a story of you—past, present, and future.

talismans possibly mean for you? Is it all just a bunch of hooey in a fancy-looking deck of cards? If nothing else, you think to yourself, it's some fun for a Saturday afternoon. Yet there's that nagging question you have about how that situation at work is going to turn out…What would the cards have to say?

From time to time, we all look for guidance. It could be a matter of grand scale, something that will affect the very course of our lives, such as deciding whom to marry or where to live. Or it could be something of smaller consequence but important in the moment. We look to a lot of sources to help us make our life decisions. Here's a list of some of the sources most of us don't think twice about consulting every day:

➤ We look to the five-day weather forecast to get a handle on whether we'll need to carry an umbrella, break out the sun block, or put the snow tires on the minivan.

➤ How about listening to the radio for the daily traffic reports? It's essential to know the most efficient and beneficial route to take to make it to the office on time.

➤ Hey, admit it. Do you check your daily horoscope?

➤ Status meetings at work or guidance counseling at school help give us a good perspective on what we've already accomplished, what needs to be done today, and how to tackle future challenges.

➤ Medical doctors and other health-care professionals tell us how to develop good life habits to keep our bodies healthy, while psychologists and therapists offer good counsel to help improve our mental well-being and promote healthy relationships with others.

➤ Many of us turn to our faith in a higher power to draw inspiration and guidance through prayer and the study of sacred texts.

We have so many choices to make every day! We're just like the guy in the Seven of Cups card: bewildered with choices. Which choice is the best one? Who can help us make our choices? And how will things turn out?

Tarot is one of many metaphysical tools that allows us to look into our lives and find out some extra information we hadn't really understood or hadn't known about before. Working with the Tarot brings to light a confirmation of things you've always known (your own inner wisdom), or adds a new perspective to a perplexing question or problem. Tarot gives the guy in the Seven of Cups a context for understanding not only what his choices are, but how he feels about them.

Are you like the guy in the 7 of Cups—faced with too many choices and not enough perspective to decide which is the right choice to make?

Meet Your Magician!

To help you understand how to use the Tarot, just consider us your Magician. Throughout this book, we'll be your teacher and guide, unlocking the creative power of the cards and showing you how to interpret their many meanings.

Study the Magician card shown in the following figure. The Magician invokes the Cup, Wand, Sword, and Pentacle on the table as the instruments of his creativity. What a wonderful garden blossoms from the fruits of his efforts!

We'll be your Magician: a teacher and guide to the Tarot.

We'll let you in right now on the great secret of the Tarot: The power to make the Tarot more than just a deck of cards lies within you! That's right. With practice, you can learn to become your own Magician, your own wizard, your own *oracle*. As Glinda the Good Witch told Dorothy at the end of the Yellow Brick Road, she'd always possessed within herself the power to make her own wishes and dreams come true.

And so do you. The Tarot is an instrument of insight into your own Free Will. *You* are the one who possesses the magic. Let's find out more.

Card Catalog

Oracles are sacred objects or altars used by many cultures throughout history for the reception of divine guiding messages and holy truths. The site of the oracle is considered a holy place and often only priests or shamans can visit it. Remember the scene in the Audrey Hepburn/ Gregory Peck movie, *Roman Holiday,* where they visit the ancient Roman oracle and stick their hands in to make a wish?

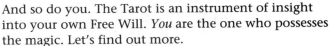

A Tarot Primer

The Tarot reveals what's *really happening* below the surface of events around us. The Tarot is a visual medium; those of you who love pictures, art, music, design—anything picture-related—can appreciate all the rich colors, symbols, numbers, and archetypes present in the Tarot cards. It doesn't take a degree in math or science to work with this wonderful medium of enlightenment and personal awareness. It's easy! The 78 Tarot cards represent every element of life, every emotion we will experience, every lesson that needs to be learned, and every condition possible to know. The story the Tarot tells every time you receive a reading allows you to know more, and gives you the decision-making edge that extra knowledge can provide.

You're in the Cards

The Tarot opens your intuitive sense. Its pictures stimulate your "gut" feelings. Do you already have a Tarot deck? Start shuffling. The Tarot cards absorb the thoughts, ideas, and curiosity of the person who shuffles the deck. By shuffling and concentrating on the question at hand, it's your energy that's being reflected through the deck of the Tarot. Your subconscious wisdom is shuffled into the cards. When the cards are thrown into different patterns, or *spreads*, the relationships between the cards reveal your personal wisdom as you infused it into the deck.

Card Catalog

Tarot spreads are different methods of laying out the cards during a Tarot reading. *Tarot readings* occur when the cards are laid out to reveal a particular story.

The 78 cards of the Tarot deck are divided into 22 *Major Arcana* cards that lead us through the archetypal passages in life's journey, and 56 *Minor Arcana* cards that illustrate the various things that happen to each of us from day to day. We'll look at the Major Arcana in Part 3 and the Minor Arcana in Part 4, but you can sneak a peek at them now.

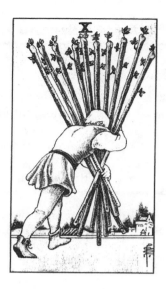

Strength, a Major Arcana card, and the 10 of Wands, a Minor Arcana card, represent two ways we meet our challenges. Strength depicts a mythological motif, while the 10 of Wands shows one way we deal with everyday challenges.

The first difference you'll notice is that the Major Arcana seem to represent mythological motifs, while the Minor Arcana show more everyday events. That's exactly the case: the Major Arcana cover the "big stuff," while the Minor Arcana are the everyday cards. The Minor Arcana are further divided into four suits:

➤ Wands

➤ Cups

➤ Swords

➤ Pentacles

These correspond to clubs, hearts, spades, and diamonds in a regular deck of cards. Each of the four suits has 14 cards: ten numbered cards (the Ace through ten), and four royal cards (a Page, Knight, Queen, and King).

The four suits of the Tarot deck—Wands, Cups, Swords, and Pentacles—correlate to the four elements of the astrological signs of the zodiac, and for good reason: They're the four energies of life. You'll find out more about the fascinating relationship between the Tarot and astrology in Chapter 25.

Card Catalog

There are 22 *Major Arcana* and 56 *Minor Arcana* cards in the Tarot deck. The Major Arcana cards depict an archetypal journey through life, while the Minor Arcana cards show everyday events.

Life Energies: The Tarot Suits and Their Astrological Elements

Suit	Element	Meaning	Corresponding Astrological Signs
Wands	Fire	Beginnings, action	Aries, Leo, Sagittarius
Cups	Water	Emotion, intuition	Cancer, Scorpio, Pisces
Swords	Air	Communication, mental activities	Gemini, Libra, Aquarius
Pentacles	Earth	Possessions, the physical	Taurus, Virgo, Capricorn

You can think about the Tarot in a number of ways: as a tool for connecting you with the universal unconscious, as a way to get in touch with your sixth sense of what's true, or as an unfolding story revealed in pictures. Any way you look at it, interpreting the Tarot is fun!

Card Catalog

A Tarot *reader* makes interpretations of cards for a *Querent*: a person who asks a question of the Tarot.

Card Catalog

Querent comes from the Latin word *quaero*, meaning "to inquire or seek, or to embark on a quest." Readers consider Tarot cards *metaphors*, rich images that hold meanings that can be transferred or carried over to the Querent's particular situation or question.

The Reader and the Querent

People who have studied the Tarot for many years (like Arlene, the co-author of this book) are called Tarot *readers*. As with any method of fortune-telling, reading the Tarot is much more than merely memorizing what each card or symbol "means." In addition to understanding Tarot cards, Tarot readers have strong backgrounds in disciplines ranging from psychology to mythology, and recognize that a reading opens up life's possibilities rather than narrows them down to an inevitable course of action.

Just as there are natural painters and those who can't draw a stick figure, there are people who are naturally good at reading the Tarot. The best Tarot readers understand that no card has any one meaning, but rather is a *metaphor* for a variety of interpretations.

The person asking the reader a question is called the *Querent*. Querents may ask specific questions: "When will I meet my soulmate?" or "Will I win the lottery?"; or they may ask about the world: "What's going to happen in the year 2000?" or "Will any film ever top *Titanic*?" Specific Tarot spreads can address different types of questions, such as how to set a goal, make a decision, or find a solution to a problem. Readings can span a time frame ("What's going to happen in my life this year?") or reveal a message ("What's my purpose or mission in life?"). You'll learn all about different Tarot spreads you can do in Part 5.

Many Tarot practitioners do a daily reading where there's no question at all. Often, they don't even interpret the cards when they select them, but merely make a note of what they are. Then, at the end of the day, they come back to them and note the connections between the cards selected and the day's events.

The reader and the Querent don't necessarily have to be in the same place. Readings today take place in Internet chat rooms, or with the absent Querent thinking about the question as the reader deals the cards.

What if the Querent wants to know about a family member, spouse or life partner, or other person? The Tarot will answer the question through the energy of the Querent him- or herself. So, whatever information is revealed through the Tarot will have to do with the Querent's own relationship to the person the Querent wants to know about. Remember, it's the *Querent's* energy that infuses the cards for a reading and that's the energy that'll come through.

Tarot Q & A

We know you've still got a lot of questions, so we'll get a jump-start on answering the five we get asked the most:

1. Does Tarot really work?
2. *How* does Tarot work?
3. Can you read your own cards?
4. Does Tarot seal your fate?
5. When can you start reading the cards?

We'll answer these questions in the following five sections. Keep in mind, though, first and foremost, that Tarot is not a magic trick. We'll say it again: The magic in Tarot comes from *you*!

Does Tarot Really Work?

Okay, if the cards indicate wealth and financial reward, should you run out and buy that new Mercedes? Maybe, maybe not. The reader's skill of interpreting the Tarot involves the ability to remain objective, to accurately describe the message of the cards, and, with the Querent's help, to put that message in the right perspective.

The cards are a great tool, but they're not so great at giving orders or pronouncing ultimatums. The message of the cards, properly understood, gently (or not so gently, depending on the situation) guides you to arrive at the correct decision that already waits in your heart. That doesn't mean it does this by providing an easy excuse to let you get your own way and buy that convertible!

Now, wait a second. If the cards are showing what you already know in your heart to be true, why bother? The answer is that the cards are in touch with a universal intelligence—our human collective unconscious—something that we Westerners are not always good at tapping into. Like the dream world that opens your mind as you sleep (Sigmund Freud called dreams the "royal road to the unconscious"), the Tarot cards awaken that place deep within you that is in touch with your human nature.

Tarot works when you look closely enough to "get" the real message, to both receive and understand it for what it really is. This means coming to the reading with an open and unprejudiced mind. Don't assume anything—either as reader or Querent—and be ready for anything. The true message of the Tarot may surprise you!

How Does the Tarot Work?

We'd like to call on a really smart guy, psychoanalysis pioneer Carl Gustav Jung (1875–1961), to answer this question for us. Jung was fascinated by the patterns of life and the way seemingly unconnected events were in fact connected. He noted that every day of human experience is filled with what could only be called meaningful coincidences, or *synchronicity*.

Jung's study of synchronistic events led him to examine ancient occult practices from astrology to the *I Ching*, and the Tarot was no exception. He found that the mysteries revealed by these practices were in fact not mysteries at all, but events common to each of us on our paths of life.

Card Catalog

Synchronicity is the principle of meaningful coincidence, studied in depth by psychoanalysis pioneer Carl Jung. Jung also postulated that human experience could be categorized into common *archetypes*, typical patterns, situations, images, or metaphors that recur among all humankind.

Jung called our common situations (and common recurrent characters), *archetypes*, and believed that ancient fortune-telling methods revealed these archetypes to us symbolically. He noted that while modern science "is based on the principle of causality," occult methods look to a "picture of the moment." Jung concluded the pictures on Tarot cards are "descended from the archetypes of transformation."

We agree with Jung that Tarot cards are a way for us to connect to the archetypal wisdom of the human collective unconscious. The Tarot deck in its entirety is a portrait of the human condition, its potential, and its possibilities. Shuffle the deck and deal the cards: Your Tarot reading is a reflection of those possibilities inherent in *your* life and present situation.

In the Cards

What have dreams got to do with the Tarot? A whole lot, it turns out. The metaphors in our dreams and in Tarot cards have a lot in common. Jung asserted that all humans share common archetypes, but that most of us can get in touch with them only through our unconscious. Dreams are one way of tapping into our unconscious thoughts, feelings, and awareness—and the Tarot is another. (See Chapter 24 for more about the connection between the Tarot and dreams.)

Can You Read Your Own Cards?

Most Tarot readers read their own cards every day. Yes, they're pros, but how do you think they got to be pros? A serious student of the Tarot devotes a lot of time to reading her or his own cards—and coming to understand intuitively what those cards are saying.

Likewise, the best way for you to begin to study the Tarot is to pick a deck that appeals to you (there's more on Tarot decks in Chapter 4), and then live with those cards for a while. Spread them out. Pick them up and look at them. Lose yourself in the pictures. Work through the exercises in Part 2 that are designed to help you become familiar with the Tarot and to explore your own emotions and reactions to the deck.

Don't read ahead to the "meanings" of the cards we give in Parts 3 and 4. Those meanings are only launching points for your study of the Tarot, and you shouldn't let yourself be limited by them—not now at the beginning of your journey, and not later on either, when you know the cards well. Ultimately, Tarot cards are a tool to unlock your imagination, and how you read the cards—alone, or with someone else—is up to you.

Does the Tarot Seal Your Fate?

No. Nothing "seals" your fate. Your life path is a series of possibilities, branching off in one direction or another with each decision you make. A Tarot reading may suggest to you what could happen if you continue along a certain path—but it's up to you to take the responsibility of choosing your own direction, if you dare.

Much of the fear and superstition associated with the Tarot—and with all the occult sciences—is that they somehow *do* foretell the future and seal your fate. *Nothing* about the Tarot is inexorable or inevitable. *What you do with what the cards show is up to you!*

The Tarot reveals possibilities and probabilities, not certainties. In fact, the only thing that's certain about life is that nothing's certain. Fate is what you make it.

When Can You Start Reading the Cards?

When can you begin giving readings? Today! One of my (Lisa's) first readings was for a friend. After the first five cards, my friend said, "Now, wait a second, all these cards are saying the same thing." I thought that was pretty weird, too, so when we finished that reading, we did mine. All *those* cards said the same thing, too—but not the same thing that my friend's cards had said! Practice and have fun.

Do You *Really* Want to Know the Future?

Sometimes, what we're looking for may be not so much a glimpse of the future, but a glimpse of our true selves. The better we know ourselves, the more likely we are to have the confidence and self-esteem to work through our life decisions fully and with the care essential to produce splendid outcomes.

The Tarot can be a wonderful tool to help you get in touch with yourself. Instead of waiting passively for life to happen *to* you—reacting to events and emotions without fully understanding or appreciating what's going on around you—you can use the Tarot to enhance your experience and active participation in the events and emotions of your life.

Fools Rush In

Are you secretly looking for an oracle to divine your true path and tell you what to do? Avoid that temptation and listen to your own inner voice. When you take responsibility for your decisions into your own hands, heart, and mind, Tarot can become a wonderful tool for personal exploration and growth. But it's not a substitute for your Free Will. Don't be a slave to the cards!

How proactive are you? Let's imagine your apartment lease is up in six months. You're not happy where you are, but can't decide where to move. You:

➤ Wallow in indecision for months and end up extending your lease to put off the move for another year.

➤ Muse about moving to a city you've always loved, like Los Angeles or New Orleans—you've been talking about it for years, actually. But you wait until the last minute to take it seriously and lose the opportunity to plan a move to that dream city.

➤ Embark on a diligent search for a new apartment without addressing your feelings about where you'd really want to live or why you'd want to live there. Just moving anywhere is progress enough.

➤ Pack up your belongings and move back in with your parents or another family member. It's really just temporary.

The Tarot is only one tool you can use to make your life decisions resonate closer and closer to your heart's true desire. It's not about surrendering to fate, or being handed a one-way ticket to the future. It's about making choices that are honest and that feel right for you. It's about getting in touch with your own life energy and using that energy to live up to your fullest potential as a human being.

What road should you take? What future lies in store for you? How will you grow and learn? Come on the journey through the Tarot with us, and you'll find yourself a Fool for the World!

Make a Fool of Yourself

The Fool is the first card of the Tarot deck's Major Arcana. Its number is zero: innocence and experience, beginning and end, joined in the great circle of life. The adventurous youth of the Tarot deck, the Fool sets off on the journey of life. Just like you! With his little white dog, the knapsack on his back holding all the tools he needs for the trip, and a lovely white flower lifted joyously, the Fool sets out to discover the world. He holds his face up to the sun shining upon him, taking no notice of the mountain crag under his feet.

The Fool embarks on the journey of life.

The Fool is full of expectation and openness to what is available, to all of human experience. "What a beautiful day," he says out loud. The dog follows anywhere the Fool wishes to go, his best friend and companion on the road. And they are off to learn all of the lessons, feel all of the feelings, know all that is knowable.

Are you ready to make a Fool of yourself?

The Least You Need to Know

➤ Tarot cards are a tool for understanding ourselves and connecting to a great universal wisdom: the human collective unconscious.

➤ There are 78 Tarot cards. The 22 Major Arcana cards describe the passages of life's journey. The 56 Minor Arcana cards describe everyday issues and events.

➤ The Minor Arcana cards are divided into four suits: Wands, Cups, Swords, and Pentacles.

➤ The Tarot reveals the possibilities and presents a forum for self-exploration, but does not "predict" or "tell" your future. *You* choose your own fate.

➤ Make like a Fool and get ready for an exciting journey!

Chapter 2

Back to the Future

> ### In This Chapter
>
> ➤ The images of the Tarot are ancient history
>
> ➤ Gypsies really *are* fortune-tellers
>
> ➤ Tarot and psychology

Arlene's grandmother always said, "Many things are around us, if only we look," and when we look at the history of the Tarot, we find that not only does every picture tell a story, every picture tells *many* stories. While no one can say for certain, the Tarot seems to have appeared in similar guises in different parts of the world at different times throughout history. What *is* clear, though, is that humans have been using pictures to tell their stories—past, present, *and* future—for a very, very long time. In this chapter, we'll learn some of the ways we've told stories with pictures—and what Tarot's got to do with it.

From Cave Painters to Tarot Card Artists

From the ancient cave paintings discovered at Lascaux, France, to the *petroglyphs* found throughout the American Southwest, artist wannabes have been using rocks as their canvasses for thousands of years. Pictures, in fact, are quite probably the earliest form of symbolic communication, and were used by neighboring tribes who had no other language in common. After all, a stick boar eating a stick man could explain far more than mere grunts and frantic gestures—and people who understood the pictures lived to pass them on another day.

Card Catalog

Petroglyphs are a form of ancient carving on stone which use representative pictures to tell their stories.

Think for a moment how it would be if you had to communicate with someone who didn't speak *your* language. What would *you* do? Use hand signals? Charades? Twenty questions? Or would you draw a picture?

Even if you're not an artist you can draw simple symbols: stars, crosses, or the moon, for example. Then you could add a little color to help get a feeling across. White, red, black, and yellow are some of the colors used in early Tarot, and we'll discuss some of that color symbolism in Chapter 4.

Pictures tell a thousand stories, and for those who came before us, even a temporary drawing on the sand could be the best way to get the message across. While symbols such as arrows, fertile seeds, the sun, the moon, a child, king, priest or priestess, shaman, bird, rose, or wild animal each meant something unique to different tribes, they also had a universal type of meaning that often transcended particular nuances and interpretations. This general quality was often the only way tribes with different languages *could* understand each other.

Like their cave-dwelling ancestors, Tarot artists use pictures to communicate the symbolic meanings of Tarot cards. As you'll learn in Chapter 4, there are Tarot decks for every taste, from the traditional Marseilles deck to the Mother Peace deck, a modern feminist deck with its perfectly round cards (edges, after all, are masculine).

A Picture's Worth a Thousand Words

The documented roots of Tarot date back to China, the Middle East, and Egypt as many as 15,000 years ago, in seemingly unconnected occurrences. And yet even today we can understand the collective meaning of a cross or a star, or the color red or black used in those ancient drawings and pictorial *hieroglyphs*.

Card Catalog

Like petroglyphs, *hieroglyphs* are another form of ancient carving on stone. Hieroglyphs are a more symbolic system, using ancient alphabets (rather than the pictures of petroglyphs) to tell their stories.

To see exactly how a picture's worth a thousand words, though, let's take a closer look at the Major Arcana card, the Magician. First, look at the figure itself: The Magician holds his hands in an attitude of power and command, creating from his table of elements the gifts of life, and the potentials of creation. He's the artist who will draw on an empty canvas.

His physical presence, or his attitude, reveals one hand pointing toward heaven, and the other hand pointing to earth, while a Wand conducting energy from above reaches for divine guidance and inspiration to create what he desires.

Heaven has always been looked upon as a somehow magical place where all energy comes from. Even in early times, the sun was an obvious light- and heat-generating globe in the sky. From this, a further assumption was made: There must be something else out there that keeps other energies flowing.

The Magician (key 1)

So the fact that the Magician is pointing toward heaven sends a message, as if he were searching for something higher, brighter, or more insightful—as if he were reaching, maybe, for a Divine Understanding, *just like you.*

When you look at a *Tarot spread*, you add all the pictures together to create a story. So if the Magician were your the first card in your spread, your story might begin with the magic of creation or a divine message. Most spreads are arranged chronologically, telling stories that begin in the past and progress to the future, but you shouldn't limit yourself to this linear way of storytelling any more than a good book does.

In a way, Tarot readers were the original storytellers, and today's Tarot readers continue that storytelling tradition. The Tarot deck's pictures can relate images, feelings, conditions, worldly issues, a sense of destiny, or describe conditions yet to be. And you thought it was just a deck of cards!

Reaching for a Divine Understanding

Perhaps because of its roots in the Hebrew Kabbalah, Tarot was often seen as a way of talking to God, and so a right reserved for kings and queens—never serfs. Indeed, until the 19th century, non-royals caught using Tarot were often put to death. Historical Tarot decks can be found dating back to the 14th century, but it wasn't until the invention of the printing press that they became widely accessible. With the advent of modern science, Tarot was relegated to the *esoteric* or "unexplainable," and its use became another pawn in power struggles. Some believe that Roman Catholic priests, aware of the power of the Tarot, were very careful to keep it away from the common people.

Fortune-telling became popular throughout history precisely because it was a great way to "see" if there would be a wedding or a new king or queen coming. Tarot could predict droughts and wars, too, so that people could take steps to avoid the worst of those threats.

In the Cards

Where does the word *Tarot* come from? Here are a few possibilities:

➤ Egyptian: *tar*, a path + *ro, ros*, or *rog*, royal

➤ Hungarian Gypsy: *tar*, a pack of cards

➤ Hindustani: *taru*, same meaning as above

It's easy to see why Tarot was seen as a way of talking to God; it *does* get us in touch with things we can't seem to see without "divine" intervention. Tarot cards seem to have a magical way of picking up our unconscious and conscious minds at once, and in so doing, reflect how we feel about a given situation. In other words, Tarot cards confirm the conditions and events around us—*even if we're not aware of them ourselves!*

Seeing It in a Dream: Prophecies and Portents

It should come as no surprise that the Tarot has close connections to dream theory. Both, after all, are symbolic systems, and both are subject to a variety of interpretations.

In ancient Greece, the Oracle at Delphi was the most popular of all the Oracles because her predictions always came true—even when people took extraordinary steps to avoid them. In Greek mythology, the hero Perseus's grandfather, for example, went so far as to set his daughter and Perseus adrift in the sea after the Oracle predicted Perseus would bring about his grandfather's death. Although Perseus never knew his grandfather, this prophesy came true: Perseus's grandfather was killed many years later by a wayward discus, thrown by the grandson he never knew.

Tarot imagery is like dream imagery—we can't always immediately figure out just what it's trying to show us. But also like dream imagery, Tarot reveals itself when we stop "thinking" about it, and let the images reveal themselves to us.

Scientists, philosophers, and psychologists all argue about the true nature and function of dreams. Even as we enter the 21st century, there is no definitive understanding of what dreams are or why we dream. Some modern researchers believe dreams are no more than a way to purge the brain of excess information and prepare for a new day of input, while others on the opposite end of the spectrum are busy exploring the connection between dreams and psychic intuition.

Throughout history, though, powerful, evocative dream images have captivated and consumed us. Dreams are the seeming bridge between conscious understanding and unconscious understanding, between the known and the unknown that lives together in each of us. At the very least, dreams prod us toward something internal, and allow us to become familiar with a particular fear, joy, truth, or enlightenment.

Some people say they dream in color, while others dream in black and white. Some don't remember their dreams, while others do. Some people claim they don't dream at all. The long and short of it is that everyone is unique in the way they dream—and there's no right or wrong way. Dreams are as individual as we are and reflect the particular things that we're working or musing on or worrying about at any particular moment. (Read more about Tarot and dreams in Chapter 24.)

East Versus West

The Chinese *I Ching* and Tarot are both ways of looking at a particular moment in time from its past, present, and future angles. Unlike Tarot, though, the *I Ching* is rooted in Eastern philosophies, where collective understanding is taken for granted. We Westerners (and not just those of us west of the Mississippi) take a far more individual approach to our lives. The symbols of the Tarot deck reflect this.

In the Cards

Even the myth of the *I Ching*'s origin has a decidedly collective bend: The Emperor Fu Hsi's revelation was a pattern that would encircle all knowledge. A Westerner probably would have kept it to himself .

Humankind's Insatiable Curiosity About the Future

It's important to remember that the *I Ching* is not a "wrong" way any more than Tarot is a "right" way. What *is* important is that they're both tools we can use to get in touch with ourselves. We humans have always been curious about our futures—we, your authors, think it has something to do with our knowledge of our own mortality.

On the other hand, we may just want to know if there's going to be a tall, dark stranger coming into our lives. And, as one of Arlene's students requested recently, "Can I get his phone number and e-mail address, too?"

The Mystery of the Mystical

By the 19th century, Tarot, along with other esoteric arts like astrology, the study of the relationship between the heavens and earth; palmistry, the study of the hand; and numerology, the study of the meaning of numbers; began enjoying a renaissance. Science, after all, hadn't provided all the answers that people had been seeking, particularly about foretelling the future, and it had become clear that it probably never would.

It was during this time that members of the Hermetic Order of the Golden Dawn began to research the Tarot in depth. The deck we're using in this book, in fact, is the one commissioned by a leading member of that society, Arthur Edward Waite. *The Pictorial Key to the Tarot*, written by Waite and published in 1910, is still used to interpret the cards—though his meanings are often too limited in scope.

In the Cards

A.E. Waite commissioned artist Pamela Colman Smith to draw the deck you see illustrated in this book (called the Universal Waite Deck) around the turn of the century. Not only was Smith the only female member of the Hermetic Order of the Golden Dawn, she also had the unique honor of drawing the deck of Tarot cards. Waite insisted she do the drawing, despite the prevalent idea that "a woman couldn't do it." Well, you see the results—they speak for themselves. The Universal Waite Deck, published by U.S. Games Systems, Inc., features the beautiful coloring of artist Mary Hanson–Roberts, adding yet another dimension to a classic Tarot deck.

What the Gypsy Said

Many believe that the Gypsies were entrusted with various forms of ancient knowledge when the peoples who had that knowledge, like the Hebrews, Moors, and Egyptians, began to be persecuted during the Crusades and the Spanish Inquisition. The Tarot and fortune-telling cards were among these methods, and were considered by the Gypsies as ways to prove their psychic powers.

Transient in nature, Gypsies were considered very mysterious people, and they were often outcasts in whatever society they migrated into. Their token, "Cross my palm with silver and I will tell you your fortune," has become emblematic of the way most people view them. Gypsies, in fact, continue to be stereotyped in ways that other ethnic groups have long overcome.

Actually, though, the Gypsies did have psychic gifts, handed down through their families, generation after generation. They were so good at "reading people well," in fact, that they were often blamed for "creating" the very situations that they foretold.

If a Gypsy said, "The king looks to be in bad health and may not live the year out," when the king did die, guess who got blamed? Because they were both so different and so psychic, the Gypsies were terribly feared: People actually believed that *they* created the king's death by their powers or rituals. In reality, of course, the Gypsies only knew it was the king's time—but their knowledge got them into trouble time and time again.

What's in the Cards?

The desire to know one's fortune is as old as time, and will always be of interest to the curious—which is just about all of us. Humankind is always seeking more information, more knowledge, and more power. More, at any rate, of something.

In today's Tarot lexicon, the term "getting a reading" is used more often than "fortune-telling." Having your cards read can mean finding out more information or empowering yourself with the extra knowledge a reading can give you.

Among the things people want readings to tell them are:

➤ How can I handle this situation?

➤ How can I help my children?

➤ How can I get a new job?

➤ How can I improve my financial situation?

➤ Will I win the lottery?

➤ What is my spiritual path?

➤ How can I improve my life?

➤ When will I get married?

> **Fools Rush In**
>
> Don't ask the cards questions you don't want to know the answers to—and don't ask the cards to tell you things when your mind's made up. You won't read the cards the way they advise, but instead will see what you want to see! You have to watch your personal biases and be objective to read the cards correctly. Ask the Tarot for help or advice, but always do so with an open mind.

You get the idea. But we're sure you've got questions of your own as well.

Tarot and Psychology

A lot of modern Tarot readers have also studied the humanities, psychology, hypnotherapy, or other areas of human relations, making them talented observers of human nature. Tarot has long been a remarkable tool for helping the Querent, or questioner of the cards, understand events and how to handle them, but this additional training adds another dimension to a reading. Tarot readers can read a person's attitude or state of mind at the time of a reading, psychoanalyze a situation, or help the Querent see the spiritual reason behind a not-so-obvious spiritual situation.

We humans learn lessons in everything we do and with everyone we make contact with. One of Arlene's teachers used to tell her, "Everything happens for a reason." "But what's the reason?" Arlene always asked. Now that Arlene's been studying the Tarot for a long time, she's got some possible answers. For example, if you were in a relationship that didn't end well, it may have been to let you know about disharmony or challenges that you needed to work with. When we have disharmony around us, the counterbalance is to find harmony for ourselves.

Think about it: When you feel uncomfortable about anything, your natural desire is to get back to feeling comfortable again. We call that "learning about the dark side of an issue," and it can make us look for or seek the light or a more peaceful side.

More than anything, it's important to know both sides of a story, and that includes the pros and cons of a relationship. You can ask yourself some questions:

➤ What is the root cause of this difficult condition?

➤ Is it the other person or is it me? Or is it something in our past conditioning?

➤ Did we learn some difficult patterns and now we have to work them out with each other in order to grow?

Card Catalog

Our *shadow side* is our archetypal hidden self, our secret nature.

Sounds like a lot of work, doesn't it? We assure you that your growth and development come from challenging your *shadow side*. Looking at a weakness and working with it will turn it, in the end, into a strength.

The Shadow Knows: Archetype and Myth

Card Catalog

Myths are the stories we tell ourselves to explain the unexplainable, and archetypes are the various types common to all our stories. Jung called archetypes "mythological motifs."

Carl Jung's detailed analysis of the relationship of archetype and *myth* to human understanding will surely go down as one of the major revelations of the 20th century. Remember Jung's archetypes from Chapter 1? Jung explained that there are certain types, or what he called archetypes, common to us all.

Here are some fun "modern" examples to connect you with the archetypal characters.

Archetypes (According to L. Frank Baum and George Lucas)

Archetype	*Wizard of Oz* Example	*Star Wars* Example
The Wise Old Man	The Professor	Obi-wan Kenobi
The Trickster	The Wizard (Yes, we know it's the same guy)	Han Solo
The Persona (or the Hero)	Dorothy	Luke Skywalker
The Darkness	The Wicked Witch (Can't you just hear that music?)	Darth Vader
The Divine Child	Toto	R2D2 and C3PO
The Animus and The Anima (or the male and female spirits, respectively)	The Scarecrow, the Tin Man, and the Lion	Luke and Princess Leia
The Great Mother	Glinda the Good Witch	Yoda!

You're probably wondering what all this has to do with the Tarot, and the answer is, everything! The archetypes we've listed here in fun are engaging to all of us precisely because they're familiar mythological motifs most of us can relate to. Luke Skywalker's and Dorothy's journeys concern us because we recognize that they're *our* archetypal journeys, too. The Wicked Witch and Darth Vader frighten us because they're our shadows as well. Our shadow side, according to Jung, consists of the archetypes we hold in our unconscious self—along with thoughts and feelings we'd rather not acknowledge in the light of day.

But, more importantly for our purposes, the archetypes Jung committed to paper are the same archetypes that can be found in every Tarot deck. The Fool is the child in all of us, the High Priestess our anima, and the Devil our secret terrors. If archetypes are about the journey of life, then Tarot cards are a vehicle to help us on our way.

Card Catalog

In Jungian psychology, the *anima* and *animus* represent the female and male soul of a human being, respectively, while the *persona* represents the way a person presents him- or herself to the world.

Symbol and Metaphor

While we'll be using the term "symbol" in this book, we'd like to take a minute now to clarify what we mean by this. Lisa insists her students use the word "metaphor" instead of symbol, in fact, and here's why: If you've taken any English class, you probably know that symbols tend to get clichèd and predictable.

But when we talk about symbols, we don't want you to think this way. Symbols are as diverse and individual as we are, and if one thing must always "stand for" another, then the real meaning of symbols gets lost in the process.

**Spinning the Wheel
of Fortune**

"A thing *is* a phallic symbol if it's longer than it's wide," the singer-songwriter Melanie sang years ago. We'd like to remind you that just because something's longer than it's wide, it's not necessarily a phallic symbol: It may be simply—the Washington Monument. Or a pencil. Or a sword or a wand! As Freud himself once said, "Sometimes a cigar is just a cigar."

So let's think of symbols as metaphors. The rich images of metaphors open up meaning rather than close it down. Instead of standing for just one thing, a metaphor invites you to think and feel the connection. A train can be a train. Or it can be something else entirely—from the one you took with your Grandma when you were a child, to the "lonesome whistle blowing all those miles down the track." Your symbols, in other words, are *yours*.

Tarot for the 21st Century

Let's talk about virtual reality. Sometimes we wonder if people still need people—in the flesh, that is. Is it possible that someday soon we'll communicate only via computers with no human contact at all?

Of course, while it's hard to say for certain if people will ever rely solely on computer connections instead of human ones, we do know that we're in greater need of spiritual insight than ever before. This should be no surprise: Our society is far more complex than societies 300, or even 50, years ago. And these days, there's a drive to take care of our material conditions first and our spiritual development second.

The truth is that all worship is a form of spiritual development, and there's a constant need to maintain a balance in our lives between the material world and the spiritual world. Sometimes that's not so easy—with college for the kids, or the higher stress levels that come with trying to get things done for every member of the family. Employment changes happen more rapidly than in years past, too.

In short, most of us feel as if we've been speeded up—or as if, at the very least, the world is moving along more quickly than it used to. Tarot has its place in the 21st century, because it can help us maintain a positive approach to the many changes and transitions that the century is sure to bring. Tarot helps us to keep our spiritual center and gives us the faith that everything *does* happen for a reason. Life *is* a continuum.

The Least You Need to Know

➤ Tarot can be traced to Egyptian hieroglyphics and the Hebrew Kabbalah.

➤ The need to know the future is as natural as being human.

➤ Tarot cards' pictures use symbol, archetype, dream, and myth to tell their stories.

➤ Tarot can get us in touch with our neglected spiritual selves.

Chapter 3

What Tarot Reveals About You

In This Chapter

➤ How Tarot can help you answer the Big Questions

➤ Let the pictures do the talking

➤ Tarot and why you are the way you are

➤ Tarot and your relationships

The Tarot is more than a tool for answering your questions—it's also a tool for becoming more aware of why you behave the way you do. You can also use the Tarot to learn how another person feels about you, how your boss feels about your work, or what to make for that big dinner party you've got planned for Saturday night.

In other words, you can use Tarot's symbols on every step of your journey of self-discovery, just as a therapist can help you use your dreams for the same purpose. You gotta admit, though, Tarot's cheaper—and it's a lot more fun, too. In this chapter, we'll show you how you can use the Tarot on your own journey of self-discovery.

Where Do We Come From? What Are We? Where Are We Going?

You're not the only person who ever asked these questions: This is the actual title of a painting by the great Impressionist mastery Paul Gauguin (1848–1903). Human curiosity is as old as humankind, and what we like to call the "Big Questions" have been debated as long as we humans have been around.

The Tarot reminds us that everything *is* interconnected, that there's a synchronicity in events that is more than mere coincidence. With this in mind, we can use the symbols of the Tarot to begin to find some personal answers to those Big Questions. Lisa calls her personal answer "Ol' Man River," who "just keeps rollin' along," and Arlene likes to call it the ebbs and flows of life. Life, Arlene believes, has its up and downs. The wheel of life is constantly turning to bring us luck or a challenge. In other words, it's all about serendipity, yet, at the same time, everything happens for a reason and everything is interwoven.

The neat thing about Tarot is that you can figure out the reason something has gone on. Whatever your spiritual system, though, Tarot can help you stay in touch with yourself.

From One Artist (Gauguin) to Another (You!)

Gauguin's painting, "Where Do We Come From? What Are We? Where Are We Going?" is from his island phase, and his use of color imagery reached its peak during that time. Unfortunately, we can't show you this painting in color, but we *can* show you its vivid imagery, and we'd like to use it to illustrate how *you* can make a conscious connection between art, pictorial explorations of inner truths, feelings and emotions, and the Tarot.

"Where Do We Come From? What Are We? Where Are We Going?" by Paul Gauguin, 1897. (Tompkins Collection. Courtesy, Museum of Fine Arts, Boston)

We think Gauguin's painting is a perfect forum to open this discussion, as the questions in the title are the ones we *all* ask ourselves when we come to the Tarot. You could think of this painting as an *allegory*, exploring possible answers to these difficult questions by telling a story.

Painted late in Gauguin's life, "Where Do We Come From?" is a panorama of human figures, deities, and landscape. It seems hard to tell the people from the gods and the two live together in a world of exotic mysteries—mysteries that are accepted, spiritual, and deeply natural.

The answers to the complicated and abstract questions of the painting's title live in the hearts of those who inhabit the world of the painting—and that includes us, as viewers drawn into this harmonious place. Where then, is the allegory? It's in us! Gauguin might have had this painting in mind when he spoke of his own painting style as an evolution "toward complication of the idea through simplification of the form." He might as well have been describing the images of the Tarot.

Card Catalog

An *allegory* is a symbolic system where words or images represent a much larger story than is shown. The allegory of the prodigal son, for example, represents a parent's love for his child.

Sister Wendy Finds Herself in Art (and Tells Bill Moyers)

Maybe you've heard of Sister Wendy, the popular Roman Catholic nun who delights in celebrating and contemplating great works of art and sharing her thoughts with us. In 1992, she did a fascinating television interview with Bill Moyers called "Sister Wendy's Odyssey," in which she talked about using art as a forum for people to discover their "true" selves. Sister Wendy Beckett hosted the wonderful PBS series on the history of art, "The Story of Painting," and published a book based on the shows. She's also the author of several other art books and books on spiritual subjects, such as *Meditations on Silence*.

According to Sister Wendy, your "true" self emerges when you have the courage and concentration to look at a great work of art and react to it on a pure and personal level. She urges you not to "fake" a response by saying what you think you should, but to truly consider the difficult and often perplexing emotional reactions that a great masterpiece can move you to if you're honest and open to its message. In other words, you can't come to an image with preconceived notions or ideas about how to respond. If you do, you're not allowing the image to reveal itself, to challenge, and, perhaps, to change you.

Just as you can come to know a work of art in this way, you can learn about yourself on a "higher" emotional level. Sister Wendy suggests taking postcards or reproductions of paintings and meditating on the image from time to time, until you feel you've really understood the painting—and also understood your own position and emotional reaction to it.

Just as you can develop this personal connection to a painting, you can learn to find personal meanings in each Tarot card. Let's find out how.

In the Cards

When a Tarot artist paints a picture for a particular Tarot card, she is representing what core issues are going on within that card's meaning. And if you allow the picture to speak to you in the way that Sister Wendy suggests, then each card's own particular story will be personalized for you in your own unique way.

Using Tarot Cards to Learn About Yourself

Tarot cards are reflections of you and your feelings or ideas at a particular time. One of the things that comes out of getting a reading is self-awareness, and, in addition to reminding you of the things you already know about yourself, Tarot can help you to awaken some new concepts or ideas about yourself that you may never have thought of before.

With the Tarot, you can see your psychological profile, emotional condition, and what you're feeling at the time of the reading. The insights that you get from a reading—perhaps just a little change of consciousness or some added information—can lead you to change how you feel about things. And when your feelings change, so, too, do the meanings of the cards for you. Because the Tarot cards are a *reflective* tool, *they* change each time *you* change, perhaps initiating a progression of changes.

Spinning the Wheel of Fortune

How do the cards know what you haven't told them? The Tarot deck hears more than your words—it's in tune with your feelings and energies—even the ones you haven't acknowledged yourself yet! Be honest with the Tarot, and the cards will be honest with you.

Here's an exercise on how to use the Tarot to learn about yourself:

Begin by taking all 22 of the Major Arcana cards out of the deck. Put the rest of the deck aside, and then, as you're shuffling the 22 Major Arcana cards, ask: "Tarot, show me my present lessons I am learning right now."

You should shuffle several times, concentrating on allowing the Tarot to reflect where and what you're learning now.

When you're finished shuffling (and that's whenever you *feel* you have), divide the 22 cards into three stacks, and either pick one card off each of the three stacks, *or* three from one of the stacks. You, the seeker, are in control here. The three Major Arcana cards you select will reflect you and your present lessons. Try it and see for yourself! Write down what each picture looks like in the space below. Don't worry about identifying each of the cards in any other way other than by describing the images on them.

Card 1._____

Card 2._____

Card 3._____

What did you see? People? Trees or flowers? Images you can't yet define? What's important about this exercise is *your* initial reactions to the cards: We want you to learn to trust your instincts.

Holding Up a Mirror

Looking at Tarot cards really *is* like holding up a mirror. How you might feel about a subject or person at the time you ask the cards is always shown exactly by the cards. In other words, even if *you* don't know how you're feeling, the cards will reflect aspects of yourself that you've been unaware of.

How Adventurous Are You?

We want to know if *you're* ready for the Tarot adventure—and so we've designed this little test to see just how adventurous you are.

1. You walk into a party, and you don't know a soul. You:
   (a) Walk up to the first person you see and introduce yourself.
   (b) Scan the room for *any* familiar face.
   (c) Head for the bar
   (d) Head for the nearest potted plant you can fit behind—and stay there until everyone's left.

2. Your friend Jackie calls to tell you she's got an extra ticket for the South Pacific, leaving tomorrow, and she wants *you* to come along. You:
   (a) Turn on your answering machine and head out to meet her at the airport.
   (b) Call your boss to see if she can spare you for a few weeks.
   (c) Pace, bite your nails, and try to decide what to do.
   (d) Tell her you can't. You've got responsibilities, after all. You can't just pick up and leave. What would people think of you?

3. While driving in an unfamiliar city, you come over a rise and see that traffic's backed up for miles. But to your right, there's an exit, and if you change lanes *right now*, you can make it over there before you get to the stopped traffic. You don't know anything about this neighborhood, but you:

(a) Go for it!

(b) Try to change lanes and read your map at the same time to make sure it's okay to get off there.

(c) Dig in your purse for a tranquilizer.

(d) Brake and bear it. Better safe than sorry, you always say.

4. Your best friend wants to fix you up with someone he works with. You:

(a) Put on your dancin' shoes.

(b) Ask for more information.

(c) Agree to meet—as long as you can take your own car.

(d) Tell him thanks, but no thanks. Blind dates never work out.

5. You're about to read your Tarot cards for the first time. To prepare yourself, you:

(a) Shuffle 'em and spread 'em.

(b) Read *The Complete Idiot's Guide to Tarot and Fortune-Telling* from cover to cover, and then shuffle 'em and spread 'em.

(c) Decide "tomorrow's another day," and put the cards away.

(d) Follow an instruction manual step by step so you don't miss anything important.

Scoring

Mostly (a)s: We can tell you're rarin' to go. You're probably a *fire sign*, always ready for new adventures. You'll love what the Tarot can reveal about you. Fire signs are always the first in line, ready to try everything from bungee jumping to signing on for the next space shuttle. The fire signs of the zodiac are Aries, Leo, and Sagittarius. The fire element is associated with Tarot's Wands.

Mostly (b)s: You're practical and careful, willing to try new things as long as you know what you're getting into. You're probably an *air sign*, and you can use the Tarot as one more tool to keep everything organized. Air signs are the great thinkers, always applying their mental capacities to any problem they encounter. The air signs of the zodiac are Gemini, Libra, and Aquarius. The air element is associated with Tarot's Swords.

Card Catalog

Fire, air, water, and *earth* are the four elements of the universe. Each of us has the energy of each element, but we lean more toward one element than the others.

Mostly (c)s: You're a sensitive and emotional water sign, and because of that, you may find that the Tarot is just the tool you need. Are you a *water sign*, by any chance? (It's okay…one of us is.) Water signs understand the need for solitude and meditation because they're the intuitive among us, ruled by their emotions, changing with the tides. The water signs of the zodiac are Cancer, Scorpio, and Pisces. The water element is associated with Tarot's Cups.

Mostly (d)s: Okay, so "Adventure" is not your middle name. You're probably an *earth sign*, who knows there's nothing wrong with the way things are right now. So why not use the Tarot to keep yourself from being surprised? Earth signs are, as their name implies, down to earth. They're not, as a rule, big adventurers. The earth signs of the zodiac are Taurus, Virgo, and Capricorn. The earth element is associated with Tarot's Pentacles.

Counting Your Blessings

Here's a "quickie," a positive affirmation exercise for you to use to count your blessings. Take your Tarot deck and start shuffling. When you're finished shuffling, divide the deck into three stacks, and as you do, ask: "What good things are around me?"

After you've divided the deck into three stacks, pick one card off each of the three stacks, or three from one of the stacks (as always in Tarot, the choice is yours). The key cards are any of the Aces (there are four in the deck), or the 9 of Cups (the wish card). All of these cards are a resounding *yes!* to any condition around you or an affirmation of a good condition developing. These five cards will show that things are happening for the better soon.

The four Aces and the 9 of Cups are all positive, affirming cards that show good things are happening.

Now, if you don't get these key cards, don't worry. What message do the images on the cards you *did* get seem to be giving you? The cards will reveal what's around you that's up and coming.

Your Relationships with Other People

The Tarot can show the reason that someone is upset with you, or why your boyfriend or girlfriend doesn't want to get too close to you. Maybe the reading will show he or she had trouble with past relationships and is leery of getting that close to another person again.

At the very least, through the Tarot we can see some of the reasons people act the way they do. Then, instead of judging them, we can begin to understand *why* they behave that way. One of Arlene's clients hadn't had a relationship in a long time. Her reading showed that she would not only be involved in a relationship within the next six months, but would be married within a year and a half! The client found it hard to believe, but it turned out to be true.

Do you have a relationship question? If so, the Tarot can help you discover the best way to answer it.

When Everything Blows Up

Here is a real week in Lisa's life (the week she was writing this chapter, in fact). It began when she woke up one morning with severe intestinal pain, and the you-know-what that comes with it. It got so severe that by that night, she was in the hospital emergency room, hooked up to an IV line that poured three liters of fluids into her arm (and Lisa's not a very big person).

The next day, Lisa's husband went to the cleaners to pick up her favorite skirt, but the cleaners couldn't find it. And then, he took her new camera on a trip and broke it. Lastly, the house they had a contract on to buy had a few more technical difficulties than anyone had anticipated.

Meanwhile, Lisa's daily readings continued to show "everything coming up roses": the 2 of Wands, the Magician, the 6 of Wands. But when Lisa looked back over her readings from the previous week, she discovered the 4 of Swords hiding back there. She'd ignored its message—to take a break—at the time the card had appeared.

Of course there'd been a lot going on in Lisa's life, just as there is in all of your lives. But if she'd paid attention to the cards, perhaps she could have avoided what ultimately came to be diagnosed as stress-induced colitis.

So when that "negative" or "counseling" card appears, take heed. And, oh yes, here are all the happy endings: Lisa's feeling much better, the cleaners found the skirt, the store replaced the camera, and the seller agreed to fix the house's technical difficulties. Everything *is* coming up roses for Lisa now.

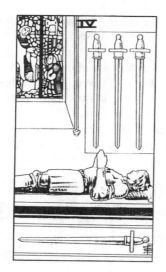

The 4 of Swords is a counseling card: It means take a break!

Letting the Tarot Help You

How much would *you* like to know through the Tarot? Some people are a little fearful, shy, or unsure about what they want to know. It's possible, too, that when you learn about something, it will be very different than you thought it would be.

Here are some questions to help you decide if you're ready for the Tarot to help you:

➤ Do you want to dive into the mystery of a relationship—or of life?

➤ Do you want to find out more about what you're really learning—or not learning—from your career?

➤ Are you unhappy about a situation around you—or worried that your happiness might come to an end?

➤ Are you worried about your health—or someone else's?

➤ Do you want some help with a difficult decision, or need some input from another source?

The Tarot can help you know more about these things so that you can get your life moving in the direction you want. Sure, it can be a little scary to think that you have a new job coming, another move (just ask Lisa, who's had over 50 address changes in 25 years), or that you may have to end a long-term relationship.

Sometimes, clients come to Arlene and say they really want something new. But then, when the Tarot cards reveal they *will* soon have a new job or house, they freak out and say, "Wow! I don't know if I'm ready for that yet."

Fools Rush In

Never use the Tarot to spy on someone, or to ask for information that could harm someone else! We always ask for the highest good to come through in a reading, and we as readers want to assist the Querent on his or her journey of life by allowing the Free Will of the individual to play out. The reader informs, enlightens, and empowers *you* to your highest good and potential.

Card Catalog

The *key* numbers of the Major Arcana cards can be thought of literally as keys to opening up a card's meanings and possibilities.

Even when we think we want something to happen, sometimes we're afraid of it, or sometimes, it seems too good to be true—and we just *can't* believe it. But remember, life has its cycles and ebbs and flows—and Tarot seems to pick up on them, good cycles as well as the more difficult ones. Do you dare venture in a particular direction? Why not? After all, life is a journey of many avenues. You've had new jobs before, new relationships, changes of residence. Why couldn't they happen again—but this time, with the added help of a Tarot reading?

Understanding Your Mission and Purpose in Life

As with so many areas the Tarot can help you with, this is another where a Tarot exercise is the key. This exercise can help you to understand your mission and purpose in life.

Take the 22 Major Arcana cards from the deck, and then set aside the rest of the deck. Mix these 22 cards without looking at their faces. Keep them moving in your hands and concentrate on this question: "What is my mission or purpose in life?"

There are not 22 cards of the Major Arcana by accident. Twenty-two is a significant number in symbolic systems ranging from the Hebrew Kaballah to numerology. According to the Kaballah, for example, there are 22 paths on the Tree of Life—and there are 22 letters in the Hebrew alphabet.

Numerologically, the number 22 is considered one of two Master Numbers (the other is 11), a number imbued with divine power and possibility. Each Major Arcana card has a number, called a *key*, which represents its position on the archetypal life journey represented by the cards. In the Universal Waite Deck, this number is at top center of the card, in Roman numerals, and the name of the card appears on the bottom. Of course, numbered Minor Arcana cards have numbers, too—their own numbers, which also appear at the top, but no title appears on the cards.

When you're ready, fan the 22 Major Arcana cards face down and then pick three of them, one at a time, and place them face down in front of you. Then put the rest of the Major Arcana away.

Now, take the rest of the deck you had put away (the 56 Minor Arcana cards) and start mixing or shuffling these, asking this question: "How will I fulfill my purpose?"

When you're ready, fan these cards out in front of you as you did for the Major Arcana cards, then pick four cards, one at a time, keeping these cards face down as well. The idea is that you will pick or gravitate toward cards whose pictures you don't yet see. We want the subconscious to pick the images for you.

Now you have three Major Arcana cards—your mission or purpose in life, and four Minor Arcana cards—how you will fulfill your purpose. Remember, the cards you pick today are for present and near-future events you will soon learn about and hopefully accomplish. Now turn all seven cards over and place them in their upright positions. What have you got there? Write down the cards here:

Major Arcana Cards: *What is my mission or purpose in life?*

Card 1:_____

Card 2:_____

Card 3:_____

Minor Arcana Cards: *How will I fulfill my purpose?*

Card 4:_____

Card 5:_____

Card 6:_____

Card 7:_____

Now, using the images of the cards, tell a story about yourself. You can be anything or anyone in each of the cards; the important thing is that this is *your* story.

When you've read more about the cards themselves in Parts 3 and 4, you'll want to come back to this exercise and look at the cards again. For now, though, you should just note the cards and your initial impressions of them.

The Therapeutic Relationship

Have you ever seen an episode of the television show *Mad About You,* in which Paul and Jamie Buchman visit Sheila, their shrink? She's just so *wrong* for them! In one episode, they even try to fire her, but in the end, they end up back on the couch in her office. She may be wrong, but she's all they've got. Your relationship with your Tarot reader—or with your Querent—is the same kind of therapeutic relationship that occurs between a therapist and client, but it should *never* be the kind of dysfunctional relationship *Mad About You* depicts so well.

Who's Reading Your Cards?

Who's reading your cards can be the single most important decision you make about a Tarot reading. Just as Sheila is all wrong for Paul and Jamie, the wrong Tarot reader can leave you with the wrong impression of Tarot.

Your personal reaction to a particular Tarot reader may have nothing to do with his or her skills as a reader. What's important in a reader/Querent relationship is chemistry, and, as with any relationship, you "click" with some people, and you don't "click" with others.

But how do you go about finding the reader who's right for you? Here are a few suggestions:

➤ Ask your friends if they have a reader they like.

➤ Check your local continuing education programs for Tarot classes and get to know your teacher if you take a class.

➤ Talk to people at your local metaphysical bookstore and get to know the owner and the salespeople. Ask them about Tarot readers they know and like.

➤ Take advantage of any local metaphysical publications and read the stories they print on local Tarot readers, as well as read the ads for ones that "connect" to you.

How Much Should You Tell the Reader About Yourself?

Would you go to a therapist and ask her to cure your problems without telling her your story? Would you go to a doctor and make him tell you what's wrong without telling him your symptoms? In the same way you talk to your therapist or doctor, we think that the more a reader knows about you, the better she or he can interpret your cards.

Those of the Skeptical School will immediately say, "Well there, you see? You tell them what you want to hear, and then they tell it back to you." But that's not how the Tarot works at all. You may tell your reader your heart's desire, but the cards reveal the what, when, and if of how it may or may not unfold. "Telling" the Future? Or Counseling Hearts?

We'd like to ask you a few questions, and we'd like you to look into your heart of hearts to answer them.

1. Do you believe your future is in your hands?
2. Do you believe the rest of your life begins today?
3. Do you believe that "telling" the future is really the same as counseling hearts?

If you've been following along with us so far, you already know our answers to these questions. But let's go over them again to make sure we're all playing with the same deck.

1. Your future is in your hands.
2. The rest of your life begins today.
3. Tarot, like all esoteric methods that get you in touch with your heart of hearts, can both "tell" your future and counsel your heart.

The rest is up to you—with the cards' able assistance.

Maslow's Hierarchy of Needs: A Journey of Self-Actualization

Abraham Harold Maslow (1908–1970) was a leading proponent of humanistic psychology. Calling Freudian psychology too focused on illness, humanistic psychology concentrates instead on the individual, and his or her progress through the stages of life. This progress is called Maslow's hierarchy of needs.

Maslow's hierarchy is one of several psychological models developed to represent the personal journey in archetypal symbols. In Maslow's definition, we progress from basic needs such as food and sex to the highest needs of self-actualization, which can ultimately fulfill our greatest human potential.

The Tarot can be a rewarding tool in your own journey toward self-actualization. By studying the cards and their images, you begin to explore your own feelings, your ideas about the life you're living, and the ways in which you'd like to grow and evolve. In contemplating the cards, you're really contemplating yourself, your own very human nature.

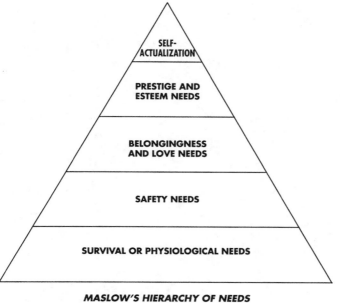

Maslow's Hierarchy of Needs.

MASLOW'S HIERARCHY OF NEEDS

The Least You Need to Know

➤ The pictures of Tarot are works of art meant to open up your imagination.

➤ Tarot cards can reveal things about yourself that you haven't known or realized.

➤ The Tarot can help you better deal with your relationships and life changes.

➤ The more your Tarot reader knows about you, the more she can help you understand your needs and desires.

➤ The Tarot cards are all about the journey of life—*your* journey of life.

Part 2
Getting to Know the Cards

It's time to take a closer look at Tarot cards. Tarot decks come in a variety of shapes and sizes, with one to suit every taste (and budget). How you respond to different decks is a highly individual affair, and which deck you feel most comfortable with is a matter of intuition as well. As you get to know your Tarot deck, you'll want to start recording its messages in a Tarot journal of your own.

Chapter 4

Contemplating Tarot Cards

> **In This Chapter**
>
> ➤ Tarot decks and cards
>
> ➤ Tarot colors and imagery
>
> ➤ Tarot mythology

If you've never gone to the Tarot section of your bookstore and looked at decks, do so soon. You'll be amazed at how many different decks there are. The best bookstores will let you examine each of the decks before you buy one, so that you can find the one that's right for you. But before you make that deck-shopping trip, we'd like to talk a little bit about just what it is you're seeing.

All About Tarot Decks

The most often-used Tarot deck is the *Universal Waite Deck*, which is the one we're using to illustrate this book. We'll explore that deck more in a minute, because we're going to want to spend some time with those particular cards. But first, we want to talk about what most Tarot decks have in common—and what's different among them.

The Most Common Decks

U.S. Game Systems, Inc., is the company that manufactures many of the Tarot decks in this country, including the Universal Waite Deck we're using here. Among the decks they sell are the *Angel* deck, the *Aquarian* deck, the *Cat People* deck, the *Marseilles* deck, the *Morgan-Greer* deck, the *Native American* deck, the *Witches* deck, and *Zolar's Astrological* deck, to name just a few.

All modern Tarot decks contain 22 Major Arcana cards and 56 Minor Arcana cards, for a total of 78 cards. And all of their artists use symbols, colors, and imagery to convey their ideas. But those symbols, colors, and imagery have as many different manifestations as there are decks themselves.

Different Strokes for Different Folks

People like different decks for different reasons. Lisa was quite taken with her used Mythic deck when she found it, in its little brown leather box, at a metaphysical bookstore in Albuquerque. It was the Moon card that grabbed her initially, quintuple Cancer that she is. She loved the blues, purples, and yellows, as well as the three-headed dog that so reminded her of her many dogs—and the three-headed woman who reminded her of herself!

Arlene is equally fond of her Aquarian deck. Arlene's an Aquarius, after all, and this deck is named after her sign. She loves the beautiful pastels; they're more romantic, she feels, nice and flowing, softer. Arlene found this deck when her first Tarot teacher was discussing the different zodiac sign decks. Arlene picked the deck for her sign, and ever since, it's been her favorite.

To help you understand the differences between decks, we're going to discuss how the High Priestess (key 2), varies from deck to deck. We'll look at symbolism, imagery, and colors, and tell you what we personally like and why. Remember that this is a very subjective account. How *you* feel about the High Priestess can—and should—be very different.

The High Priestess in the Universal Waite Deck, which we're using in this book, is sometimes called the Papess. She's sitting on her throne, waxing crescent moon at her feet, a cross on her breast, the Hebrew Torah in her lap, and a pillar on either side of her. The letter on the black pillar to her right is "B," and the letter on the white pillar to her left is "J."

According to Tarot authority Leo Louis Martello, the black pillar is Boaz, the negative life principle, and the white pillar is Jakin, the positive life principle (the names come from the pillars of Solomon's Temple in Jerusalem). The Torah symbolizes hidden knowledge; the moon, ancient witchcraft-based religions; and the cross, the Church.

THE HIGH PRIESTESS

The High Priestess from the Universal Waite Deck.

When *we* look at this card, we're drawn first by the colors: the pure blue and white of the High Priestess's gown; the rich red pomegranate seeds bursting from their bright yellow pods. We're struck by the flow of the High Priestess's skirt, the way it seems almost liquid as it approaches the moon. We don't worry about what any of this symbolizes; we just feel a strong feminine current of intuition, the immortality of the life force, and the emotional knowledge that exists just beneath the surface.

But different decks depict this card in different ways. Sometimes you'll find the High Priestess shown as a young woman all in white. Maybe she stands at the base of a long black stairway, carrying in her left hand five-pointed, star-shaped flowers and in her right a pomegranate. Or she may be depicted in a decidedly modern way, or in some variation of the huntress archetype. She may be more witch-like in some decks, or the two pillars may appear as trees, or poles of some kind.

What's most important to consider about the High Priestess is that she represents our intuition or Third Eye—our all-knowing, all-seeing aspect. Yes, we all need both our male and female sides (the black and white pillars) to function. But the High Priestess sits *between* the two pillars. She *is* intuition—or Third Eye, those "gut feelings" that come when we need more than just emotion and/or logic. When the High Priestess appears in your reading, she's asking that you go within and listen to that inner voice of intuition.

So what does this mean to you? If you're artistically inclined, you might want to draw your own image of what the High Priestess represents to you. Or you can examine how she appears in various Tarot Decks (see Appendix C) and find the one that feels right to you.

The Deck You See Illustrated in This Book

We're using the Universal Waite Deck in this book for a number of reasons, the main one being that it's the most common Tarot deck in this country today, and therefore the one you're most likely to find and see illustrated in other books.

In the Cards

A.E. Waite, who supervised the design of the Waite deck, is primarily responsible for the Fool beginning the Tarot deck today. He felt that its "unnumbered" key 0 naturally belonged before the Magician, at the beginning of life's journey. It's hard to believe the Fool could be anywhere else.

A. E. Waite's Tarot decks were the first to use symbolic design rather than stylized drawing to depict each card. This is especially evident in the Minor Arcana cards, which in earlier decks look much more like the common playing cards we see today. The early 3 of Cups, for example, had, literally, three cups on it. In the Universal Waite Deck, though, this card has the three dancing women who appear in various guises on this card in most modern decks.

The 3 of Cups has a symbolic design in the Universal Waite Deck.

So What Do All These Cards Mean?

Have we told you often enough that what the cards "mean" is ultimately up to you? While it's true that each card has a number of divinatory meanings, and that many Tarot authors, including us, will try to "explain" those meanings, Tarot is at heart an instinctual art, and as such is at its best when its meanings are found intuitively.

The High Priestess, for example, whom you met earlier, has a different meaning according to each expert you consult, as shown in the following table.

What Does the High Priestess "Mean"?

Meaning	Authority/Book
"Subconscious knowledge"	Leo Louis Martello in *Reading the Tarot*
"Intuitive awareness"	Anthony Louis in *Tarot: Plain and Simple*
"A card of waiting and gestation"	Nancy Garen in *Tarot Made Easy*
"Hidden influences"	Eden Gray in *The Complete Guide to the Tarot*
"Secrets, mysteries, the truth not yet revealed"	A.E. Waite in *The Pictorial Guide to the Tarot*

What all these differences of opinion confirm is that you shouldn't think of a card's meaning as cast in stone, but rather as a door that opens to a variety of possibilities. To us, the High Priestess is a card about those very possibilities, about listening to your intuition and following its lead. But what this card means to *you*, well, that's up to you.

Sharpening Your Powers of Observation

Are you wondering how we "saw" all those images in the High Priestess cards we just showed you? Did you have to go back to the Universal Waite card to find the pomegranates, the moon, or the Torah scroll?

If so, you're not alone. We're all inundated with so much information that everyone uses some sort of selective filtering to get them through their days. If you read the license plate number of every car that passed you on the freeway, for example, you wouldn't be able to pay much attention to traffic. So you selectively filter out the extraneous information, like license numbers, in order to get on with the job of driving.

The problem is that we've become *too good* at selective filtering, and so when we first encounter the rich imagery of Tarot cards, we look at them the way we're used to looking at everything: We just read the headline. This means that when we look at the High Priestess this way, we see a lady in a blue cloak with a funny pointed hat.

One of the first things you'll want to do in your encounter with Tarot cards is to turn off your selective filtering system and let all that imagery in. To help you on your way, we've designed an exercise to get you started.

The Star: A Tarot Exercise

For this exercise, you should select the Star card from your Tarot deck. (If you don't have a deck yet, you can use the following picture, but remember that the colors are missing.) Place the card comfortably before you, and let it tell you its story.

The Star (key 17).

As you study the details of the card's design, write down what you see, using the following questions to guide you.

Are there animals? If so, what are they?

_____

_____

Are there shapes? If so, what are they? Are they large or small? Realistic or stylized?

_____

_____

Are there elements (fire, earth, air, water) present? If so, how are they depicted?

_____

_____

Are there human figures? If so, how are they depicted?

_____

_____

What about vegetation? Are there trees or flowers? If so, what are they?

_____

_____

What colors are in the card? What do these colors mean to you?

_____

_____

What other symbols do you see in the card? What do they mean to you?

_____

_____

Rather than tell you what *we* see in this card, we suggest that you have someone else do the exercise, too. After you've both finished, compare your notes. Did she see things you didn't, or vice versa? Did you see things she's certain aren't even there? Are there images that you absolutely disagree about?

For now, just note all of your and your friend's thoughts about this card. Save them for Chapter 11, in which we discuss the Star card in more detail.

Tarot Cards and Color Theory 101

Just as we may not consciously be aware of archetypal symbolism, so we confront color symbolism on a daily basis without giving it a thought. But think about it: What color cape gets tossed before a bull? Red, the color of anger. And what color are those ubiquitous happy faces? Yellow, the color of optimism.

At the same time, remember that to think that each color can be only the meanings we suggest is to limit its potential. With that in mind, let's look at some traditional color symbolism in the following table.

Spinning the Wheel of Fortune

The key to studying any Tarot card is to *relax*. Don't demand that the card show you everything at once. Don't worry that you're missing something that someone else may have seen. What you see in the card is what is there for you—and that's what *is* important.

Color Symbolism

Color	Possible Meanings
White	The soul (white light), innocence, purity, naïveté, faith.
Yellow	The sunny yellow kitchen, vitality, good energy, healing, enthusiasm.
Orange	Healing powers, playful, fun, flirtatious (red + yellow).

continues

continued

Color	Possible Meanings
Red	Passion for life, aggression, danger, power, desire, lust, stop sign.
Green	Prosperity, growth, money, springtime, the Emerald City.
Blue	Tranquillity, thoughtfulness, peace, calmness, deep as the ocean, high as the sky.
Purple	Problem-solving, intuition, the psychic realm, resurrection, royalty, red + blue = passionate problem-solving.
Brown	Earthy connection, grounded, serious, thoughtful, subtlety, quietness, solid commitment, the brown bear, perseverance.
Black	The beginning and the end, the abyss, the culmination of things, the completion of a cycle, the void, termination, the unknown. All colors are included in black, the universal color, which used to be considered bad luck, evil, darkness.

There may be other things that certain colors mean to you. If so, you can record them here.

Personal Color	SymbolismColor	Personal Meanings
_____	_____	_____
_____	_____	_____
_____	_____	_____

Fools Rush In

When is a bull just plain bull? Tarot artists clearly rely on many different mythological systems. If you're not familiar with one, will you miss its meaning? For the answer to this question, we repeat from earlier in this chapter: The most important meaning of a card is what it means to *you*. So, if a bull is just plain bull to you, then that's what it is.

A Matter of Mythology (Greek, That Is)

Now, we don't expect all of you, or even very many of you, to be steeped in mythology the way someone with a classics background like Lisa is. We know that the most you may know about Hercules is that Disney made a movie about him a few years ago—or that he's played by that hunky guy on the Fox network.

But the mythology that Tarot symbolism uses comes from more than just those old Greek stories. There are, for example, Christian-era angels, such as Raphael, Michael, and Gabriel; Egyptian gods like Ankh and Anubis; wiccan (witchcraft) symbols like black cats and roses; and Hebrew letters such as the "YHVH" that stand for the Hebrew God, Yahweh.

You don't have to be a classics scholar to recognize the inherent meaning in any of these symbols. But just in case you want a little background, the following tables list some of the more common mythological symbols used in Tarot.

Symbols From Christian Mythology

Symbol	Meaning
Angels: Raphael	Angel of the air ("superconscious")
Michael	Angel of fire (consciousness)
Gabriel	Angel of water (subconscious)
Cross	Union of God and Earth
Crown	The will vs. cosmic purpose
Devil	Spiritual blindness, temptation

Symbols From the Hebrew Kabbalah

Symbol	Meaning
Lightning	The life power from the Tree of Life
Scroll (Torah)	Divine law; hidden mysteries
Stone	Unity of father and son, spirit and body

Symbols From Egyptian Mythology

Symbol	Meaning
Ankh	Life; male + female
Anubis	Jackal-headed god representing the mind
Sphinx	The mystery of life

Symbols From Greek Mythology

Symbol	Meaning
Bull	The element earth
Moon	Emotions and intuition
Ram's Head	Mars, the planet of action

These four mythological systems are just a few of the many that Tarot artists have used. The Universal Waite Deck alone also includes numerological, mathematical, and astrological symbolism, for example. Other popular Tarot decks use Native American, Goddess, and African myths, to name but three. If a particular mythological imagery appeals to you, learn more about it. Your local library will have a wealth of information on any mythology you want to study in depth.

Common Images in the Cards

Because we're using the Universal Waite Deck, we'd like to explore some of the common images these particular cards use before we move on to more exercises where you get to know the cards better yourself. But remember, the "meanings" we show here are just suggestions.

Common Images in the Universal Waite Deck

Image	Possible Meaning
Banner	Freedom from material possessions
Birds	Messengers from the sky who give us warning or enlightenment
Butterfly	The immortality of the soul
Cat	The psychic mysteries of life
Chain	Self-imposed restriction
Circle	Wholeness, continuity
Crown	Mastery
Dog	Friend of humans
Eagle	Power
Flame	Spirit
Grapes	Abundance and fertility
Horse	Creating action and powerful movement in your life
Leaves	Vitality
Lily	Purity
Mountains	Abstract thought
Olive branch	Peace
Palm	Victory over death
Scales	Balanced judgment
Serpent	Wisdom
Star	Luck, good fortune, hope
Stream	The flow of life
Veil	Hidden things
Wheel	The whole of cosmic expression
Yod	The tenth letter of the Hebrew alphabet, hand of God, blessings from heaven

Now that you've got a basic understanding of some of the Tarot's symbolic systems, you're ready to take a good, long look at the cards themselves. That's what the next chapter is all about.

The Least You Need to Know

➤ There are Tarot decks to suit every taste.

➤ The colors in Tarot cards have a variety of meanings.

➤ The myths of many societies—from Greek to Native American—can be found in Tarot cards.

➤ Certain images are common to all Tarot decks—male and female, for example.

➤ What you see in a Tarot card is up to you.

Chapter 5

What Do YOU See in the Cards?

In This Chapter

➤ How Tarot can help you make big decisions

➤ Finding personal meaning in the cards

➤ Getting rid of preconceived notions

So far, we've talked mostly about symbolic systems, and the fact that Tarot is one of them. It's obvious we think this concept is very important to an understanding of "the" Tarot, and now that you've got it firmly in hand, we'd like to take that lesson and apply it to the cards. In this chapter we'll take a good, long look at the cards and at what *you* see when you look at them.

Walking the Fool's Path

Through the Tarot's Major Arcana cards, you can see the cycles that are repeated throughout your life. Each of the Major Arcana cards has a number, and that number tells what you're learning and how that lesson might express itself. (In Chapter 26 we'll talk about how numerology shows you even more about Tarot and numbers.)

The first six cards, the Fool (key 0) through the Hierophant (key 5), show us as "beginners" who have not yet been shaped by more mature societal forces.

The next six cards, the Lovers (key 6) through Justice (key 11), represent our intermediate steps, where we learn to apply our knowledge to new challenges.

The next five cards, the Hanged Man (key 12) through the Tower (key 16), show our process of wrestling with our inner demons and of beginning a process of regeneration and deeper learning.

THE STAR.

THE MOON.

THE SUN .

JUDGEMENT.

THE WORLD.

The final five Major Arcana cards, the Star (key 17) through the World (key 21), mean that we've achieved group consciousness, that we're pretty advanced life journeyers.

Along our journey in life, all of us wonder what's ahead of us. Your questions might include:

➤ What is my future?

➤ Whom will I meet?

➤ What is my calling?

➤ Is there someone out there for me?

Fools Rush In

The Tarot can warn you of possible events that might not be so pleasant, and foretell new hope of things to come that will change your life for the better. How you walk the Fool's path, though, is up to you.

Card Catalog

Your *life lessons* reflect both the lessons that all of us learn as we go through our lives (the Major Arcana), and the lessons you must learn yourself in your own life (the Minor Arcana).

You can think of the Tarot as a wonderful journey where you're seeking the opportunities and possibilities we've all longed for. Tarot can reveal a new start in life after a difficult phase, or tell you of new relationships on the horizon. It can direct you toward a new career opportunity you hadn't thought of, or reflect new skills, new people, and new conditions up ahead. Just follow the Yellow Brick Road of the Fool's journey through the Major Arcana: Your dreams are at the end of the rainbow!

Tarot and Life's Cycles

It's interesting to watch how the Tarot reflects exactly what *life lessons* you might be going through at any given time. People who have had regular readings throughout their lives, for example, note that in their 20s, Temperance (key 14) and the Hierophant (key 5) come up over and over again to represent their life's lessons.

Why do these cards show up at this particular time in peoples' lives? Well, in answer to the question, "What do I need to learn now?", Temperance answers, "Great patience with life and a tempering of energies. Adaptation to current conditions." The Hierophant's response to this same question is, "Learn to deal with the institutions or conventions of society."

For people in their 20s, these cards show up again and again, making it clear that these people need to learn these particular lessons. The funny thing is, most of them don't want to hear it! While these cards reflect what lessons 20-somethings usually need to develop and integrate into their lives, like all of us, they'd rather see the Sun (key 19), the Lovers (key 6), and other cards showing great personal success and good relationships.

Later, in their 30s, these same people receive the cards of marriage, prosperity, and good relations. Temperance and the Hierophant no longer appear in their readings, but the Sun and the Lovers do. By this time, they are ready for these lessons, and no longer wonder why these specific cards appear.

Tarot cards, such as Temperance (key 14) and the Hierophant (key 5), are common in Tarot readings for people in their twenties. By their thirties, cards such as the Sun (key 19) and the Lovers (key 6) begin to appear.

What does this mean? It means that *cards will come up at certain times in your life to reflect the lessons you're able to handle at that time*. So, when you're 60 or 70, the cards that appear won't have shown themselves before. The cards you receive at any given time represent what you need to grow into—and even at 60 and 70, we're still growing.

Tarot and Life's Big Decisions

Once you understand the reflective nature of the cards, you can begin to see how they can help you with your life's big decisions. Here, it's the Minor Arcana, or daily, cards that come into play, showing you how current events have, are, or will be played out.

A client of Arlene's once came to her after putting down a hefty down payment on a condo. "Was this a good move?" he wanted to know. "Did I make the right decision?" He suspected that it wasn't, but he'd already made the down payment and signed the papers, so there was no way out of the decision he'd made.

The cards revealed that it wasn't a wise decision—and that he still needed to learn his life lesson about hurrying into decisions without seeking counsel first. His *final* outcome wouldn't necessarily be negative, but he'd already set the wheels in motion for current difficulties, and there was no way around them.

Naturally, the client was angry with Arlene, when all she'd done was read his cards! If he'd come to her first, *before* he'd signed those papers and made that down payment, she might have been able to warn him. But chances are, *he wouldn't have listened anyway,* because this is a lesson he needed to learn.

What Brings You to the Tarot?

Most people who take a class or get a reading want help with making a major decision in life—and they need to know *now*! We know you can go for months or years and not really feel the need or urge to get a reading, but then all of a sudden—especially when a negative situation happens or something crashes and burns in your life—you'll want to turn to someone else to help guide you out of the "bad" cycle.

Some people seek out their ministers, their rabbis, their counselors, their mentors, or their grandmas—or a darn good Tarot reader or psychic. It usually takes a desperate or uncomfortable situation to motivate someone to get a reading, but then, it's in just such circumstances that we usually go for some kind of help.

HELP! The desperate phone calls come in, begging for readings.

HELP! I need to take a class *now* to understand my life better.

HELP! I need guidance *now*!

We hear anxiety in every voice, so we try to help everybody. We can't, of course, replace other forms of counsel or therapy you may need for certain situations. If you need a lawyer, you should see a lawyer. If you need a doctor, see a doctor. If you need a therapist, see one. But if you need a spiritual advisor or insight of a higher nature, that's when you should seek out a Tarot reader!

Looking for Personal Meaning

Each of us sees what's happening from our own particular point of view, but because of this, no two versions of any story are exactly the same. Think about it—even if you and your brother are sitting across from each other at the same table eating dinner, he's looking at you, and you're looking at him—so your points of view are different!

This is what personal meaning is all about—your own particular perspective in your own particular story. Tarot can help you understand just what your story is, but how you live your story is up to you. We all want to develop a sense of individualism and follow our own drummer instead of the band. The key to this is inside you—it's your story, and no one else's. No one else can—or should—tell you how to live your life, because it's *your* life and no one else's. Here's an example.

The middle-aged son of a wealthy family recently came to see Arlene. He'd rather be driving an old Ford pickup than his Mercedes, would rather be wearing jeans than his suit and tie. But this 47-year-old doesn't want to make his 70-something-year-old Mom mad, so when he visits his family, he puts on the suit and tie he keeps in the trunk of his Mercedes.

When Arlene did a reading for him, she told him he needed to be what and who he wanted to be. Nobody *really* cares but him, she told him. But somewhere along the line, this guy developed a pattern that told him he had to please others first, that his needs were secondary to those of his family, and that the things he needed weren't important. But that's not true for *anyone*—we all need to learn to be true to ourselves before we can be true to others.

Finding personal meaning is about learning to have the self-confidence to be true to ourselves. And where that personal meaning is can be found in the cards.

Reading for Other People

Objectivity is important in any reading, and it seems the closer you are to the individual emotionally, the less likely you are to be intuitive. Arlene can't read for her Mom, for example, because when she tries, she starts to get into her view of her Mom, rather than what the cards are really showing. If we know someone well, we'll try to make the cards fit the picture we have of them, rather than what the cards are actually saying.

So don't read for people you can't be objective about, like your best friend or a loved one. If you know too much about one's situation, have a preconceived notion about what the person is asking, or have a stake in the question, you just can't be objective—and you shouldn't even try.

Follow these tips for giving an ethical reading:

➤ Be objective. If you can't, find someone else to do the reading.

➤ Provide constructive counsel. If anything looks "negative," work with the Querent to turn the negativity around.

➤ Use the cards to empower the Querent to make his own personal judgments and decisions without you.

➤ Be aware when you're doing a reading that you're helping a person find her past more clearly, and that you have to be gentle with that process.

➤ As much as some people say they don't believe it, they're all ears when you give them a reading. Your responsibility is to give them something to go on without you, after they walk out the door.

Your Personal Response to the Cards: A Tarot Exercise

What cards you're most and least drawn to can reveal a lot about you. For this exercise, you should place all 22 Major Arcana cards facing you so that you can look at them all, individually and together. Let the cards speak to you, and listen to what they have to say.

It's possible you already know which card you love the best, as Lisa did; she was immediately drawn to her Mythic deck Moon card. And you might know, too, which card really turns you off, gives you the creeps, or you just hate to see. A businessman we know, for example, hates the Tower card and the chaos it seems to represent.

This exercise is about your *personal* response, though, so what we think of particular cards has nothing to do with it. The Tower may be the card you like best, and the Moon the one you like the least. Remember, *there are no right or wrong answers.*

What Cards Are You Most Drawn To?

There's probably one Major Arcana card that just leaps out at you. Is it the Star, pouring her dual pitchers of water into stream and lake? Is it the happy couple of the Lovers, or the cheerful, innocent Fool? Maybe you're drawn to the power of the Emperor, the Empress, or the Hierophant. Whatever card just *gets* you, though, record it here.

Favorite card: _____

Chances are, there are other cards you like as well. Pick out two other cards that appeal to you, and list them here.

Card: _____

Card: _____

Now, place these three cards next to each other in front of you. Look at the cards, together and individually. What colors are they? Are there images they have in common? Use the following space to note what you like about these cards.

What colors are in the cards? What do these colors mean to you?

_____

_____

Are there human figures? If so, how are they depicted? Why do you like them?

_____

_____

Are there shapes? If so, what are they? Are they large or small? Realistic or stylized? What is it about these shapes that you like?

_____

_____

Are there elements (fire, earth, air, water) present? If so, how are they depicted? What do these elements mean to you?

_____

_____

Are there animals? If so, what are they? Why do you like these particular animals?

_____

_____

What about vegetation? Are there trees or flowers? If so, what are they? What do they remind you of?

_____

_____

What other symbols do you see in these cards? What do they mean to you?

_____

_____

What have you found? Are you drawn to certain colors? Certain people? Certain animals or shapes? What are they? Why are you drawn to them? Think about your answers to these questions and then move on to the next part of this exercise.

What Cards Are You Least Drawn To?

Here, too, there's probably one card that just gets your goat. It could be that old goat, the Devil, in all his horned splendor, or Death peering out from beneath his visor. Maybe something about the Hermit or the Hierophant disturbs you. Whatever card bothers you the most, though, record it here.

Least favorite card: _____

There are probably some other cards you don't like either. Pick out two of them, and list them here.

Card: _____

Card: _____

Now, place these three cards next to each other in front of you and look at them. Once again note their colors, their imagery, their symbols. Use the following space to note what you dislike about these particular cards.

What colors are in the cards? What do these colors mean to you? Why don't you like them?

_____

_____

Are there human figures? If so, how are they depicted? What is it about them that you don't like?

_____

_____

Are there shapes? If so, what are they? Are they large or small? Realistic or stylized? What do you dislike about these particular shapes?

_____

_____

Are there elements (fire, earth, air, water) present? If so, how are they depicted? Why don't you like them?

_____

_____

Are there animals? If so, what are they? Do you know why you dislike these kinds of animals?

_____

_____

What about vegetation? Are there trees or flowers? If so, what are they? Why don't you like them?

_____

_____

What other symbols do you see in these cards? What do they mean to you? Are there reasons they turn you off?

_____

_____

What have you found? Do you dislike certain colors? Certain people? Certain animals or shapes? What are they? Why don't you like them? Think about your answers to these questions. After you have, we think you'll find that some of the answers to why you don't like certain cards can be found in the following section.

Life in the Tower

Did you ever have a bad experience in life that seemed to color your perceptions for a long time after? Have you ever noticed that we humans tend to remember traumas or negative events far better than we remember the pleasant or joyful ones? What's wrong with us, for goodness sake? Are we complete idiots—or just Fools?

Much about the mind remains a mystery, even with the enormous leaps and bounds knowledge has made in this century alone. For whatever reason, we're very good at hiding behind the fears or traumas *that we know* rather than taking steps that might introduce us to new ones. Without our even realizing it, we become overly cautious or fearful about the same thing happening again, so that if something comes up for the future that looks anything like a former trauma, we jump back and say, "Oh, no! I'm don't want to go through *that* again!"

Right? If a present event looks even remotely familiar, we may run in the opposite direction. "Not another guy named Ken!" or "Not another boss who tells long-winded jokes!" These things may have nothing to do with what was really traumatic about the old event, but the mind has associated the trauma with all sorts of unrelated baggage.

We call this "Life in the Tower." Take out the Tower Major Arcana card and look at it. What's happening in this card, and why is it so scary?

This card kind of looks like a bad year in California—everything from rain to lightning, from mud slides to fires. What else could possibly go wrong? Maybe it would be better to just crawl off somewhere and hide—that way, nothing can find us.

But what about the *good things* that happen unexpectedly? What about that tall, dark stranger, or that chance encounter? Remember the cleaners who lost Lisa's skirt back in Chapter 4? The woman who accidentally took it home turned out to be a book publicist. Talk about *karma*!

There is no growth without risk. You've got to break through the old destructive patterns before you can develop more constructive ones. You've got to get rid of your excess baggage and learn that life in the Tower isn't always a bad thing.

The Tower (key 16).

Breaking Through Preconceived Notions

So how do we stop these destructive patterns? First of all, we learn to use our intuition about every new event in our lives, rather than assume, because of our bad experiences, that it will come out the same as it did the last time. No matter what went wrong in the past, it is just that: *in the past.*

In the Cards

We all get into patterns in our lives—they make things easier, and keep the unexpected from knocking us for a loop. But sometimes the very patterns we think are protecting us can be keeping us from living our lives to their greatest potential. The Tarot can help you separate the good patterns from the destructive ones, so that you can get your life moving in a direction that's right for you.

It's years later now. You have a new opportunity to try again. Let's say you went through a messy divorce and now you've met someone new. "Oh wonderful, I finally found the right person. This is so great. I can't wait to get started in this new direction." And then, *boom*! Fear and anxiety creep over you. "Oh no. It could happen again. I don't want to go through another loss." So halfway through this promising relationship, you cut it off. Because of your experience and its associated bad memories, instead of looking at the possibility that this relationship could be good for you and help you heal from the old one, you run.

But you know, "You got to get up on the horse what kicked you." Fear and trauma can—and will—get in the way of finding happiness whenever they can. But if you listen to what the cards have to say, Tarot can help you separate your *real* fears from your *imagined* ones.

There's No Such Thing as Good Cards and Bad Cards

So here comes the Devil. The Devil card, that is. This is one seriously ugly dude. Just look at him—he's all hair and horns, and he's got those people in chains at his feet. The Devil is a bad card, right?

The Devil (key 15).

Repeat after us: "There's no such thing as good cards or bad cards. There's no such thing as good cards or bad cards." Now, close your eyes and click your heels three times, and before you know it, you're back in Kansas. Oops, wrong story!

Or is it? Just as Dorothy's power to get back to Kansas was inside her all along, the Tarot's power resides inside of you. Yes, these are graphic pictures—the Tarot's a very graphic tool. It uses pictures to relay messages, and some of those pictures are pretty ugly.

When the cards look difficult, they can indeed be reflecting the shadow side of a situation—but they're also sending information that it's important to pay attention to. Would Dorothy have believed the Ruby Slippers could get her home if she hadn't followed the Yellow Brick Road all the way to the witch's tower?

If a card like the Devil or the Tower appears in a reading, you should think of it as a wake-up call, not an all-points bulletin. Ask yourself, "What is this card trying to tell me? Is there someone in my life that's not good for me? Or a situation that I should think twice about before I leap into it?"

It's always better to be prepared or forewarned, so that we might be able to change our course of action. And no matter what cards come up for you, all the Tarot cards in the deck should be welcomed as having some information that can help you avoid unnecessary difficulties. So, if a card looks scary, it's there to warn you rather than predict what's coming. Taking heed is using your head!

Take Nothing for Granted

Sometimes, you'll put out a spread of cards and decide, "This is not answering my question. I don't like what I see." Okay, we'll tell you, reshuffle the cards, and see what comes up. See if you can get a "better answer." Guess what? The same cards come up, or, if not, you'll get something with a similar meaning! What's going on here?

Even when the cards don't seem to be answering the question you asked, they're probably answering something you should know about or that your subconscious is chewing over. When certain cards appear, you should take nothing for granted. Even if you don't know—the cards do! So pay attention to what they have to say.

The Least You Need to Know

➤ The Major Arcana cards can show the lessons you need to learn at this point in your life.

➤ The Minor Arcana cards can show the lessons you need to learn today.

➤ You shouldn't wait for a crisis to consult a Tarot reader.

➤ What cards you're most and least drawn to can reveal a lot about you.

➤ The Tarot can help you break through your destructive patterns and ideas.

➤ There are no such things as good cards or bad cards!

Chapter 6

Putting the Cards Together

In This Chapter

➤ "Wearing in" your Tarot cards

➤ Upright and reversed cards

➤ Your Tarot journal

Your relationship with your Tarot deck is the beginning of a beautiful friendship, and, like any friendship, a little mutual respect and care will go a long way. In this chapter, we're going to explore ways to enhance the energy you and your Tarot deck will share, so that your beautiful friendship will move beyond that beginning into a long and exciting future.

Your Personal Energy and the Tarot Deck

When you do a Tarot reading, it's important to be objective. This means opening yourself to the possibilities of the Tarot and not allowing your preconceived notions to sneak in.

Let's say, for example, that a client of Arlene's, a Querent, asks her, "Will I win the lottery tonight?" Lots of people *do* ask questions just like this one. But let's say Arlene thinks gambling's a waste of time. She doesn't let her judgment cloud a reading. Instead, she might let the Querent know why she's obsessed with winning the lottery. She might tell her, if a Major Arcana card comes up, that there could be a deep soul level issue that she's working through.

The most important thing is to let the cards talk. Let them come out. Read what they say, not what you feel about them. Let people experience their own souls, even if it means they have to go "to the edge." Take *yourself* out of it, in other words. The information you provide should help the Querent instigate her own power. Your role is to channel information constructively: Be the High Priestess, sitting between logic and emotion—objective.

In the Cards

Doing a Tarot reading is a lot like teaching: You can learn a great deal from the readings you do for other people by connecting to their personal energy. After you do a reading, you may feel a tingle, and that means you've gotten in touch with your own higher energy, that healing psychic power we all possess.

Rather than judge if someone's concern is "good" or "bad," you should always bear in mind that the Querent should be allowed to pursue her particular issue. That's how she'll get to learn, in the case of gambling, for example, that she can't always win—and that she can't use a medium, like Tarot, to make herself win.

When people put too much stock in something, their very obsession with obtaining it can push it away. One Tarot reader we know has always been struck by people she sees at the race track, carefully marking up their tip sheets and calculating odds. When she bets on a horse, she picks it by its name or just on some hunch (if you're one of those people with the tip sheets, we know you're shuddering now!). Interestingly, she wins at least as often as those people with their tip sheets—and sometimes, more often.

The lesson here is sometimes called "beginner's luck." What beginner's luck really means is that, if it's not a big deal to you, you win. Beginner's luck occurs because you approach something with no preconceptions, with the honesty and innocence of the Fool. Such pureness of intention, uncolored by fear or bias, can result in big payoffs, while obsession can result in misdirected or negative energy. Think about it!

Can You Read Yourself from Your Own Deck?

When you read from your own deck, again, the most important thing is to be objective. Take your time, and don't demand that the cards reveal some meaning to you. Preconceived ideas can result in missed messages—so it's important to not let them color what you see.

The reader—even when it's you reading for yourself—should always tell the truth, and always do so in a non-threatening way. You may know on a subconscious level what's going on, but it's the cards that will show you the truth. With a good ear and a good heart, you can find a new way of seeing, for yourself as well as for others.

"Wearing In" the Cards

Part of getting all you can from your Tarot deck is helping the cards help you and the Querent, and one way to ensure that this happens is to "wear in" or "season" your cards on a weekly basis. Arlene does this affirmation exercise every Sunday evening, before she begins another week of readings.

Separate your deck into its four Minor Arcana suits and its one Major Arcana group. Your cards won't necessarily be in order, but Wands will be with Wands, Cups with Cups, Pentacles with Pentacles, Swords with Swords, and Major Arcana with Major Arcana.

After you've divided your deck into these five stacks, spend some time with each individual stack, clearing the cards of the past week's readings and opening them up for the readings to come. You should use an affirmation, which is a positive sort of prayer, to do this; here's the affirmation that Arlene recites each week as she contemplates her five stacks of cards:

> "My wish for these cards will be to read for the next person well, with confidence, the best intentions, and for the highest good."

"Season" your cards in this way at least once a week, taking the time to do an affirmation for each of the five stacks. When you're finished, reshuffle your stacks back into each other, as if they were parts of a new deck. Shuffle at least six or seven times, and the cards will be ready for another work week.

"Seasoning" your deck clears both the cards' energy and yours, renewing it so that the readings of one week will not be influenced by the readings of another week.

What's the Deal If Cards Are Reversed? (Upside Down)

You mean there's a difference between upright and *reversed cards*? Some readers say there's not, but we feel there is—but it's not necessarily a negative thing. Reversed meanings can mean the lessons of a particular card may be more challenging for this Querent, or that he is fighting himself on this issue. The Querent will also need to evaluate his issues when a reversed card appears in his spread.

All the cards—both the Major and Minor Arcana—have both upright and reversed meanings, and this can scare people. For one, reversed cards don't "look right" to us; they don't sit right with our brain, which seeks to put everything in order, or upright, so it feels "normal." Anything "reversed" seems scary to us, as if its energy were somehow negative instead of positive. (Reversed cards are usually noted in Tarot texts, including this book, with a capital "R" following the cards' names.) But once you

Card Catalog

Reversed cards occur when the lessons of a particular card are more challenging for a Querent, or when a Querent is fighting himself on an issue.

realize that reversed cards allow you to know where you might have delays, false starts, indecision, ambivalence, or frustrations, you begin to see that they're helpful rather than dangerous cards. At the same time, they can let the reader know when a Querent is having difficulty handling a particular situation, and so help her help you—or you help her, as the case may be.

So although reversed cards might *appear* to be negative, in fact they're just another way the cards tell us what's happening or could happen. Reversed cards are crying, "Pay attention!" loud and clear, and we should listen to their message.

When we turn Strength upside-down, it looks as if the lion is in control instead of the woman.

All in a Day's Energy: A Tarot Exercise

We like to do daily spreads and record them in a Tarot journal to review later. If you'd like to try this, too, you should use a Three-Card Spread like those we've mentioned in earlier chapters, or the one that follows.

In the morning, take out your Tarot deck and shuffle it, asking the question: "How's my day going to go?"

Think about this question as you shuffle, and then, when you feel you're ready, divide the deck into three stacks. Select three cards, either all from one stack or one from each, and put these three cards out, face up. Write the cards down in your journal, and also write down the date. Don't look up the cards' interpretations now. Just let them speak to you, without demanding any meaning from them.

You can do this daily, for a week, a month, or forever. The purpose of this exercise is to look for patterns. If you miss a day or two or three, don't worry about it. There's nothing rigid about this exercise; it's meant to help you understand yourself.

To help you see how this works, here are five days from one person's daily readings:

Date	Card 1	Card 2	Card 3
23 March	8 of Wands R	7 of Wands	High Priestess R
24 March	Queen of Pentacles R	2 of Cups	Knight of Wands R
25 March	8 of Cups R	9 of Swords R	Fool R
26 March	7 of Wands	6 of Swords	4 of Wands R
27 March	Queen of Swords	King of Wands	8 of Swords

Take out your own Tarot deck and assemble the readings as above to "get the picture" of the week. Don't look up the interpretations of these cards. Instead, look at the patterns you see here. There are quite a few 8s and 9s, for example, and a lot of reversed cards (those followed by "R"), including the two Major Arcana cards that appear. By the end of the week, though, the reversed cards have disappeared, and there are two Swords in that daily reading. In fact, Wands and Swords seem to be the energy of this particular week. Remember this reading when we talk about the specific energies of the Minor Arcana suits in Chapter 12.

Your Own Daily Readings

Now it's time to start doing your own daily readings, if you'd like. Use the following table to record the cards you find for any five consecutive days.

Daily Readings

Date	Card 1	Card 2	Card 3
(Day 1)			
(Day 2)			
(Day 3)			
(Day 4)			
(Day 5)			

Again, don't look up the interpretations for these cards. Instead, wait a few days, weeks, or months, and then go back and look at what you've recorded. You may want to take the cards themselves back out and place them as they first appeared, so that you can note their visual impressions on you.

Note, too, any patterns you see, whether they're suits, numbers, or reversed cards, for example. As you get to know the cards, you'll intuitively know what these patterns mean to you, and you'll be able to come back to these first daily readings and understand just what they meant for you then—and now.

Feeling the Synergy of Card Combinations

For this exercise, we're going to put out our first Celtic Cross Spread. We'll be discussing this spread in detail in Chapter 19, so if you'd like to know more about it now, sneak a peek ahead. Here's a form for recording the cards, which we'll be using throughout the book to record this particular spread.

The Celtic Cross.

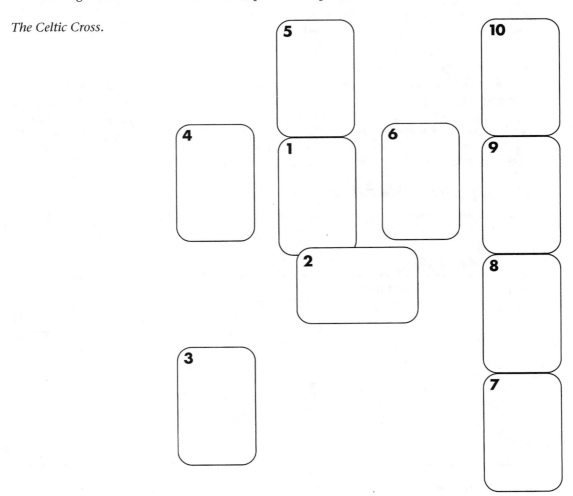

Shuffle the deck as many times as you wish, asking whatever question you wish. Your question can be as general as, "What's going to happen in the next six months?" to a more specific, "Will I find the job I want?"

When you're ready, select ten cards from the deck, either from the top of the deck or from a fanned-out spread. Lay the cards you choose face up in the pattern the form shows, placing the first card at "1," the second card at "2," and so on.

After you put out the ten cards, take a moment to study them. We want you to *feel* them first, noting how they mix, match, or alternate. Try to answer these two questions as well:

➤ Do the cards seem to belong together?

➤ Do the cards feel as if they don't combine well?

Look at the pictures first before checking the cards' interpretations—that's where you'll find the synergy (the energy of the cards together) of the cards.

Sit back and spend at least five minutes considering how you feel about these cards and this combination of pictures. If they "feel" confusing to you, your answer is about confusion. If you feel a harmony, then the answer's harmonious.

Be sure you feel the cards' energy before you check what this book has to say about them in later chapters. Open up your intuitive sense to the cards, and see what they have to say. Don't be surprised that you're not surprised when you look them up—you may already have found what you needed to know.

In the Cards

If five or more cards in a Celtic Cross Spread are Major Arcana, something's going on at a karmic level that's destined to be learned or to happen in your life. When this occurs, you're working with other forces or people for these things to happen—and they're going to happen no matter what—so you may as well cooperate. Such a spread helps explain why you can't seem to get your mind off certain people or situations at times. Some things are bigger than we are, and we need to accept them when they come along. But it's not necessarily something to worry about!

A Sample Spread

Let's turn to one of Lisa's sample spreads, which happens to have a lot of Major Arcana cards in it. That means that a lot of what's happening in Lisa's life is destined to happen, and beyond her control—which of course aggravates her no end!

Lisa's Sample Spread

Celtic Cross

23 February 1998

Question: "What's happening?"

Card 1   *3 of Pentacles*

Card 2   *The Sun*

Card 3   *High Priestess*

Card 4   *King of Cups*

Card 5   *The Empress*

Card 6   *The World*

Card 7   *The Star*

Card 8   *Queen of Swords*

Card 9   *5 of Wands*

Card 10   *4 of Pentacles*

Without looking up these cards, and ignoring for the moment the five Major Arcana, which we've already mentioned, what do we see here? There are two Royal Minor Arcana—the King of Cups and the Queen of Swords, which Lisa immediately "knew" were she and her husband. That leaves three Minor Arcana: the 3 of Pentacles, the 5 of Wands, and the 4 of Pentacles. Two Pentacles and one Wand. Take these cards out and put them into this spread, if you want, and see what it looks like to you.

Now, what are the Major Arcana in this spread? The Sun, the High Priestess, the Empress, the World, and the Star. Even without looking up these cards' meanings, we can just feel the positive feminine energy this reading has. Lisa knows it's got good energy just from looking at it!

Now, It's Your Turn

But you don't want to look at Lisa's reading, do you? You want to do one of your own. So shuffle the cards and lay them out, using the Celtic Cross form we provided earlier. If you already did a Celtic Cross Spread in the earlier section, "Feeling the Synergy of Card Combinations," you can use those cards for this exercise. But if you want to do another, you may be surprised to see how closely it resembles that first spread. Either way, record the cards you choose here.

Your Celtic Cross Spread

Name:_____

Date:_____

Question: "What's happening?"

Card 1   _____

Card 2   _____

Card 3   _____

Card 4   _____

Card 5   _____

Card 6   _____

Card 7   _____

Card 8   _____

Card 9   _____

Card 10   _____

Now, look at these cards. What do you notice?

➤ Are there a lot of Major Arcana cards?

➤ Are there more of a certain suit or number?

➤ What about the pictures themselves?

➤ Are there a lot of men, or women?

➤ Do certain pictures or shapes occur more than once?

➤ Does there seem to be a pattern of harmony, or of conflict?

After you've spent some time contemplating the cards, go ahead and look up what we have to say about them later in these pages. You may very well find that it's not so very far from what you already knew yourself!

Start Your Own Tarot Journal

Keeping track of Tarot spreads is as important as the spreads themselves. Writing them down means you won't lose any of the spreads you have. Even Cancers like Lisa can't commit that many cards to memory, after all.

Where do you want to record your Tarot journal? You can choose whatever book you want, from a spiral notebook to that pretty journal you got for Christmas. A word of warning about those pretty journals, though: You may be hesitant to write in them. At one time, Lisa had seven or eight of them people had given her, and she hadn't written a word in any of them—and she's a writer!

Then she realized she thought they were too perfect to mess up with her terrible handwriting, half-formed thoughts, scribbled notes and ideas, so she was leaving them all unused and empty. That's when Lisa decided to assign them each a use: one for her dream journal, one for her Tarot journal, another for her car journal (if you see Lisa driving toward you with a notebook balanced on her steering wheel, take cover!), one for her idea journal, and so on. These books weren't any more "perfect" than what Lisa had to put in them, and when she allowed them to be what they were, they became valued companions instead of pretty things that couldn't be touched.

Spinning the Wheel of Fortune

Get creative with your Tarot journal. Make it a picture journal! Photocopy your spreads and collect them in a three-ring binder, or draw the cards in your journal. (You might want to write down the name of the card, too, especially if you're no Picasso!)

Keeping Track of the Cards

You don't have to use pretty books; an 8 × 11-inch sheet of paper, with the date and time you did the reading, your question, and a line for each card, is fine. You can make 40 or 50 copies of the form we have here and then save your recorded readings in a spiral notebook. You can even set up a database in your computer and record your daily cards there. You can use any format you want, in other words, but be sure to save each reading as you do it.

When you return to look at these spreads three, or six, months later, you'll find that the cards say much more than you first realized or imagined. Saving a page for each reading provides a visual record and assists your memory—which has enough to remember, after all. With your journal in front of you, you can pull the cards out again and see what they have to say to you now. When you record every spread you do in some form you're sure to learn a great deal when you look back, and you'll be recording your own history in the process.

Daily Tarot Reading

Date: _____

Question: _____?

Card 1 _____

Card 2 _____

Card 3 _____

Thoughts: _____

_____

_____

_____

_____

_____

_____

_____

_____

_____

_____

_____

_____

_____

Recognizing Patterns

One of the things you should record in your "Thoughts" section for each daily reading is what's going on that day. Do you have a doctor's appointment? Are you behind in your bills? Did your daughter bring home a straight-A report card? Was your Christmas bonus much bigger (or smaller) than you'd been expecting? Just scribbling down a few words about what's going on will bring the emotions you were feeling at the time of the reading back for you—and, with the perspective of three or six months, you'll begin to see a pattern to which cards appear when you're feeling certain things.

At the same time, when you look back at readings you did over a period of time, you'll begin to notice that certain cards seem to recur much more often than others. One of us, for example, seems to have a lot of Queens show up, which she attributes to all the positive feminine energy of her co-authors, her book producer at Amaranth, and her friends.

If a certain Major Arcana card appears frequently, whether upright or reversed, remember what we said in Chapter 5: That card represents a lesson you need to learn. If the card is upright, you're doing just fine, but if it's reversed, it could be that you're resisting its message—or the messenger.

Practice, Practice, Practice

We'd like to close this chapter with a little story. This one is about Lisa and her husband Bob, who's a very talented guitarist. Now Bob's always claimed that the reason he's such a good guitarist is "practice, practice, practice." He supports this claim by doing just that, practicing every day.

Lisa says he wouldn't have practiced in the first place if he didn't have some innate talent for the guitar before he ever began. She supports her claim by pointing out that his mother's a concert and jazz pianist, his brother also plays guitar, and his grandfather died as he was getting his bass out of his trunk—at age 70-something.

This particular discussion has been going on for years—Lisa and Bob love "arguing" about it, and whenever something comes along that seems to support one or the other position, they start it up all over again. But the truth is, they're both right. Bob wouldn't be such a good guitar player if he didn't practice every day. But he wouldn't have picked up a guitar if he didn't have that innate talent.

In the same way, lots of Arlene's students ask her if they'll ever be as good a reader as Arlene is. Arlene always tells them, "You might be even better." Because Arlene knows that as much as any of us practice, some of us are natural Tarot readers and some of us are natural guitar players (some of us may be both!). You can be a good Tarot reader, with practice—and some of you will be great ones, if you've got that innate Tarot talent. Time—and practice—will tell.

The Least You Need to Know

➤ Think of your Tarot deck as a friend you want to take care of.

➤ Objectivity for yourself and for others is key in any Tarot reading.

➤ A reversed card can mean you're resisting that card's lesson. You designate reversed cards with an "R," as in 3 of Pentacles R.

➤ Record your Tarot spreads in a daily journal so you can go back to them again and again.

➤ Practicing with your Tarot cards can help make you a better reader.

Part 3
The Major Arcana: A Fool for the World

The Tarot cards themselves are divided into 22 Major Arcana cards and 56 Minor Arcana cards. By the time you've traveled through the 22 Major Arcana cards, you've completed a journey from beginning (the Fool) to end (the World), and encountered both the best and worst of life in the process.

Chapter 7

Don't Be an Idiot, Be a Fool

In This Chapter

➤ The Major Arcana cards

➤ The significance of lots of Major Arcana in a reading

➤ Some Major Arcana in combination

➤ Destiny versus Free Will: Who's in charge here?

Where are you in your journey of life? From those first baby steps to the wisdom of maturity, every day of life is a celebration, and we find ourselves participants in an arc of experience. As Muhammad Ali (The Greatest!) once said, "The man who views the world at 50 the same as he did at 20 has wasted 30 years of his life."

The *Major Arcana* cards of the Tarot deck are visual metaphors for each step in the experience of human life, for each lesson to be learned in a continual movement toward self-actualization. These cards represent your life's journey toward enlightenment and depict situations of major significance: Think of them as the many forks along your own particular road. How, when, and if these archetypal cards appear in a reading can show you where you are on life's highway, what you already know about life, and what you still have to learn.

Take the 22 Major Arcana cards out of your Tarot deck and examine their names. As you'll notice, these names alone, like the Emperor, the Empress, the Chariot, the Hermit, and the Tower, suggest ancient mysteries and myths. What do they have to do with you? Everything! These "mysteries" are as relevant today as they ever were!

Through the Universal Waite Deck, let's take a look at the pictures, symbols, colors, and numbers of each of the Major Arcana. Come along with us and enjoy the beauty, color, awakenings, and challenges of experience that we're sure to find.

The Fool Looks for Signposts of Experience

Sometimes, just realizing that we don't know everything or understand everything there is to know and understand about life can open us up to whole new worlds and ways of thinking and growing. As the Fool (key 0) sets off to learn about the World (key 21), he's full of confidence and anticipation—but it's clear he's not the most practical observer. Ah, youth! This guy's not afraid of falling into the valley beneath him, or even aware that there might be any danger at all. He's dazzled by the strong light of the Sun (key 19).

Little by little, as we grow older and accumulate experience, we learn life's lessons and achieve the compassion and empathy we need to guide others. The strong light of the Sun enters our souls and we become the shining signposts for the youth who stands bedazzled on the mountain crag, poised to fly and fall—that is, if we're willing to fully experience the journey of life ourselves. We can be wise guides if we dare to challenge our notion of ourselves, to question the ways of the world, to push the envelope of what we know, to face life's darker side (both in ourselves and in others), to tear it all down and build it all up again.

THE FOOL .

THE MAGICIAN.

THE SUN .

From 0 to 21

The path of life is indeed exciting, and the Major Arcana's archetypes contain a variety of metaphors for unlocking it. Whether you think of it as the Yellow Brick Road or Luke Skywalker's odyssey through space (move over Homer!), a metaphor can help you better understand your own travels. We'd like to take you on a tour of the Major Arcana, following a progression of Jungian archetypal signposts.

The Fool, key 0. Here's where the journey begins, with the Divine Child archetype. In this myth, an infant, such as the Baby Jesus, is sent by God to enlighten the human race.

The Magician, key 1. Here's where the Fool discovers his creativity and talent for using various tools to achieve his goals. The Jungian archetype for the Magician is the Trickster, such as the Native American coyote.

The High Priestess, key 2. While the Magician can control the material world, there's another world out there—the hidden, intuitive side of everything. The High Priestess sits between logic and spirit, and is associated with the Jungian archetype of the Wise Woman, such as Grandmother Spider in Navajo myth.

The Empress, key 3. Now that he's learned about his own two sides, the Fool meets the first of the parental archetypes. The Empress represents the Earth Mother, and so fertility, healing, feeling, and giving. According to Jungian theory, the Empress is the anima, or the feminine side of the self.

THE EMPEROR.

The Emperor, key 4. *Just as the Empress is the feminine, the Emperor represents the masculine side of each of us, the animus. This card is about responsibility, authority, and reason—all ideas we associate with a father figure. Picture Hamlet's father, the king of Denmark, from the famous Shakespearean tragedy.*

THE HIEROPHANT

The Hierophant, key 5. *Societies larger traditional values are represented by the Hierophant, sometimes called the Pope. Jungian psychologists assign the archetype of the persona to this card, the social mask we all wear when we are out in the world. This concept is also associated with your astrological ascendant, or rising sign. For example, if you're Libra rising, the "mask" you wear for the world will have a Libran balance and sense of diplomacy.*

THE LOVERS.

The Lovers, key 6. *It's time for the Fool to learn about sex! The Lovers represent Yin and Yang, attraction, desire, and romance. There are a variety of archetypal equivalents for this card, including Romeo and Juliet and Tristan and Isolde. Mythological lovers are often fated to heartache because even love is not without its difficulties, as we all know.*

THE CHARIOT.

The Chariot, key 7. *Here's where the Fool encounters the two sides of any issue, and learns about compromise and balancing conflicting forces. In Jungian terms, the Chariot represents the struggle between light and shadow. We all possess Luke Skywalker's heroic goodness, for example, but Luke's shadow, Darth Vader, lives buried in our hearts as well.*

Strength, key 8. *After encountering his dark side, the Fool needs to learn to trust himself and to develop self-confidence. This card can be equated with the Jungian hero or heroine, the mythological self.*

The Hermit, key 9. It's the Fool, but instead of looking skyward while he walks toward a cliff, he's looking inward, where he'll learn about the benefits of meditation and reflection. The archetypal equivalent here is The Wise Old Man, or Star Wars' *Obi-wan Kenobi.*

The Wheel of Fortune, key 10. *Having completed the personal aspects of his journey, the Fool now encounters the outside forces associated with it. The Wheel of Fortune is all about destiny, the things of life that are beyond his control. Remember the saying, "God grant me the courage to change the things I can, the serenity to accept the things I can't, and the wisdom to know the difference."*

Justice, key 11. Some aspects of life may seem beyond the Fool's control, but at the same time, justice does prevail. This card is about learning our lessons, being rewarded for the good that we do, and punished for the evil.

THE HANGED MAN.

The Hanged Man, key 12. Hanging by a thread, the Hanged Man is learning the lessons of letting go, of not being ruled by the material or the mundane. Here's the Fool searching for spiritual enlightenment and psychic revelation.

DEATH.

Death, key 13. Here's one of the hardest lessons the Fool must face—the knowledge of his own mortality. But this is also where he will learn that death is not an ending but a beginning, and that new things cannot be started without old ones coming to an end.

TEMPERANCE.

Temperance, key 14. With transformation come the lessons of moderation and perspective. Temperance is all about tolerating differences, learning patience, and waiting rather than rushing in head-first.

THE DEVIL.

The Devil, key 15. Even with all his newfound knowledge, the Fool continues to harbor internal demons, petty things that could undermine his existence, such as obsessions, doubts, or impulsiveness. This card is to remind us once again of our shadow side, and the evil we can do to ourselves.

The Tower, key 16.
Without warning, lightning can strike, and the Tower serves to remind us that sometimes change can come out of the blue. Sometimes it's change for the good, and sometimes it can be more difficult. Here's a wonderful haiku that puts the Tower into perspective:

> *Until I lost my rooftop*
> *I could not see how*
> *The Moon floats along the sky.*

The Star, key 17. *The last five Major Arcana cards can be found in the heavens, and, as the haiku of the previous card reminds us, there's always hope no matter how dark the road may seem. The Star represents that hope, courage, and inspiration will bring the promise of better days to come.*

The Moon, key 18.
By the light of the Moon, things aren't always what they seem. The Moon reminds us that illusions and hidden forces can obscure what's really happening. But this card also represents our psychic, imaginative side, the Pisces in us all.

The Sun, key 19. *The darkest hour is just before dawn, and in the light of the Sun, the Fool has come out of that darkness into a new awareness and strength. He is revitalized by the power of life's journey and at his strongest, ready to shine.*

Judgement, key 20. Archetypally, Judgement means resurrection, the rebirth that comes with spiritual awareness. Arriving at this step on his journey, the Fool understands the possibilities of transformation that can come with change. The Fool reaches for enlightenment.

The World, key 21. At the end his journey, the Fool has achieved wholeness and understands his place in the world. This is the card of achievement and success, where the Fool understands that there is much more to life than himself and his own journey. He is ready to begin again on a new cycle of learning: the process of reincarnation from the world of experience to the innocence once again of the Fool.

Where Are You on the Journey?

We asked a friend to take the Major Arcana cards, mix them around and shuffle them well, separating the cards into three piles. Then we asked her to pick three cards that would indicate where she stood on the Fool's journey. Here's what came up: the Hanged Man (key 12), Justice (key 11), and the Fool (key 0). Then we asked her to pick another card to represent her current challenge: Death (key 13) reversed.

Like the Hanged Man, our friend is in a state of questioning everything, barely hanging on to the old order of things. With the exuberance of the Fool, she needs to trust her intuition and let go—with the assurance that Justice will prevail and she won't fall on her head! She needs to resist the temptation to fight against the rebirth that will come if she has the courage to let go and allow herself, and her life, to change. Notice the numbers of her cards: 11, 12, 13, with a return to 0 for a little bit of courage of heart to keep moving on the path, and to find the new beginning that awaits her.

Try this exercise yourself. Record the cards in the space below.

Your Current Signposts

Card 1 _____

Card 2 _____

Card 3 _____

Your challenge _____

_____

_____

What do the cards tell you about your position on the Fool's journey?

THE HANGED MAN.

JUSTICE.

THE FOOL.

DEATH.

The Universal Mysteries of Life

Life. Death. Sex. Violence. Rock 'n' roll. (Well, maybe not rock 'n' roll.) But certain things in life remain mysteries despite science's greatest efforts to explain them. But are they really "mysteries"? Let's look at a few of them from a mythological point of view and see if they begin to make a little more sense:

➤ *Birth.* We've seen those *Life* magazine pictures, too: The mystery of birth revealed in living color! But do we *really* understand how a little fun on Saturday night can lead to a little bundle of joy nine months later? If you've ever been present at any birth—whether an animal's or a human's—you probably use the word "miracle" to describe this event.

Being born is a lot like the Fool beginning his journey—we arrive innocent, with clean slates, waiting for our lives to write our lessons. Myths from Adam and Eve to the birth of Venus on a half-shell explore this innocence, too, helping to demystify this particular mystery.

➤ *Death.* Yup, that horseman of the Apocalypse. That nasty skeletal face you can just make out under that black cowl—the grim reaper. The black-armored skeleton on a white horse at key 13(!) of the Tarot deck. All these images and ideas share a common theme—that after we die, we go somewhere else.

Now, sure, science can't "prove" that. And yet every great religion—both modern and ancient—insists that this is so. Some call it "heaven" and some call it "Valhalla," but the fact remains that our myths provide an "answer" to death's mystery; namely, that it's not an end, but a beginning.

➤ *The Unexplained.* Why did Harry meet Sally, anyway? Why did John F. Kennedy meet his destiny in Dallas on November 22, 1963? Myths incorporate the unexpected under various names, most often something like the Fates of Greek mythology. Now, meet the Tower (key 16) in the Tarot deck, and expect the unexpected. Or read the Warren Commission report, and get bogged down in contradictions.

As you can see, while science is still trying to answer these mysteries, our myths explained them a long time ago. We think Tarot can help, too. Its images, after all, are rooted in these very myths.

In the Cards

Joseph Campbell (1904–1987), the master of comparative mythology, showed how seemingly unconnected societies share the same mythological motifs. There are "creation stories," such as the one at the beginning of the Judeo-Christian Genesis and the Navajo story of how The People came up from The World Below. There are flood myths, like that of Noah in the Bible, and of Pyrrha and Deucalion in Greek tradition. It's written in Ecclesiastes that "There's nothing new under the Sun," and when we look at the myths of various peoples, we find that this is definitely true.

What Do a Lot of Major Arcana Cards in Your Reading Mean?

As we discovered in Chapter 6, when a lot of Major Arcana cards show up in a reading, much of what's going on is fated to happen, whether you work with it or not. A reading with many Major Arcana cards infers that the answer to the question at hand is not under your, the seeker's, control. Instead, many other surrounding circumstances are affecting its outcome.

When this happens, you really can't change what's already in motion, because the cards reflect a process that has already started before you even asked. In other words, the wheels are in motion, so you're just gonna have to go along for the ride!

The particular Major Arcana that show up are the particular lessons you're learning about the question at hand. Major Arcana tell you that there's something going on that you need to pay attention to—even though you won't be able to control the whole outcome. In fact, the outcome is usually in someone else's hands, such as the court case you'll read about next.

**Spinning the Wheel
of Fortune**

Upright, a Major Arcana card shows that you've been successfully mastering the card's particular lesson; you're ready to accept it. Reversed, the lesson is meeting resistance, and so setbacks, delays, or other difficulties may be occurring.

The Major Arcana in Combination with Minor Arcana Cards

When you look at a Tarot spread, you should look at the whole spread, because meanings of cards can change depending on the surrounding cards. If Temperance R is next to Judgement, for example, you may be impatient for the answer you're waiting for. Here are two spreads with Major Arcana in combination for you to contemplate.

How Will My Court Case Go?

Here's an example of how Major Arcana in combination can reveal an outcome that's not in your hands. "Flo" came to Arlene and asked how her court case would come out. This was after the judge and jury had already been picked, and Flo and the lawyers were already going to court.

Who are all those Major Arcana? Well first, there's the obvious Justice card. Then we've got the Emperor, the authority figure; the Chariot, representing compromise; the Star, the card of the Querent's hopes for this case; and the Sun R, representing partial success.

Now clearly, this case was already up to others before Flo posed her question to Arlene. Ultimately the jury and the judge would make the decision in this drama. In the end, Flo came out pretty well—she didn't get any jail time, though she was required to perform community service and pay a fine. This is precisely what the lessons of the combined Major Arcana showed when Flo came to Arlene for her reading!

Celtic Cross
for Flo's Court Case:
"How Will My Case Go?"

Card 1   Ace of Wands R

Card 2   Page of Swords

Card 3   Justice

Card 4   10 of Swords

Card 5   The Emperor

Card 6   The Chariot

Card 7   The Star

Card 8   The Sun R

Card 9   8 of Cups

Card 10   6 of Pentacles R

Will I Have a Baby?

Here's another example of Major Arcana in combination. "Mary" was told by her physician that she might never get pregnant because of very low fertility, but Mary and her spouse wanted to continue to try to conceive without using drugs or any other artificial means. Mary's question: "Will I get pregnant within a year?"

Not only do the Major Arcana clearly answer Mary's question, but the Minor Arcana get into the picture as well. Look at those three royal Wands: the Queen (Mary), the King (her husband), and the Page (a child!). And the Major Arcana here conspire for a resounding answer: the Moon R (confusion ends); the Fool (a baby) + the World (culmination); Judgement R (the authorities are wrong); and the Lovers—clearly the happy parents!

In answer to your question, yes, she had a baby! This couple had been married for ten years. In the eleventh year, the child arrived.

Celtic Cross for Mary:
"Will I get pregnant?"

Card 1   5 of Swords

Card 2   Page of Wands

Card 3   6 of Cups

Card 4   The Moon R

Card 5   Queen of Wands

Card 6   King of Wands

Card 7   The Fool

Card 8   The World

Card 9   Judgement R

Card 10   The Lovers

Destiny Versus Free Will

Looking at the previous two sample spreads, you're probably wondering who's in charge here? Whatever happened to the idea of Free Will? Don't we have *any* control over our destinies?

Of course we do, and when we talk about the Minor Arcana cards, you'll see how those choices are shown in the cards. Some things, though, are *karmic lessons* we're destined to learn, and, although we have choices about whether we learn these lessons the easy way or the hard, we're going to learn them no matter what.

Fools Rush In

You can run, but you can't hide! When something is destined to happen in your life, no matter how hard you try to avoid or deny it, it's going to happen anyway.

Travelers on the Road of Life

We're all travelers on the road of life, just like our archetypal counterparts Luke Skywalker, Dorothy, and the Fool. The journey the Major Arcana illustrate is nothing to be afraid of; no matter what shows up, you can handle it!

As we discussed in Chapter 6, a reversed card doesn't necessarily equal a reversed meaning. Major Arcana represent your life lessons—and if a card appears reversed, it could be because you're resisting that particular lesson.

Until you learn that lesson, in fact, that card will show up again and again. Sometimes it will be upright—"Ah, you're really trying," it says. Then it will appear again, reversed—"Fighting your lesson again, aren't you?" Both of us seem to get Temperance pretty regularly when we're waiting for a situation that's out of our control to resolve itself. "Patience," it says, "patience." If only we could actually learn that lesson!

So, if the Devil appears in your spread, upright or reversed, don't worry. The Devil's a lesson you'll learn as you travel along the road of your life. Pay attention to what that card has to say, and soon you'll be the Star!

The Least You Need to Know

➤ The Major Arcana cards reveal the things that are destined to happen in your life.

➤ The Major Arcana cards show how events that are already in motion will play out.

➤ The Major Arcana cards reveal the lessons you must learn in your life.

➤ A lot of Major Arcana in a reading mean the outcome of a situation is not in your hands.

➤ Each Major Arcana card is a step along the journey of your life.

Setting Off on the Life Path

As any Fool knows, all enterprises and/or adventures require a beginning, and the first six Major Arcana cards depict all the things that can happen whenever we start anything new. Whether it's the spontaneity of the Fool or the constraint of the Hierophant, though, the lesson of each card will be what you make of it.

At last—it's time to set off on the life path of the cards themselves! First Lady Hillary Clinton wrote that "it takes a village to raise a child." In this chapter, we'll learn about the Major Arcana cards that nurture and guide the Fool in those crucial early years of childhood development.

Let the Cards Tell You What They Mean

We've provided you with keywords and archetypal characters for each card, but we encourage you to let each card "tell" you what it means as well. Here's a *meditation exercise* for you to do just that.

Before you read about each card, find that card in your deck, and place it in front of you. Don't even look at the keywords or archetypes we provide. Instead, just look at the picture. What do you see? Consider any or all of the following:

Card Catalog

Meditation exercises are ways of helping us to use more than our logical, analytical left brains to look at things. Looking at Tarot cards without preconceived ideas and allowing the images to "tell" us what they mean is one such exercise.

➤ Colors

➤ Figures (both human and animal)

➤ Shapes

➤ Landscape

➤ Vegetation

➤ Heavenly bodies

➤ Symbols

Write down what each card seems to be showing you. Only then should you go on to read what we say about it. We bet you'll be pleasantly surprised when you find just how in tune your own High Priestess is—before you even read a word!

The Fool (Key 0): The Open Mind of Innocence

The Fool (key 0).

Your initial reactions to the Fool:

_____

_____

Keywords: Beginnings

Innocence

Naiveté

Look before you leap!

Archetypes: Toto

R2D2 and C3PO

Charlie Brown (especially when Lucy's holding the football for him)

"A Babe in the Woods"

Upright Imagery: A carefree young man in yellow boots and a flowing tunic looks up at the bright yellow sky, about to step off a cliff. In his left hand, he carries a white rose; in his right, a satchel on a pole. His little dog dances at his feet, just as happy, carefree—and unaware—as he is.

Upright Meanings: What you do with this particular adventure, whether it be life, a new job, or a new relationship, is up to you. You're entering into the situation with excitement and childlike wonder: The Fool is full of optimism, hope, and the freedom to explore without any preconceived notions. Upright, this card means a fresh start, a clean slate, and a wonderful beginning.

Reversed Imagery and Meanings: When we look at the Fool reversed, we see the same desire to seek new freedoms, start new beginnings in life, and explore different horizons, but reversed, the journey could be unsatisfying, or fraught with "foolhardy" actions. Look at the imagery in this reversed position: Upside down, the satchel will lose all of its contents, the rose will fall out of the Fool's hand, and the sun is setting instead of rising. This Fool looks like he'll fall off the cliff head-first. And the little dog, poor pup, can't help his master, because he's falling along with him!

Spinning the Wheel of Fortune

Reversed cards don't necessarily mean the opposite of upright ones. A reversed card can indicate delays, more difficulties than expected, or a lesson that needs to be worked on. The reversed card reminds you that you'll grapple with this particular lesson again and again—until you get it right. "If at first you don't succeed, try, try again!"

The Fool reversed can represent that the path you're now on will have delays and troubles, or that you'll make unwise choices along the way. Foolhardy or thoughtless actions can lead to unsatisfactory experiences, and wanting freedom—or anything—too fast or too soon can mean you won't be able to handle what's coming into your life later on down the road.

103

The Magician (Key 1): Unleashing Your Creative Power

The Magician (key 1).

Your initial reactions to the Magician:

_____

_____

Keywords: Creative power

Manifestation

Turning an idea into reality

You already know the magic words!

Archetypes: The Wizard of Oz

Obi-wan Kenobi

Georgia O'Keefe

The artist in us all

Upright Imagery: The Magician stands with his wand pointing toward heaven and his left hand pointing toward earth. All the tools of his trade are on the table in front of him, and also represent the suits of the minor Arcana: the Cup, the Sword, the Wand, and the Pentacle. And, these are the same items he carried in his satchel as the Fool. Note, too, the figure eight, which represents the continuum that is life, and the red roses of passion and white lilies of thought that surround him.

Upright Meanings: The Magician represents our ability to create our own reality. Because of the Magician in all of us, we're able to turn ideas into something tangible, so the writer writes it down on paper (or inputs it into the computer!), the architect draws the design to build that new house, the artist paints the watercolor, the mathematician figures, or the musician sounds it out on her instrument.

Sometimes, the Magician comes up for someone who wishes to create a baby or find a new direction in life. This card always indicates that something great is developing, because something is being created. Ask and you shall receive.

Reversed Imagery and Meanings: Turned upside down, all the Magician's tools fall off the table, which leads to scattered ability and inadequate use of talent. Your Mom might say, "You can do better than that!", and she's right. The reversed Magician indicates that your ability lies hidden, and that you're not using your hidden talent— or not using a talent that's visible, either. At the same time, the roses and lilies can't grow as well upside down, and the Magician's wand is pointed down instead of up, indicating wrong use of power.

With nothing to hold them to the Magician's table, the Cup (imagination), the Sword (ideas), the Wand (enthusiasm), and the Pentacle (hardware) all fall down. The Magician is upside down as well. Like any of us, he can't get much done standing on his head. This means that you haven't yet realized your full potential. Sometimes, the Magician reversed can describe a situation that's not developing correctly, or one where there's a lack of enthusiasm for following through on the original idea. This card may also show up reversed to describe mediocre workmanship.

The High Priestess (Key 2): Trusting Your Own Intuition

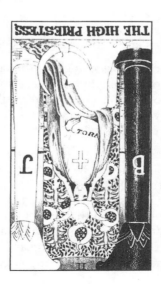

The High Priestess (key 2).

Your initial reactions to the High Priestess:

_____

_____

Keywords: Intuition

Developing your psychic skills

The sixth sense

Go with your gut!

Archetypes: Glinda, the Good Witch

Yoda

Shirley MacLaine

Your psychic self

Upright Imagery: Sitting between the pillars of Boas and Joachin with pomegranates and palms on her silkscreen, the High Priestess represents the world of the unseen and the mystery of what's "behind the veil." She holds out toward you the Torah of Divine Law, representing truth, half-hidden and half-exposed to your view. The crescent moon at her feet and the full and crescent moons on her crown represent the power and the ability of your own intuition: Through your third eye (the High Priestess), you can know more than what's visible to your other two. The High Priestess represents the lesson of psychic development at its beginning stages.

Upright Meanings: The High Priestess comes into a reading to get you to open up your intuition and feel energy being sent or received in ways in which you may not be accustomed. The High Priestess reminds us about our own ability to see beneath the surface of what's happening around us. She's the psychic intuition within each of us, neither male nor female, nor left brain or right brain; the High Priestess is simply the part of you that at some level knows the answer to your own question.

The High Priestess uses psychic insight to get to that answer instead of what we Westerners might call "rational thought." If you're doing too much analyzing, or are too emotionally attached to an issue, chances are you're not using your High Priestess energy. This card is telling you to listen to yourself, because the High Priestess just knows—and so do you, if you listen to her.

Reversed Imagery and Meanings: Reversed, the High Priestess creates an image of confused psychic energy. Now she can be less than honest about the information she's about to give you because the pillars are on the opposite sides of the card. Sometimes students of the Tarot see these reversed pillars and feel that the black pillar is more dominant or ominous in this position than when it's on the left. In any event, the High Priestess reversed can't give accurate information; instead, information may be delayed or, worse, because the Torah is dropping away from her, the truth leaves her entirely, so that what you see may not be what you get.

Superstitious, cautious, and not very trusting, the High Priestess reversed represents that things are not right or not accurate. Here, she teaches us that all that "appears" may or not be true or real: There's more to this than meets the eye. So be cautious when you get the High Priestess reversed; she has the power to manipulate psychic energy toward personal gain—and not necessarily your own.

In the Cards

The High Priestess is the first incarnation of the goddess figure in the Tarot. You'll find this imagery again in cards like the Lovers, the Star, and the Moon. Here, the goddess is represented in a practical way, as the beginning of your connection to your higher self.

The Empress (Key 3): Abundance and Fertility (i.e., Mom)

The Empress (key 3).

Your initial reactions to the Empress:

_____

_____

107

Keywords:	Abundance
	Fertility
	Nurturing
	Your garden runneth over!
Archetypes:	Aunt Em
	Princess Leia
	Mother Teresa
	Your Mom

Upright Imagery: The Empress sits on her cushioned chair with a scepter in her hand. Her crown of twelve stars represents the twelve signs of the zodiac, and Venus, the planet of affection and love, is represented in her heart-shaped shield. The Empress is surrounded by wheat, trees, and all that Mother Nature has to offer. She's clearly content and ready to bring forth abundance, new life, and prosperity.

Upright Meanings: Happiness to come! From her chair, the Empress assures that she can be of help and service to the earth and humankind. The archetypal Earth Mother, she represents fertility to would-be parents, a happy home and marriage to couples, and contentment with life to all. The Empress brings comfort and a peaceful lifestyle, along with the help of supportive women and the nourishment in all its forms they can bring.

When the Empress appears upright, it can mean a cycle of prosperity is about to begin. This could mean a new home or new conditions in the home that are peaceful and filled with an abundance of the good things in life. The Empress indicates good resources from the land and agriculture. It's harvest time!

Reversed Imagery and Meanings: Reversed, the Empress sits decidedly uncomfortably in the same field. Nearly earthbound, the power of her scepter is no longer strong, and growth and development have stopped. When this card appears reversed the lesson may be one of poverty or a lack of security. The heart-shaped shield of Venus is not as prominent and hence has less power.

A reversed Empress can indicate infertility, or that the home or environment is lacking in some way. There may be a troubled home or marriage, inadequate resources, low income, environmental pollution, or contaminated land or environment. This card could mean a bad year for the farmer, a loss in the family, or a lack of understanding between family members. Dissatisfaction with the family or a dysfunctional family could also be indicated. The lesson here may be to pay more attention to one's home life before it becomes a problem.

The Emperor (Key 4): Authority (i.e., Dad)

The Emperor (key 4).

Your initial reactions to the Emperor:

_____

_____

Keywords: Leadership

Problem solving

Male energy

Logic

Strategic planning

Archetypes: The President (of the United States, or of anything)

Your doctor

Colin Powell

Your Dad

Upright Imagery: The regal Emperor sits on his throne wearing the emblems of war (rams' heads and the planet Mars), with the Egyptian *ankh* in his right hand and the globe of dominion in his left. Everything about this card suggests power and authority, from his determined visage to his suit of

Card Catalog

The Egyptian *ankh* (shown above in The Emperor's right hand) is an ancient symbol of wisdom.

armor. Behind him are mountains—pillars of strength—and his red robes and purple throne are the colors reserved for royalty.

Upright Meanings: The Emperor dominates the patriarchal world and is the active father archetype (the Empress is the active mother archetype). When the Emperor shows up in your cards, he represents the need to develop leadership, and the lesson of using good logic and reasoning ability. The Emperor is a thinker, a problem solver, and analyzer. He leads the organization or groups into whatever confrontations may be necessary for their own good.

When the Emperor shows up, you'll learn to develop your leadership skills and the masculine side of your nature. This card gives you the power to use logic and reasoning well, and to receive good counsel and advice. The Emperor upright means you can use your authority to gain positive recognition and are learning to develop your powers.

This card may predict government connections or authority figures you'll need to deal with, whether it's your boss, your doctor, the president, or your father. Women will come up with this card as well as men, because don't we all have to master our ability to lead, govern, or analyze situations? Concrete knowledge is as essential a tool as the nurturing the Empress provides.

Reversed Imagery and Meanings: The reversed Emperor is falling from his place of comfort and can't hold on to the position any longer. When you turn the card over, you can see how the armor on his legs is more evident, and with good reason—he's much more cautious now, more guarded and careful.

This card can indicate immaturity in dealing with positions of power, or with being dictatorial because of a fear of losing power or of being out of control. The Emperor reversed is emotional rather than logical and is not always following his head. Character can become weak here (or at the very least, timid) in the face of problems. A lack of leadership, abusive conditions, or the feeling of being put in a very uncomfortable situation may be present. The Emperor reversed is cautioning you to take a careful look at things to make sure you're safe before proceeding.

The Hierophant (Key 5): The Lure of Conformity

The Hierophant (key 5).

Your initial reactions to the Hierophant:

_____

_____

Keywords: Conventional wisdom

              Conformity

              Traditions

              Don't rock the boat!

Archetypes: The Empire

              Kansas

              The Pope

              Public education

Upright Imagery: The Hierophant (or Pope) sits in an attitude of blessing the two priests kneeling at his feet. The crossed keys between the priests represent the kingdom of heaven and earth in communion. Note, too, the gold of his mitre, or triple crown (the kingdom of heaven), and the red of his sacred vestment, or robe (the kingdom of earth). The vestment's white trim symbolizes the purity of God, while the triple cross in his left hand, the *crosier*, represents the Trinity.

Upright Meanings: The Hierophant is the educator or the rabbi, who teaches the tribes one common language so all can communicate. He also teaches a common way to deal with philosophy and religious practices. The main idea of the Hierophant upright is to connect the masses through one common language, religion, or even one common denomination of money for trade.

Card Catalog

In the Roman Catholic Church, the *crosier* can be traced back to the walking staffs used by the twelve apostles. Ancient Roman astronomers also used staffs similar to those carried by bishops of the early Church.

Fools Rush In

If you've ever stood in line for your driver's license, waited in your doctor's lobby, or argued with your parents or your children about anything, you've confronted the Hierophant we all must deal with in our day-to-day lives. What this card is trying to tell you is that it does no good to butt your head against authority—it's there for a reason. Remember, father knows best!

At the same time, this card represents the need for social approval. If this card appears in your reading, you're learning how to conform to a given situation, whether it's the ways of the present society or culture you live in, or living with conventional ideas. Marriage, public education, and traditional medicine are all ruled by the Hierophant upright, too. We do a lot of things in life to be accepted by others and so we all get to learn how to be conventional at different times in our lives. What's good for the whole is good for you, this card says—sometimes, whether you like it or not!

Reversed Imagery and Meanings: How does the Hierophant feel to you when you put him upside down? Feelings of the card are very important. Suddenly, the two priests are at the top of the card. Are they questioning the Hierophant and his authority? What are those upside-down "Y"s at the top of the card? Those were the priests' vestments when the card was upright. Is the Hierophant hanging by a thread?

The Hierophant reversed indicates unconventional behavior and unorthodox ideas—the flower child, the rebel, and the nonconformist. Non-traditional circumstances can be found when this card appears, as well as unconventional ways of going about your life. You may have a different focus than the rest of society. Non-traditional practices such as holistic medicine, metaphysical studies, and unconventional marriages or partnerships are also indicated by the Hierophant reversed. Are you bohemian? A rebel? A "defiant youth"? Or are you just going to the beat of your own drummer?

The Least You Need to Know

➤ The first Major Arcana cards represent your early life lessons.

➤ The Fool stands for the innocence of new beginnings and the start of your journey.

➤ The Magician represents the tools and creativity that will help you on your way as you aim to reach your full potential.

➤ The High Priestess gets you in touch with your intuitive side, your psychic power, and your hidden talents.

➤ The Empress is your mothering instincts; your nurturing, feminine side; and the abundance of nature.

➤ The Emperor represents your masculine, paternal instincts as well as power and authority.

➤ The Hierophant is about understanding the need for and conforming to social values. It's all about how you deal with authority.

Chapter 9

What Kind of Fool Are You?

In This Chapter

➤ The Lovers (key 6)

➤ The Chariot (key 7)

➤ Strength (key 8)

➤ The Hermit (key 9)

➤ The Wheel of Fortune (key 10)

➤ Justice (key 11)

There's a lot more involved in getting through life than those first baby steps—and there are a lot more issues to consider as well. We're faced with choices and decisions every day, and how we deal with those choices will help determine just what kinds of fools we are—and aren't.

The second six cards of the Major Arcana represent the many choices we all must make as we journey through our lives. From relationships (the Lovers), to reflection (the Hermit), to the vagaries of chance and society's rules (the Wheel of Fortune and Justice), this sequence of cards reminds us that learning can only come with experience. And that the best way to learn a lesson is sometimes to first make a mistake.

Gaining Knowledge Through Choice and Experience

As you did with the first six Arcana cards, look at these, one by one and, and see what you can see. What discoveries do you make in their colors and images?

The people in these six cards include lovers, strong men and women, and solitary men and women. There are also choices present, especially in the Wheel of Fortune card. This part of life's journey represents the choices we all must face as we gain more and more experience about our lives.

The Lovers (Key 6): Choices in the Garden of Eden

The Lovers (key 6).

Your initial reactions to the Lovers:

_____

_____

Keywords:	Choices offered
	Romance
	Inspiration
	Temptation
Archetypes:	Princess Leia and Han Solo
	Romeo and Juliet
	Jack and Rose (from *Titanic*)
	George and Mary Bailey (from *It's a Wonderful Life*)
	You and your soul mate

Upright Imagery: A nude woman and man stand beneath the arms of *Raphael, the angel of Air*, who gives them his blessing. Behind the woman is the Tree of Knowledge, and behind the man is a tree bearing the twelve signs of the zodiac. The man, who looks toward the woman, represents the conscious mind and reason. The woman represents the subconscious and emotion, and so it is she who can look up to the angel Raphael.

Upright Meanings: The Lovers card upright is about making choices in love and romance. With this card, there's always the possibility of a new romance or a new direction for the heart. The angel Raphael indicates inspiration from above, and so, love at all levels—spiritual, physical, and emotional.

This card also points toward harmony with others around you. Family and personal relations are very important to you, and you want all your relationships to be balanced and intimate. You may be trying to make choices and decisions for the highest good in your life. Or you may find new love, or the love of something new starting out in your life. The Lovers card is all about learning the ways of the heart, attraction, and the desire for cooperation.

Reversed Imagery and Meanings: When we turn the Lovers upside down, the mountain becomes prominent and seems to divide the couple, and so represents obstacles or division. The upside-down angel has no power to give the couple energy from above, and so the relationship is hard to develop. Consequently, you might find delays in attaining a desired result with someone or something you love.

This card may indicate indecision, or that you're making a choice that won't fulfill you. You may be involved in an unsatisfactory relationship. The lesson of the Lovers reversed is to learn how to make the right choices for where you are now in your life. Make sure you're ready for this; it could be a difficult or rocky beginning.

Card Catalog

Raphael, the angel of Air, is one of three archangels who appear in Tarot imagery. Thee others are *Michael, the angel of fire and the sun,* and *Gabriel, the angel of water.*

The Chariot (Key 7): Victory Through Adversity

The Chariot (key 7).

 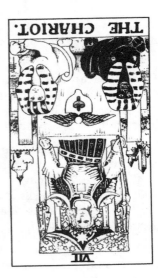

Your initial reactions to the Chariot:

_____

_____

Keywords: Success and conquest

Victory after hardship

Stamina

Good health

Archetypes: Luke Skywalker

John Wayne

Wonder Woman

"My hero!"

Upright Imagery: In this card, a prince rides in a chariot under a starry canopy, carrying his wand of will and authority, and is protected by celestial influence. The astrological symbols and celestial hieroglyphics indicate he has protection from above, but he must use his own will and fortitude to win the day. The black and white sphinxes represent the negative and positive energies that are in the world, and the charioteer has control over them for now. But notice there are no reins: His control comes from his stamina and focus on the goal at hand.

Upright Meanings: The upright Chariot indicates success and victory through hard work and effort, and triumph over enemies of any kind. When this card appears in a reading, it shows you have a responsible and kind nature but may be very intensely focused on your goal and concentrating on victory. You have the perseverance to maintain focus and the inner strength to achieve the desired success.

This card often comes up in relation to travel. After the journey, the hero, like Homer's Odysseus, is welcomed home safe and sound. Excellent health and the ability to overcome adversaries are also indicated when the Chariot appears upright.

Reversed Imagery and Meanings: When the Chariot appears reversed in a reading, you may have difficulty maintaining focus and stamina. Perhaps you're too weak to fight or feel like just giving up. Maybe the battle has been too long and too hard, and you're finding it tough to stick with the program. Sometimes, the Chariot reversed can represent poor health or a lack of vigor, or mentally giving up the fight. You may feel at loose ends, as if you can't find your way out of the situation.

Despite the desire for change, there's just too much that overwhelms the Chariot reversed. But take heart: "Tomorrow is another day." Rest, recuperate, and regroup before you go out to fight this one again. Once you relax, you'll be better equipped to decide if the battle is worth it. So stay calm and retreat, give yourself time to think about further action, and the Chariot will soon be traveling forward again.

In the Cards

We all must struggle to control the light and dark in our own natures. Jung called this the "balance of shadow and light," and the Chariot, in both its upright and reversed positions, illustrates this principle beautifully. Even the black and white pillars you see in this card represent this idea.

Strength (Key 8): Learning Fortitude and Compassion

Strength (key 8).

Your initial reactions to Strength:

_____

_____

Keywords:	Love wins over hate
	Unconditional love
	Calmness
	Compassion
Archetypes:	The Cowardly Lion
	Chewbacca
	Indira Ghandi
	Your best friend

Upright Imagery: The woman of Strength has flowers in her hair and around her waist. Calmly, she closes the lion's mouth, and actually seems to be petting him. This card is showing us unconditional love and spiritual courage by teaching us how to face our fears. The lion represents our fears of the unknown or anything that's wild to us. The cosmic figure eight above the woman's head (remember the one above the Magician's head in Chapter 8?) represents her confidence to calm a fear.

In the Cards

The Cowardly Lion as a symbol of Strength? Yes, we say, exactly. This card is all about overcoming fears to find the courage to face what may seem at first too frightening to consider. Does that sound like a lion we all know from our annual journeys down the Yellow Brick Road?

Upright Meanings: Strength is what we all need and courage is what we desire so that we can face our fears, whatever they may be. And love is always stronger than fear or hate, and out of that comes the ability to develop courage and face conditions that seem to be overwhelming. Facing your fears can help you evolve: As you free yourself of your fears, you become freer to do more with your life.

Strength upright is all about unconditional love and understanding. The woman of Strength doesn't need physical force to make her point—and neither do you. Like her, you have inner strength already. This card reminds you to use it.

Reversed Imagery and Meanings: As several students have said, the lion's in control now! He's at the top of the card, representing a fear that's getting to you. Of course you feel out of control when Strength is reversed. The woman has the power, but it seems to be leaving her in this position. You may be feeling out of control because fear has taken over. You need to be careful that discord and confusion don't result.

Strength reversed can also indicate fear of overwhelming passions, or intense emotions leading to uncontrolled action. You may be paying too much attention to the material or physical side of life, or lack the courage to face a problem. This card is telling you to pay attention to that lion. Calm him down, and get yourself back upright again. Remember, that lion's just a kitty cat at heart!

The Hermit (Key 9): Time Out for Inner Truth

The Hermit (key 9).

 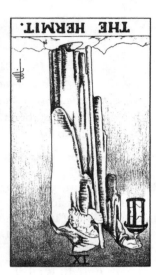

Your initial reactions to the Hermit:

_____

_____

Keywords: Seeking truth

Wisdom offered

The inner voice

Silence is golden

Archetypes: The Dalai Lama

Hal (the computer in *2001*)

Mentors

The voice of Obi-wan Kenobi telling Luke Skywalker, "The force is with
    you!"

Upright Imagery: The Hermit stands alone, high on a snowy peak, waiting and
watching for others who come along the path. He holds the Lantern of Truth, which
contains a six-pointed star. Look at him closely: He's the Fool who's gotten much
older—and wiser. "Where I am, so shall you be," the Hermit seems to be thinking. He
has experienced many lessons and now wishes to share them with you. Even though
he's alone, he's not lonely: Even though we're often surrounded by others, we always
must follow our own paths.

Upright Meanings: The Hermit upright indicates silent counsel and wise advice given and received. You've learned many lessons thus far, and now have the experiences under your belt to know much more clearly which way to turn in your life. This card also shows open-mindedness and a willingness to be of help, and can represent that you will seek counsel or that someone wishes to help you on your path of life. Either way, you have the maturity and wisdom of your own truth to decide for yourself.

Like the solitary Hermit, you may need to withdraw to meditate about what's going on in your life. Patience is a virtue and leads to a studied conclusion rather than a hasty one.

Reversed Imagery and Meanings: When the Hermit is reversed, the Lantern of Truth is about to go out. As the light fades, the Hermit feels the cold in the air, and the snow comes down upon him. Then the light goes out, and when this happens you may need to review a few lessons you might have missed. Upside down, no one is listening to the Hermit and he truly feels alone in the darkness; even his walking stick can't balance him anymore.

In his reversed position, the Hermit suggests that wisdom is disregarded. Perhaps you're not listening to your own advice, or paying attention to others who have been there before. History can repeat itself, remember, and your refusal to learn from your past can lead to foolish decisions. There's also a tendency to daydream or wish for something to happen without taking any action when this card appears. The Hermit reversed can mean your head's in the clouds, so you're unaware of how dark it really is outside.

Wheel of Fortune (Key 10): Taking Your Chances

Wheel of Fortune (key 10).

Your initial reactions to the Wheel of Fortune:

_____

_____

Keywords: Luck

The ups and downs of fate

The dartboard of life

Fortune

Archetypes: The gambler

Beginner's luck

Pat and Vanna

You've won the lottery!

Upright Imagery: Life keeps turning as this wheel does, and the Wheel of Fortune represents the ebbs and flows of life. The four creatures represent the four fixed signs of the zodiac: Aquarius (the angel), Scorpio (the eagle), Taurus (the bull), and Leo (the lion). These show that spiritual reality is unchanging even though your personal life changes constantly. Also on the wheel are the letters TARO. Now where have we seen those before? The mystery of life through the tool of the Tarot shows that TARO destiny is at work.

Upright Meanings: When the Wheel of Fortune appears upright in a reading, you're entering a lucky period or cycle in your life. You get to turn the Wheel of Fortune and have great things come up. You're very lucky now no matter what you wish to do; things just seem to go your way. In fact, nothing can stop you now!

There could be new conditions in the home or business, or the possibility of financial improvement, or a change in environment for the better. No matter what, the Wheel of Fortune always indicates a change for the better, whatever it is. When this card appears in a reading, the laws of chance are in your favor.

Spinning the Wheel of Fortune

"Can I buy a vowel?" Or get a different card? The answer to both questions is yes, but you shouldn't ignore what the cards are trying to tell you. If the Wheel of Fortune reversed comes up and tells you your luck has turned, you need to relax and wait for it to come back up again. The wheel never stays in one place for long—it's a wheel, after all.

Reversed Imagery and Meanings: When the Wheel of Fortune is reversed, what comes up must go down. The four fixed creatures are about to lose their books of knowledge, which are falling away from them. The wheel itself has come to a grinding halt, and not even the snake, jackal, and sphinx can keep the wheel moving with the correct momentum. Situations are in disarray, and the lucky cycle has come to a halt.

Chances are you've got a feeling of stagnation, where there's no action or momentum anymore. Because the cycle has turned downward, it's best to relax and slow down. Remember, the Wheel of Fortune will eventually come back up again. It's wise to know when to stop action and when to start up again. Have the courage to pull away and say better luck next time—or at least know there will be a better time later.

Justice (Key 11): Being Fair and Honorable

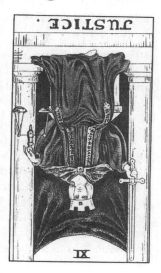

Justice (key 11).

Your initial reactions to Justice:

_____

_____

Keywords: Fairness

Pros and cons

Balanced judgment

Equilibrium

Archetypes: The Wizard of Oz

Supreme Court Justice Sandra Day O'Connor

Mediators

Your own sense of fairness

Upright Imagery: Justice holds a sword in her right hand and the balance scales in her left, and she has no blindfold so she can see everything clearly. Behind her are the same pillars we've seen in the High Priestess and the Hierophant cards. Justice sits between them to give us balanced and fair judgment.

Upright Meanings: Fair and honorable, Justice will make certain the right thing is done in the end. Lawsuits will be fair and the system will give an honest assessment with no preconceived notions. With Justice in a reading, there will be the open-mindedness to weigh the pros and cons, and fair decisions will be made to the satisfaction of all parties.

125

Fools Rush In

If you come to your Tarot reader and ask about the outcome of a court case that's already in progress, chances are the Justice card will come up in your reading. But don't assume that just because it comes up upright that things will go your way—or that if it comes up reversed, things won't. There are many factors involved in any case—and sometimes, Justice belongs to the other party.

All things being equal, Justice will say, "This is the decision I have made." She comes to a conclusion with all the evidence present, and so her decisions will always be just ones.

Reversed Imagery and Meanings: When Justice is reversed her sword is pointed downward, the scales are no longer balanced, and everything upside down leads to unwise decisions and unfairness. It's difficult for her to keep the sword and the scales in her hands, after all.

A variety of factors may be at play when Justice appears reversed in a reading: Inadequate counsel, unwise decisions, or unfairness when dealing with the system. The outcome of events might not be fair, or a lesson in dealing with an authority might have a prejudicial nature. There could be opinionated, unfair treatment, or discrimination or legal complications. Things will seem unfair at the moment, and that's because they're not equal. Justice seeks a balance in all things—and so should you.

The Least You Need to Know

➤ The Lovers reveal what's going on in your love life and with all your relationships.

➤ The Chariot gives you the fortitude and energy to achieve success and reach your goals.

➤ Strength is all about finding power and courage you may not have known you possessed.

➤ The Hermit gives you time for the solitude, reflection, and soul-searching that are necessary to make better decisions.

➤ The Wheel of Fortune represents the hand of Fate in your life, your lucky cycles, and your not-so-lucky ones.

➤ Justice comes into play when there are decisions to be made. Justice will prevail with a verdict of honesty and fairness.

Chapter 10

The Fool in Dante's Dark Wood

In This Chapter

➤ The Hanged Man (key 12)

➤ Death (key 13)

➤ Temperance (key 14)

➤ The Devil (key 15)

➤ The Tower (key 16)

No experience is without its problems and setbacks, and Major Arcana cards for keys 12 (the Hanged Man) through 16 (the Tower) metaphorically represent the various ways such issues may manifest themselves. Whether it's the transformation of Death, the tolerance demanded by Temperance, or those hits into left field represented by the Tower, the cards in this sequence signal questioning, spiritual grappling, and coming to terms with our demons. It's time for the Fool's mid-life crisis.

"Midway upon the Journey of Our Life..."

Up until now, the Major Arcana have pretty much let us go our own way. With the innocence of the Fool and the tools of the Magician, our path was cleared for the success of the Chariot (whose charioteer seems so adept at balancing the light and dark sides), and the luck of the Wheel of Fortune. Now, though, we come to the dark, middle part of the journey, where we encounter "lions and tigers and bears"—and Death, the Devil, and the Tower.

Written seven hundred years ago, Italian poet Dante Alighieri's (1265–1321) profoundly beautiful poem, *The Inferno,* continues to challenge us, even as we move into the 21st century. It was translated by Henry Wadsworth Longfellow in the 19th century, and again recently, in a collaboration of 20th-century poets who include Seamus Heaney, Mark Strand, Amy Clampitt, Robert Hass, and Robert Pinsky, among others. At the beginning of the poem, Dante finds himself lost:

> *Midway upon the journey of our life*
>
> *I found myself within a forest dark*
>
> *For the straightforward pathway had been lost.*

To reach enlightenment, Dante (the Fool) must journey through the underworld, with the ancient Greek poet Virgil (the Magician) as his guide. At some point, we all stumble upon Dante's dark wood. How we find our way through it can make all the difference on our life journey. Are we ready to look deeper?

Dante in the dark wood.
*Engraving by Gustave
Doré, 1861.*

Those new to the Tarot often find this sequence of cards frightening, and we'll be the first to say we can well understand why. But Death doesn't mean death literally, and you can't meet that tall, dark stranger without experiencing the unexpected events the Tower represents. Change isn't easy, especially major, transforming change, but with the Tarot tools we've already acquired, we can make it past those lions and tigers and bears—and witches and Evil Empires, too.

As you did in Chapters 8 and 9, look at the cards here and let them speak to you before you read more about them.

The Hanged Man (Key 12): Sacrifice and Release

The Hanged Man (key 12).

Your initial reactions to the Hanged Man:

_____

_____

Keywords: The gift of prophecy

Self-sacrifice

Hanging by a thread

Letting go

Archetypes: Dr. Martin Luther King

Jesus

Confucius

Yourself at the crossroads

Card Catalog

A *nimbus*, represented by a halo or bright disk around someone's head (this is often seen around the heads of saints in religious paintings from the Middle Ages), stands for someone's spiritual aura. People crowned with a nimbus are blessed and protected by a higher power.

Upright Imagery: The Hanged Man is being held on a T-cross of living wood with one leg free. His position looks similar to the yoga tree pose, which lets God come in. At the same time as he contemplates his former life, he desires a more uplifting or spiritual one. Around his head there's a *nimbus*, or white light (yeah, we know it's yellow, but it's a nimbus, okay?), and his face expresses contemplation or meditation of some kind.

The Hanged Man is contemplating making sacrifices for a higher good, and he's certain that Heaven will lead the way. Whatever comes will come, after all, and the Hanged Man is ready to accept the next direction in his life for the highest good of himself as well as others. The color red represents his passion about life, the blue his deep thoughts and contemplation, and the yellow and white about his head are vitality and spiritual desire.

Upright Meanings: In its upright position, the Hanged Man card represents spiritual growth and surrender to a higher wisdom. By accepting the situation he's tied to, the Hanged Man is finding his enlightenment. Heaven has many things to offer, and the Hanged Man is ready for the new direction being shown to him. He could be looking toward a complete reversal of lifestyle, or he might be making sacrifices that he hasn't in the past. In any event, he's definitely giving up and letting go.

Put another way, the Hanged Man means that you're finding your place in the spiritual universe. You wish to stay on the earth plane to do good work to benefit others, but you may develop psychic or prophetic ability in order to do so. The Hanged Man tolerates every other person's ideas and philosophy—this is a card about being open to possibility and ready for it as well.

When this card appears in your reading, you're at a point where it's time to leave the past behind in order to move on to the future. You could think of the Hanged Man as a present moment of stasis—but you can't remain there forever, or even for very long.

In the Cards

The archetype the Hanged Man represents tends to be reserved for those we hold in high spiritual acclaim, like Jesus, Buddha, Mohammed, and Mother Teresa. To move on to a new phase one must first accept what's come before, and acceptance of what we're going to leave behind is one of the hardest things we do. It's no wonder we revere those who've accomplished it.

Reversed Imagery and Meanings: The Hanged Man reversed stands on one foot, and so is still quite literally in touch with his former life. He can move his hands away from his back, and he can come off the living T-cross of wood and walk away. He wants to change, in other words, but he's still holding on to the past—he's not quite able to totally let go and let things be yet.

Reversed, the Hanged Man delays himself from the eventual outcome. When this card appears in your reading, you need to remember that it's okay to let go. You don't need to worry about the past anymore; once you really change consciousness, you can't go back there anyway. That's what growth is all about.

The desire of the Hanged Man reversed is to slow down the progress of events that are in the end inevitable. He's hung up (pun intended) on the past and hung up on the future, indecisive and vacillating between them. The Hanged Man reversed is stuck on maintaining his old image, rather than what he's become. He has a fear of making a sacrifice, a fear of letting go and letting God or the other side help. This card can also indicate a resistance to spiritual teachings or other lessons that may help you.

Death (Key 13): The Power of Regeneration

Death (key 13).

Your initial reactions to Death:

_____

_____

Keywords: Transformation

               Rebirth

               Renewal

               Time to move on

Archetypes: The Wicked Witch of the West

               Darth Vader

               The King is dead! Long live the King!

               Your big move

Upright Imagery: A black-armored skeleton rides an armored white horse toward a priest, a woman and a child, and the fallen king. He carries the banner of life, and the five-petalled rose in the banner signifies change and rejuvenation. Note that while there is death and destruction at the horse's feet, the sun is rising yellow and hopeful, and the priest seems to feel that death offers the promise of a new day.

In the Cards

"Oh no! The Death card!" If you haven't said this yourself, you've probably heard it from someone else when this card came up in a reading. The truth is the Death card comes up a lot whenever people are going through a change of attitude or lifestyle, who are realizing that their old way is truly obsolete. Death signifies that it's time to move on, for the old to make way for the new. We never predict the death of a loved one or the Querent in a reading, and neither does the Death card. We don't want to add unwanted fears that could harm in some way.

Upright Meanings: When Death appears upright in a reading, it signifies renewal, transformation, or a total change in your life cycle. An old chapter is coming to a close when this card shows up. For one thing to live, another must die, and what Death is really about is major change, and the leaving behind that comes with it.

You can't live in the past if it no longer has any substance or application to where you are now. After "Death," the birth of new ideas follows. You'll take off in your new direction, and the horse will go between the two pillars and find the sun again. When Death appears in a reading, we can truly say that the old will be gone, and the new will follow.

The Death card depicts the cycles of life and death, and the ebbs and flows that go along with these cycles. The symbolism here is the constant circulation of the life force. Life has a constant flow of change, even if we aren't aware of it, but it's a circular flow, always returning to its source.

Think, for example, about how people say, "When I was a child, we didn't do things this way. My, how things have changed since my generation!" Your parents said it; their parents said it; and soon, if you haven't already, you'll be saying it, too. That's because this cycle repeats itself all over again, from generation to generation. The Death card reminds us that, "The more things change, the more they stay the same"— but sometimes it takes major transformation to get there.

Reversed Imagery and Meanings: When Death is reversed, the horse can no longer move well, and his lack of action means there's no movement ahead. The skeleton will fall off the horse, and then his banner won't be seen by anyone.

Death reversed indicates stagnation, inertia, stalemates, complications, political upheaval, or that what you're doing seems to have come to a standstill. Revolution or strife may be indicated by this card. The crisis continues, it says, and there seems to be constant battling, with no end in sight. When Death reversed appears in your reading, you probably have the desire to call it quits, but the event itself won't quit. Instead, the war goes on, the tension continues to mount, and the horse isn't dead, but instead sick or immobile, and you meet blockages at every turn.

This card suggests that you regroup and see if you really want to take this particular path. Perhaps you should just stop, camp out, and rest until dawn. For now, the warrior (you) is tired of trying to initiate a change. Death reversed can mean the future is delayed, but a new start, new treaty, or new direction is coming. Sometimes, this card comes up when someone is very enthusiastic about something. When this happens, it may mean there will be delays and stagnation in the projects they wish to initiate.

Temperance (Key 14): Patience and Adaptation

Temperance (key 14).

Your initial reactions to Temperance:

_____

_____

Keywords: Patience

Adaptation

Self-discipline

Cooperation

Archetypes: Penelope (Odysseus's wife)

Aunt Em

Hillary Rodham Clinton

Your dog

Upright Imagery: In the Temperance card, Michael, one of the archangels, is pouring the essence of life from a silver cup to a golden one. Symbolically, the water flows from the subconscious to the conscious, from the unseen to the seen and then back again. The archangel is coordinating the flow of the past to the present into the future. The square on the angel's breast is four-square reality (earth), and the triangle with the square is that of spirit manifest on earth. Michael is well balanced, with one foot on the water and one foot on land. Water (emotions) and earth (logic) are perfectly balanced in this card.

Upright Meanings: When Temperance appears upright, it indicates self-control or a good sense of balance with people management. Temperance is able to coordinate the work of many and to work in harmony with others. This card indicates good management skills and an understanding of other people's skills.

When this card appears in your reading, its lesson is to have patience with others and work with and not against them. Harmony can prevail if we all work together, after all. To have good balance in your feelings about life, you need to learn patience and develop an understanding of where other people are coming from. Temperance tells you to learn to go with the flow. Patience and perseverance are what's at stake here—learn them and prosper.

Reversed Imagery and Meanings: When Temperance appears upside down, the rainbow around the angel's head is not strong and the wings no longer have their power to take flight. The balance of land and water has changed, too; the water, which represents our emotions, seems to be the focus. The water will fall from the two cups as well, again representing water (emotions) out of control.

Temperance reversed can indicate impatience or intolerance of others. There may be poor business management due to not listening to other people's complaints, or unfortunate combinations in business or personal life. A lack of good judgment may be present.

Perhaps you want everything to move fast, or you're getting pushy in order to get things done your way. Others may seem to be in the way of your ideas, or it may appear to you that they're moving way too slowly. Maybe there's a lack of follow-through if it seems like things are taking too long. Remember, though, if you run too fast, you might miss something great. Take it from two speedsters who get Temperance far too often—slow down and smell the roses!

Spinning the Wheel of Fortune

Someone we know (hint: first name, Arlene) kept getting Temperance in her readings. "Again?" she always asked her reader. Arlene kept getting Temperance because *she needed to learn its lesson,* namely, *patience.* Arlene still gets this card sometimes—so does Lisa, but she's much more patient. (Are not! Am too!) Some lessons are just particularly hard for us to learn—no matter what the cards tell us!

The Devil (Key 15): Confronting Materialism

The Devil (key 15).

Your initial reactions to the Devil:

_____

_____

Keywords:	Bondage to the material world
	Temptation
	Addictions—to anything
	Obsessions
Archetypes:	The Wicked Witch of the West's flying monkeys
	Jabba the Hut
	Mick Jagger
	Those who seek to control you

Upright Imagery: The Devil sits on a half-cube, which signifies the half-knowledge we have if we look only at the material side of life. There's nothing wrong with having a little fun, but this Devil wants to keep the couple we saw before in the Lovers chained to something, such as fear or ignorance. The Devil's bat wings and the inverted pentagram represent the sensory side of life. And those chains, well, remember Aretha Franklin singing, "Chain, chain, chain...chain of Fools"?

Upright Meanings: In its upright position, the Devil card represents sensuality, bondage to fears, or sexual energy that seems a little out of control. There could be addiction—to anyone, anything, or the way things ought to be. Maybe you're obsessed with an old boyfriend or girlfriend, or obsessed with a fear. It could be you're paranoid or somehow focused on one thing and one thing only.

This card can also indicate the wrong use of force or abusive conditions. This is where we find the dark side of humankind, controlling others for the purpose of self-gain. If there's addiction to anything from sex to drugs to rock 'n' roll, the Devil probably made you do it.

While the figures are chained to the Devil, those chains can easily be released. The Devil is really that part of ourselves that likes to delve into the dark side once in a while to find out about human nature in its most possessive form. We've all been obsessed with something or someone before—and we will be again. That's what the Devil reminds us about.

Reversed Imagery and Meanings: Reversing the Devil means letting go of obsession, letting go of your fears of the dark side, or freeing yourself of an addiction. In the Devil reversed, the inverted pentagram becomes a star, so the goodness comes back into the card. When this happens, no fear has to control you. You have the power to release the chains of bondage at any time in your life.

Sometimes this card can come up if you're being weak or ineffectual, or if you're starting to get yourself back together again after a long battle. This could be due to an addiction, fear, or something that's taken control over you in the past.

The Devil reversed gives you the freedom to go into your future with no chains, with nothing holding you back. This card means you're free of your own self-imposed prison or restrictions. It's only when you lose your fears that true freedom comes. When it does, the Devil will be just a figment of your imagination. Remember, the Force is with you.

The Tower (Key 16): Facing the Unexpected

The Tower (key 16).

Your initial reactions to the Tower:

_____

_____

Keywords: Expect the unexpected

A bolt from the blue

Surprise!

You could have knocked me over with a feather

Archetypes: Dorothy's house in Kansas (that killed the witch)

The lightning bolt of Thor

The tall, dark stranger

Your wildest dreams

Upright Imagery: Man, oh, man, look at this card. A bolt of lightning has struck a gray tower, setting it on fire, knocking off the king's crown, and sending everybody flying. Raindrops are flying, too, in the form of the Hebrew letter yod, which are emblematic of the hand of God. The symbolism of this card can be thought of as a fall from grace or banishment from the Garden of Eden. All in all, things aren't looking too good.

Upright Meanings: This card used to be called the Tower of God or the Tower of Babel. It represents the unexpected events that can change your life or your perception of things. The clearest aspect of this card is the element of surprise. The Tower indicates a rude awakening of some sort, whether it's your old way of life coming suddenly to an end, or a release from a situation in which you were stuck.

But the Tower may also forecast a wonderful unexpected event, such as a new baby. It might be "Some Enchanted Evening" when "you may see a stranger/across a crowded room." The Tower may be the accident that forces you to reevaluate your values or lifestyle, or the wrong turn that causes you to end up in Oz's Emerald City.

The Tower can also be something that no one expected, or an upsetting event of some kind. If you thought you had that new job, and then the company decided not to follow through on the offer for you, the Tower, sometimes called a reversal of fortune, is at play. You can't plan for what the Tower will offer up, though—because there's no way to know what it will be. That's why it's called "unexpected," right?

Reversed Imagery and Meanings: When you turn the Tower upside down, the people are flying up instead of down. The bolt is coming from below, from—you guessed it— the Devil in key 15. The people still don't look entirely happy, but it's quite possible that all is not lost. Something that shocked you initially may be coming to an end. Or maybe you'll soon be able to start over, putting the chaos and disruption behind you.

The Tower reversed can also indicate a feeling that life isn't giving you a fair shake. Maybe you feel as if circumstances are conspiring against you, and that no matter what you do, you'll never come out on top—as if you were, like these people, trying to fly without wings. You may feel backed into a corner, or stuck in a situation with no way out. This card is telling you to pay the piper and listen to the music. It's time to face what you've been avoiding so you can get on with the rest of your life.

The Least You Need to Know

➤ The Hanged Man slows things down while you make your decisions to move ahead. He helps you to let go of the old to make way for the new.

➤ Death represents your major, transformative, life-changing experiences.

➤ Temperance reminds you to be tolerant and patient as you go through life.

➤ The Devil stands for your base instincts, the things that are not so good for you, but that we all have to face once in a while.

➤ The Tower is all about unexpected change, both good and not so good. This card reminds us that we can't plan for everything.

Chapter 11

Good Heavens! The Fool Transformed

In This Chapter

➤ The Star (key 17)

➤ The Moon (key 18)

➤ The Sun (key 19)

➤ Judgement (key 20)

➤ The World (key 21)

By the time you arrive at the last five cards of the Major Arcana, you've earned the right to the hope and success they assure you. There's no question your journey's been fraught with trial and error, bumps and false starts, but now, you get to reap what you sowed along the way. The Star, the Moon, the Sun, Judgement, and the World are the cards of the Fool's successful return to the fold after his hero's journey into the great unknown.

Look to the Skies

Just as the ancients looked to the skies for divine inspiration, the last five cards of the Tarot's Major Arcana archetypically represent the rewards you'll find at the end of the Fool's long, arduous journey. From the hope of the Star to the completion signified by the World, here's where you'll find the fruits of your labors and the affirmation of your goals.

What do these cards hold for you? Take a few moments to respond to them on your own before you read our interpretations.

The Star (Key 17): Hope and Faith

The Star (key 17).

Your initial reactions to the Star:

_____

_____

Keywords: Hope

Faith

Over the rainbow

When you wish upon a star…

Archetypes: Dorothy from Kansas

Cinderella's Fairy Godmother

Princess Diana

Your hopes and wishes for *your* life

Upright Imagery: A beautiful woman kneels at a pond's edge, holding two urns of water. She pours one on the land (the material universe, or earth), and the other into the pond or pool of water (emotions and imagination). To dream is to create, this card tells us. The Water of Life the woman pours will bring new life through new hope.

The woman of the Star is inspired from above by the eight-pointed radiant star of spiritual energy and truth. The seven smaller stars represent the wisdom she has; she's already realized, for example, that life has many miracles, and her experiences have never taken away her faith about life or humankind. There's always hope, the Star assures us, and to confirm this, the sacred ibis rests in the tree of the mind and sends messages from heaven to focus and concentrate on her wishes.

Upright Meanings: The Star upright always focuses on affirming a positive attitude toward whatever you wish to accomplish. Courage, hope, and inspiration from above are this card's messages. She believes all things (including any wish you might have) can come into being, and that anything can manifest, simply because you wish it so. Whether it's good health, good energy, or an optimistic attitude, the Star will win the day and make things happen.

The Star also indicates that great love will be given and received. There's an insight here into the meaning of life, and with that knowledge, the Star continues to create more for everyone. She believes there are plenty of the worldly goods for all, and that everyone can share in the abundance in life—or at least have the faith that anything can change for the better.

In the Cards

The Star card is often used as a card of meditation. To calm down after a hard day, take out the Star card and meditate on it for awhile. It really does calm the heart and mind. Its cool water, tranquil skies, green fields, and peaceful, relaxed state will make you feel the same way. Say to yourself, "I believe things will improve," and just as Dorothy was whisked back to Kansas, you'll find the Star's peace and tranquility are also yours. That's because the Star doesn't just *think* things will get better. She *knows* they will. So use the Star's faith to bolster your own.

Reversed Imagery and Meanings: When we turn the Star over, the stars are now falling away from the woman, and her waters are falling back into the urns. It's almost as if good energy is being taken back, or that water and earth will mix together and create a muddy mess. The stars in the sky are dimming, too, and so there's not much hope here. It feels as if she's no longer flowing with the universe.

When the Star appears reversed in a reading, it can indicate that, at least for now, all hope is dashed. The lights fade, the bird stops singing, and it's just altogether much too quiet. The woman appears nearly sullen or moody, and it may be necessary to apply reserved energy here. Something you've hoped for might not materialize as you idealized. The Star reversed may mean you're doubtful, pessimistic, stubborn, or ill-at-ease about a situation; or you may be confused, or lack faith that things will work out. A loss of friendship could also be indicated with this card, or, sometimes, a health problem, either physical or mental.

You may feel as if nothing will ever change when this card comes up for you. But instead of becoming more despondent, let this card encourage you to read, meditate, or ask for help from others who will encourage you to a higher state of mind. You need to move past your lack of confidence and find the faith that things—and the Star card—will turn around.

The Moon (Key 18): Nurturing Imagination

The Moon (key 18).

Your initial reactions to the Moon:

_____

_____

Keywords: The imagination

Psychic development

Unforeseen changes

Things ain't always what they seem

Archetypes: Perils of Pauline

Mother Nature

The Madonna

Your hidden side

Upright Imagery: A dog and a wolf bay at the Moon in its full phase, representing the domesticated and the wild, the tamed and the untamed. The pool of water represents the imagination and the subconscious, and a crayfish crawls from the pool—is he friend or foe? Will that crayfish walk away or is he gonna bite me? In other words, is he disciplined or undisciplined?

The two pillars again represent the theme of duality, in this case, good and evil. The path goes between the pillars, because, after all, in life we walk through a lot of different emotional experiences, with the ups and downs emotion inevitably brings. In Spanish tradition, La Luna—the moon—is sometimes psychic and sometimes crazy, and this is a good metaphor for this card. It's well known that both people and animals react to the full moon every month, and that when the moon begins to wane, everything calms down again.

In the Cards

The Moon and the High Priestess are sisters in the Major Arcana. When the Moon appears in your reading, it means you've just gone a notch higher in your development. Just as the High Priestess is a young goddess archetype, the Moon represents a more mature one. You could think of the High Priestess as Dorothy before she gets to Oz, and the Moon as Dorothy when she gets back to Kansas with all her newfound knowledge about herself.

Upright Meanings: When the Moon appears upright, it can herald unforeseen events or a new turn of events already in motion. Sometimes it can mean a disagreement with the one you love or an emotional outburst over very little—making a mountain out of a molehill. The Moon always intensifies everyone's emotions, just as it pulls the tides in and out.

The Moon also reflects psychic ability, dreams, and intuitive powers. The Moon gives you the ability to prophesize universally. When you feel something big is coming, whether it's a change of residence, career, or in your own emotions, the Moon will appear to confirm your intuition. This card also indicates nocturnal activity, or things that happen at night.

Reversed Imagery and Meanings: Now here's a card that seems to do a lot better in its reversed position. That's because instead of being full, it's now a *new* moon. A new moon indicates harnessed imagination, and when this card is reversed, the moon is setting rather than rising. The dog and wolf seem to have calmed down, the crayfish goes back into the water, and the animals will rest now.

When the Moon appears reversed in a reading, it indicates that your imagination will be harnessed by good common sense. You'll take practical considerations into account, and be cautious not to make any rash decisions. Any change that occurs now won't be disruptive.

Reversed, the Moon allows all truth to come to the surface. This means that people will tell you what they're really feeling—without theatrics and without being overly emotional. The Moon reversed assures us that love and understanding will win in the end and that all misunderstandings will be cleared, thank goodness. Communications will have clarity, and there's good psychic information as well. This is a card that clears the slate.

The Sun (Key 19): Enjoying Contentment

The Sun (key 19).

Your initial reactions to the Sun:

_____

_____

Keywords: Contentment

Enjoying a peaceful life

Happy unions/partnerships

Pleasure

Archetypes: Spanky and Our Gang

The Munchkins

Your children and grandchildren

Your own inner child

Upright Imagery: A big brilliant sun shines down upon a little boy on a strong horse. The child is open, with nothing to hide, and carries the red banner of life. He holds the banner in his right hand (the subconscious) and passes it on to his left hand (the conscious). He's been successful in learning his lessons. "You did it!" this card says, and this is what we all do when we've learned a skill well.

What lessons the child (yes, the Fool, again) has finally mastered! The four sunflowers represent the four elements of the Tarot—air, earth, fire, and water—which we'll soon be seeing more of in the Minor Arcana. These sunflowers are turned toward the boy and horse to continue their development, because that's where the brightest light is. The horse represents freedom of movement, travel, and movement toward goals, and the walled garden reflects the growth and development of humankind.

Upright Meanings: The upright Sun promises happiness and success in all your lessons. You'll have a good marriage, a good home life, and success in all that you do. There's also success indicated in areas from higher education to agriculture to the sciences and the arts. You've become a master of your talent, the Sun says. Your studies in life are completed. Congratulations, you've graduated!

Happiness and pleasure come from within, so enjoy your success and happy memories of childhood past. You can reflect on the past, review how well you've done, and bask in your well-earned glory. Travel and the freedom to move around are also represented by the upright Sun, and this could mean new career offers, or simply happiness with the good life, satisfied and content.

Reversed Imagery and Meanings: The Sun doesn't shine as well when the card is reversed, and the child and horse don't have the same movement or momentum. The sunflowers can't grow and develop correctly either. The Sun reversed indicates delays in getting a lesson, and so accomplishment will seem far away, and the future clouded.

The Sun reversed may indicate trouble understanding what a delay is all about. Perhaps your home life or marriage is at a crossroads. It's likely that development and growth in this particular phase have stopped. You may be stuck in some childhood memory or suffering from low self-esteem.

The path you're on is rocky and you feel you haven't completed or mastered the situation correctly—or at least not enough to make you feel satisfied. When the Sun appears reversed in a reading, counsel and optimism are needed. The issue may require more study so that you can check out what needs to be corrected.

Fools Rush In

Is your partner not talking? Is the textbook you're studying a little over your head? Is your goal stubbornly just out of your reach? The Sun reversed is telling you to ask someone for direction. The Yellow Brick Road is not far away; all you need is for someone to point you in the right direction.

Judgement (Key 20): The Awakening

Judgement (key 20).

Your initial reactions to Judgement:

_____

_____

Keywords: A cosmic wake-up call

The great ah-ha!

Clarity

A change in consciousness

Archetypes: The Force

The Ruby Slippers

And heaven and nature sing...

I have seen the light!

Upright Imagery: In this card, the angel Gabriel is blowing seven blasts on his horn to awaken humankind from its earthly state. "Look up," he says, "All things will be known!" People rise from their coffins, aroused by the music from above to realize there's more to life than meets the eye; there's a greater purpose for everything we do and how we do it.

The cross on the angel's banner is red and white. The red represents a passion for life, and the white, spiritual attainment and purity of spirit. This banner represents balanced forces in nature and heaven. As above, so below.

Upright Meanings: In its upright position, Judgement signals an awakening, a coming alive to a change of awareness. This card indicates self-actualization, a life well lived, and work well done. You're on the verge of blending with the universe, and have renewed energy now that you're so close.

This card often comes up when you're trying to improve your health or well being. It indicates a desire for something higher or better than where you are now. We call it the great ah-ha of life because you'll be saying, "Oh, now I've got the picture," "I didn't realize that," or, "Gee, I never thought I'd learn something new, but here it is." All these statements reflect your own awareness toward life and its mystery. Judgement represents that you'll understand something you hadn't, or that you'll suddenly realize something existed that you'd never thought of before. Whoa! Cool!

Reversed Imagery and Meanings: Judgement reversed is a card where the people don't seem to have control over the ocean, the coffins, or whether to listen to the seven blasts of the horn. This indicates that they can't hear the true calling of a situation, and that there's confusion on the seas of life.

Gabriel is still blasting away, but when Judgement is reversed, he's not being heard by the one who has this card. Are you denying the inevitable? Do you have a fear of failure, or a fear of being judged? Judgement reversed may be trying to tell you to listen.

Judgement reversed can indicate a fear of losing control or a fear that you won't find happiness. Sometimes it shows there's a lack of interest or awareness in the spiritual side of life, or possible losses or delays in realizing a higher spiritual calling. This card cautions you to take care not to be superstitious, but instead to believe that all conditions of life have a higher purpose. There's a reason, in other words, for everything—even though some of those things are not too pleasant.

Fools Rush In

Some are afraid of this card because of how it looks. Maybe it has something to do with the old Armageddon thing—the end of the world as we know it. But what is Armageddon anyway? It's a condition that's happened on earth over and over again throughout history, an old way making way for a new one. The unknown is always scary, but where would we be if brave folks hadn't ventured out into it before us?

The World (Key 21): Attainment and Self-Actualization

The World (key 21).

Your initial reactions to the World:

_____

_____

Keywords: Final attainment

Triumph in all areas

Karmic lessons complete

Liberation

Archetypes: The winner and still champion

The rebels who defeat the Empire

Dorothy getting back to Kansas

You have it all!

Upright Imagery: A maiden is dancing, holding two wands in her hands. One wand is the power of involution and the other is the power of evolution, so she has the power to connect to all the lessons previously learned. Now she's ready to understand why she's here and what she's accomplished, and is ready to grow into a new phase of life, accepting the responsibility of life on this earth.

The four mystical creatures from the Wheel of Fortune are here, too, now evolved into their full potential in the World card. The wreath surrounding the maiden represents universality and blending with a global perspective.

Upright Meanings: In its upright position, the World promises fulfillment of all desires and goals and an understanding of all the lessons you've been through. Here's the freedom to move ahead and continue your growth the way you wish to. Now you have all the talents and all the tools, so go for it.

You have the ability to make others happy or aware of what their gifts are. There could be a change for the better of home or career, or an arrival at a cosmic state of consciousness. There may be travel—in comfort, now that you've arrived. The World upright indicates the freedom to come and go as you please. You've earned the path of liberation, your karmic reward.

Reversed Imagery and Meanings: When the World is reversed, the maiden will lose her wands and her scarf will come off. Energy or power leaves, and there's a failure to learn or integrate the former lessons. Upside down, she's no longer totally aware of what's going on around her. There may be a fear of change, or the home may be threatened in some way.

The World reversed can indicate a lack of vision or a refusal to learn from your experiences. It's possible you could walk off the path you were on. At any rate, your journey is postponed or frustrated for now. It could have been better—and it still could be—but more concentration is required and more work must be done first. This is not a traumatic card or a negative card reversed, but it does indicate that more must be done, or more work must be accomplished, to attain the upright position of security. Total self-actualization—the World upright—can be yours. You're almost there already!

The most important use of the Tarot is to make us think about our lives and reach toward our goals with patience. The Tarot gives us an understanding that anything good takes time and some introspection. The lessons of the Major Arcana are lessons we learn again and again as we journey throughout our lives.

The Least You Need to Know

➤ The Star represents your wishes come true and your dreams fulfilled. This card promises hope and faith for the future.

➤ The Moon puts you in touch with your intuitive and emotional natures. It fires the imagination.

➤ The Sun promises success—a bright, sunshiny day and an optimistic outlook.

➤ Judgement helps us see things we haven't seen before. This card is one of rejuvenation and renewal.

➤ The World is the card of universal attainment and mastery. It is the journey's end, the culmination of the Fool's efforts.

Part 4

The Minor Arcana: Wands, Cups, Swords, Pentacles

The 56 Minor Arcana cards stand for the events in Everyperson's archetypal day. Through their symbolism, these cards represent everyday events and the things that you have choices about. Divided into four suits representing the four areas of life— enterprise, the material, the emotional, and conflict—together these cards add up to anything that can happen.

Chapter 12

ACE of WANDS

Everyday Cards

In This Chapter

➤ The Minor Arcana cards

➤ Free Will and your everyday choices

➤ Some Minor Arcana in combination

➤ The four suits: Wands, Cups, Swords, and Pentacles

Now that you've successfully completed your journey through the Major Arcana, you're ready to deal with life on a day-to-day basis. That's what the 56 *Minor Arcana* cards of the Tarot deck are all about. These cards deal with every eventuality a life can offer, from career to relationships, from emotions to cold, hard cash. They represent the choices we make in our everyday lives.

Where should I go for lunch? Should I buy that suit? How about a date with X? Or accepting that job in sales? All these questions are addressed by the Minor Arcana cards, the Tarot cards of your own Free Will .

The Small Mysteries

Our study of the Minor Arcana returns to the four elements—fire, water, air, and earth—that Tarot uses to represent the human condition and the use of your Free Will. The elements are also important in a study of astrology (read more about this connection in Chapter 25). Each element, and each of the Minor Arcana suits, represents an area of life:

➤ *Fire* is represented by Wands, and is connected to enterprise and beginnings.

➤ *Water* is represented by Cups, and is the element of emotions and matters of the heart.

➤ *Air* characterizes Swords, and is all about mental activity and decisive action.

➤ *Earth* is represented by Pentacles, and is the element of the material world.

In the Major Arcana cards, these astrological equivalents can be found: Leo, the lion, for fire; Scorpio, the eagle, for water; Aquarius, the angel, for air; and Taurus, the bull, for earth. We've already seen astrological signs in the Wheel of Fortune card and in the World card—and we'll be seeing a lot more of them as we make our way through the Minor Arcana.

Every Choice You Make

We know you've got questions, and we also know you often can't remember what those questions are when it comes time to ask them (we know *we* can't!). So we've devised a set of questions for you to use when you want to ask the cards to address those matters closest to your heart, your wallet, your ego, and your mind:

➤ Do you need help making a decision about your job or career? Your answer will be found in Wands, the cards of your goals and ambitions.

➤ Are you wondering whether a relationship is worth your efforts? Your answer will be found in Cups, the cards of your emotions.

➤ Does it seem as if a situation you're in is full of conflict or problems? The answer will be found in Swords, the cards of how you act and interact.

➤ Are you worried about money, or trying to decide about an investment? The answer will be found in Pentacles, the cards of the material things in your life.

There Are More Free Will Cards Than Destiny Cards

Now, out of the 78 Tarot cards, 56 cards are the Minor Arcana, which represent humankind. In these cards, you'll find your ability to choose or select conditions to work with as you live your day-to-day life.

In any life, there are many choices to be made. We like to think of these as choices along the road. Do you take the high road or the low road? The little winding lane or the freeway? The left fork or the right? When it comes to decisions like these, you have the Free Will to choose, and the Minor Arcana represent those choices that *you* make.

So while the 22 Major Arcana cards represent things that are destined to occur, or karmic issues you've got very little choice about working on in this life, the 56 cards we're looking at now allow you to make choices, to choose your fate. Using your Free Will, those choices shape the lessons you *choose* to learn. So there you have it: Not everything is written in stone. There are only a few guidelines for how to live your life; the rest, you get to choose.

In the Cards

Does it seem sometimes as if you keep butting your head up against the same lesson over and over again? When that happens, you're dealing with something you're *fated* to learn, a Major Arcana issue of karma. Whether it's consistently picking the wrong type of guy or always misplacing your car keys, if it happens again and again, it's a Major Arcana issue. While the Minor Arcana can help you learn how to make better choices about these things, they're lessons you have to learn—with or without your help.

What Suits You?

In addition to being correlated with the elements, the suits of the Minor Arcana have their equivalents in the regular deck of playing cards. Thinking about the meanings of these suits can help you identify them more easily. Each suit has a keyword and an image associated with it, as shown in the following table.

Tarot	Playing Cards	Keyword	Image
Wands	Clubs	Enterprise	Waving a magic wand
Cups	Hearts	Emotion	A cupful of joy
Swords	Spades	Action	A sword fight
Pentacles	Diamonds	Money	Counting your money

As with learning anything new, remembering what each suit represents takes time. We hope these words and pictures will help reduce that time a little bit. We'll repeat them for you as we talk about each suit individually, too.

All About Wands

Keywords: Enterprise, growth

Key Image: Waving a magic wand

Season: Spring

Corresponding Astrological Sign: Aries

Go ahead, take that Wand. Its power belongs to you.

Wands represent our ability to dive into our work world, our ambition, growth, and development. These are the cards of our enthusiasm for life and our enthusiasm for living it.

Wands were originally called staffs, which were used to carry fires at night. Wands were on fire to bring light into wherever the darkness was, and so are also a symbol of authority or personal power.

Card Catalog

Wands are the suit of enterprise, growth, and development.

Wands are associated with the element of fire, and are made out of green wood that still has a few twigs, which represents growth. In the Minor Arcana cards, Wands are used for everything from clubs for fighting, to staffs to carry victors' crowns, to walking sticks to lean on. With this in mind, it's easy to see that the position that Wands take within a reading will tell us whether they'll be used for a constructive or destructive outcome.

Wands are associated with the world of creation and ideas, with manifesting something to make it real—just like a magic wand. Poof—it appears! Wands are helping us create this book—and Wands are helping you use it for good purpose.

Each Tarot suit has a corresponding astrological sign and season. On the first day of spring, the Sun enters Aries, a fire sign, and so Wands represent the season of spring. With their Aries nature, Wands represent enterprise, growth, and new beginnings.

All About Cups

Keywords: Emotion, sensitivity

Key Image: A cupful of joy

Season: Summer

Corresponding Astrological Sign: Cancer

Drink from the Cup and get in touch with your feelings.

Cups stand for how we perceive our emotions. Here's where we find our feelings and sensitivity for others, our joys, our artistic selves—and a good, old-fashioned cry. Cups indicate matters of the heart.

The suit of Cups is associated with water, which is the symbol of the subconscious mind and instincts. Cups represent the heart-centered connections we have, such as attachments to people or animals, or to anything to which we have an emotional response.

The association of cups with water, and of water with emotional issues, is rooted the fact that cups hold water. Cups are filled with water from above, symbolically considered the wine of life. This represents the joys—and the sorrows— of living, and Cups are in fact called the happy suit—though they're sometimes the sadder suit as well because they deal with all human emotion. If you're looking for love, Cups is the suit you'd like to see come up in your spread.

Card Catalog

Cups are the cards of emotion and sensitivity.

When summer starts, the Sun enters the astrological sign of Cancer. Cancer is a water sign (and a very emotional one at that!). The suit of Cups represents summer, the season of fun for family and friends, and the season when we water and nurture our gardens as well.

All About Swords

Keywords: Action, mental ability

Key Image: A sword fight

Season: Fall

Corresponding Astrological Sign: Libra

Grab that Sword and get ready for action.

Swords represent our mind and mental ability, including how we think, our logic and reasoning, and our ability to know what to do through the use of good, old-fashioned common sense. At the same time, Swords can be symbolic of strife or aggressive behavior; but remember, these too start in the mind.

When we look at the cards in the suit of Swords, we often find fighting, acts of aggression, or people in some kind of misfortune. Sometimes these cards can be graphic, and it's for a reason. Swords can cut two ways: for either constructive or destructive purposes.

Swords symbolize what we can do to each other when we're fearful or threatened. In these circumstances, we can either act or react in a way that causes trauma instead of enlightenment.

Swords are a natural choice to represent activity as well as action. Swords represent the season of fall, when the Sun's journey takes it to the sign of Libra, an air sign of activity, both mental and physical.

Card Catalog

Swords are the cards of mental activity and action.

All About Pentacles

Keywords: Money, possessions

Key Image: Counting your money

Season: Winter

Corresponding Astrological Sign: Capricorn

Take possession of that Pentacle and count your riches.

Pentacles represent our connection to the material world and focus us on financial issues and goods, on shelter and on earthly things, including clothing, home, and financial success. Pentacles can indicate material gain and abundance of the land, or they can represent difficulties with handling finances—it all depends on the cards and their placement.

Except for the 5 of Pentacles, this suit shows people working away at developing resources or enjoying the fruits of their labors. Pentacles are actually the coin-like discs shown in these cards. They're inscribed with pentagrams, which are five-pointed stars that are symbolic of man's earthly presence.

Pentacles represent the financial success or material gains you can develop in your life. Here is where you'll find your riches or your prosperity. Labor, hard work, and industrious efforts pay off and bring Pentacles into your spreads, and these cards may appear when you ask a question about money or future money, wealth, or security. Pentacles also show up when you're gambling or thinking about investing.

Card Catalog

Pentacles are the cards of the material world, of money and possessions.

The Sun's journey through the sign of Capricorn corresponds to the suit of Pentacles. Capricorn is an earth sign, practical, down-to-earth, and concerned with the material—just like Pentacles.

The Minor Arcana in Combination with Major Arcana Cards

Between the 56 Minor Arcana and the 22 Major Arcana, you have the full spectrum of your talents and abilities, your karmic lessons and your Free Will, and the choices you'll make to try new ideas and learn the lessons of fate. How these cards appear in combination can help you understand exactly what's going on in a given situation.

As we discussed in Chapter 7, when the majority of cards in a reading are Major Arcana (five or more in a ten-card Celtic Cross Spread is a majority), the answer to the question is not in your hands. It may be in the hands of other people, or already in the works, but you can't do much about changing anything now. Lots of Major Arcana in a reading signal that you're in a learning curve, and so going with the flow is important. At the same time, the reader pays close attention to the fact that you're doing something with a higher purpose than you realize.

When the majority of cards in a reading are from the Minor Arcana, though, you have a lot of Free Will or choice in deciding which way the reading could turn or how you wish to pursue it. Here, matters are in your hands—and your fate is what *you* make it.

Even if Major Arcana cards represent karmic issues you must deal with in this life like it or not, you still have the Free Will to deal with them successfully or unsuccessfully. So, ultimately Free Will is the rule and you use it to your advantage or detriment in dealing with karmic issues of life. So, while you may not be able to choose your "lessons," you can choose how you evolve or grow through them. For example, if your lesson is to break free of destructive or addictive relationships, you can choose to develop the power to do that, or remain in that lesson, even repeating it into the next life. The choice is yours!

Spinning the Wheel of Fortune

Do you consistently receive a lot of Minor Arcana cards in your daily Three-Card Spreads? Some people think this means that nothing significant is going on in their lives, but that's not the case at all. A majority of Minor Arcana means that, at least for now, *you* hold the cards. Have a good time plotting your course!

Rising to the Challenge

Are you ready to accept the challenge of learning something new about your life? Are you ready to get to know what's happening on a deeper level than you knew before? Are you curious about what's at the other end of the Yellow Brick Road? Well, Toto wants to take you on a fabulous journey, so turn the page and let's get started!

THE FOOL.

Put your Wand, Cup, Sword, and Pentacle in your knapsack and let's hit the Fool's road with your trusty canine friend.

The Least You Need to Know

➤ The Minor Arcana cards represent your everyday choices.

➤ Wands speak for your choices about growth and enterprise, your goals and ambitions.

➤ Cups are your emotional choices, keeping you in touch with your day-to-day ups and downs.

➤ Swords point to your mental choices about action and interaction.

➤ Pentacles indicate money and your material choices.

➤ When the majority of cards in your reading are Minor Arcana, your fate is in your own hands.

Chapter 13

Wands: The Fruits of Your Labors, the Tools of Your Trade

In This Chapter

➤ Wands represent enterprise, growth, and development

➤ Royal Wands: Strength, energy, and new efforts

➤ Everyday Wands: How you work through things

The first Minor Arcana suit we'll be exploring is Wands. As we discussed in Chapter 12, Wands are the suit of your enterprise, growth, and development. Here's where you'll find the ways in which you approach anything new that comes into your life, whether it's with the excitement of the Ace of Wands, the fear of the 5 of Wands, or the impatience of the Knight of Wands.

The Royal Court

Royal Minor Arcana cards, or *court cards,* often take on more meaning than simply speaking for events. Sometimes, they can be people in your life or an aspect of yourself. Royal cards may reveal some role you're currently playing, or a role you *should* be playing in order to deal with a situation. Or these cards may represent certain times or seasons, which we'll discuss in Chapter 25.

King of Wands: A Capable Leader

King of Wands.

Upright Imagery and Meanings: What do you notice first when you look at the King of Wands? We see the lions and salamanders decorating his robe. These represent growth and new beginnings, and the lion has the pride and passion to follow through on those beginnings, too.

The regal King of Wands has the element of fire as his realm, and he holds it in a torch (wand) in his left hand. This indicates that he's a man of authority and personal power, confident in all that he does. The King of Wands has an enthusiasm for life, and encourages growth and potential in others as well. This is a king who says, "With a positive outlook and confidence, you can do anything your heart desires."

Card Catalog

Royal Minor Arcana cards, or *court cards,* can stand for various aspects of yourself or for those around you. Sometimes they stand for certain times or seasons as well. The royal cards are the King, Queen, Knight, and Page in each of the four suits.

The King of Wands is a proud, confident, enthusiastic, and kind soul, with the presence that comes with those qualities. He's also a proud father, and eager to be of help—always forthcoming with advice when someone asks. The King of Wands is passionate about all that he believes, and he carries himself well. He has excellent leadership qualities and can delegate well. Think of him as a mentor or father figure, good at getting people to see their potential.

In the Cards

The King of Wands used to be called the Country Gentleman because he loves the outdoors and all types of sports and is enthusiastic about change and development. He loves to see things grow, too, and he adores both animals and children.

Reversed Imagery and Meanings: When we turn the King of Wands upside down, we find the same power—but not the same enthusiasm. Reversed, the King of Wands can represent a lack of confidence in his ability to follow through, low self-esteem, or a lack of centering or focus for getting things done.

The King of Wands reversed has a tendency to let everything fall away because of pessimism or doubt. He's insecure and unsure of himself or others, and he may be temperamental. The King of Wands reversed can scare people away with his big roar, but, like the Cowardly Lion, he's not as harsh as he seems. All reversed court cards exhibit uncertainty and fear. There may be feelings of inadequacy, hastiness, or a short fuse. The King of Wands reversed, for example, appears to be grumpy and detached.

But remember, even though they're court cards, these are still Minor Arcana. When you receive a reversed court card, *you* have the power to right yourself if you work on the issues, because *these are free will cards.* Just because you've received a reversed Minor Arcana in a reading doesn't mean you'll stay that way. Reversed Minor Arcana indicate momentary reversals, or may be specifically about a reversal for the question asked. Unlike the Major Arcana, the Minor Arcana *can and will change to their upright positions* if and when you change consciousness.

Queen of Wands: Ambitious, Determined, Outgoing

Queen of Wands.

 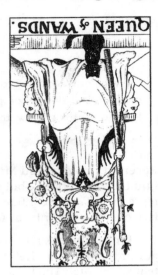

Upright Imagery and Meanings: The regal Queen of Wands has lions and sunflowers on her throne. These show her strong personality and her desire for growth and development. The black cat at her feet represents her intuition and her ability to assume a role of cat-like observation.

The Queen of Wands sits facing us and has strong features. These show us her power of command and her power to create new directions: Action and movement will take place when she's around. Ambition, growth, and development of any idea or plan are the name of the game here.

The Queen of Wands is honorable and respectable and can be a strong leader in business or at home. "Dominant" is a good word to describe her presence, and in fact you can sense her in a room. She's affable, cordial, sometimes just a little aggressive, but above all enthusiastic and motivated. The Queen of Wands is kind to animals and children and enjoys growing and/or developing anything into something greater. She has an outgoing personality, and overall is agreeable and strong.

Reversed Imagery and Meanings: When we turn the Queen of Wands upside down, the black cat is on top. The cat is the more aggressive, passionate side of the Queen of Wands, as well as the sometimes pushy part of her personality. Reversed, the Queen of Wands is almost too forceful with her ideas, words, and actions. In addition, she can be overly temperamental and easily agitated.

The Queen of Wands reversed can be quite strict and domineering. Sometimes immature emotions come through and she seems bossy, pushy, or arrogant. This kind of fire, in both the King and Queen of Wands can be hurtful. But, as with all Minor Arcana, this position can be reversed if you work at it.

Knight of Wands: Growth and Enterprise

Knight of Wands.

Upright Imagery and Meanings: The brave young Knight of Wands is going off on his own journey, and—lucky him!—he has a strong and gallant horse to carry him through all sorts of territory. The Knight's armor and robe are decorated with salamanders, which protect him as he goes on his journey.

This Knight is hasty in all that he does, and takes action where others would not. The Knight of Wands carries his wand, which gives him the power to manifest his goals, and the three pyramids in the background represent body, mind, and spirit.

In the Cards

Any time we see a horse image in a card, it signifies movement, action, or a change in the wind, and news to come of a new beginning. All knights have horses, of course, and so they are cards heralding just such things. But these are not the only cards where horses appear, so be sure to notice them when they ride into your spread.

While he's sudden and impatient in all he does, the Knight of Wands is nonetheless strong and always enthusiastic. We might call him a little hyper these days, but he just wants to get on with it and get going; he doesn't like to dilly-dally!

169

The Knight of Wands can be a generous friend or lover, and always does everything in a big way. This card can also represent a change of residence, a journey that you're about to undertake (sometimes an unexpected one), a new adventure, or that a major change in your life is approaching for which you'll want to be ready. Because it's upright, any change it heralds will be terrific!

Reversed Imagery and Meanings: The Knight is upside down! Poor horse! Everything is falling away, the horse is lame, the wand of fire falls away (the Knight's power has left him), and even the pyramids are upside down, reversing all energy that was constructive when they were upright.

The Knight of Wands reversed comes up when things are awry, disorganized, out of control, and chaotic. Perhaps the journey is postponed or not worth taking. Maybe messages are not being delivered correctly, or things are out of control at the office, in a business deal, or at home.

Jealousy, personal conflict, insecurity, self-doubt, and vulnerability are just a few of the words that describe the Knight of Wands reversed. He can be narrow-minded, argumentative, and downright ornery as well. But, as with all reversed Minor Arcana cards, *you* have the power to turn this free will card upright again.

Page of Wands: Phone, Fax, E-Mail...

Page of Wands.

Upright Imagery and Meanings: As the messengers of the Tarot, all pages relay messages of concern. This can take the form of a phone call, fax, e-mail, regular mail, or just good-old-fashioned conversation. When we look at the Page of Wands, we see that, like the Knight of Wands, he's next to the three pyramids of the body, mind, and spirit. He's studying his wand, possibly reading a message he's just received.

The Page of Wands is often contemplating and studying messages and information, and that's because he brings you good news. It may be a message confirming your new job or that you just passed your exams. When he's upright, the Page of Wands always brings news of the best kind.

This card can also represent a child or young person who's still considered dependent on family or friends. This could be a grandchild, a new baby coming into the family, or your own child, who's a good communicator.

The Page of Wands has great enthusiasm for life. He loves adventure and is often interested in travel to foreign lands. With his strong and dynamic personality, he can prove to be a good friend—one who will always tell it the way it is.

Reversed Imagery and Meanings: When the Page of Wands is reversed, the messenger isn't able to deliver his news correctly. This could mean delays in receiving the message (sounds like a certain net server we know...), or that the contacts are not made. Things may be waylaid, or delays or disappointing news may be on the horizon.

The reversed Page of Wands usually brings a message you don't want to hear, but as you know, sometimes that happens in life. This message may not arrive in time, and warnings are often being given when the Page of Wands is reversed.

If a person is represented by this card, he's likely to be theatrical, overzealous, superficial, or image-conscious. The Page of Wands reversed is trying to let you know that you should be on the alert for some delays or disappointing news. But remember—you can turn the card back up if you desire.

Everyday Wands

The everyday Minor Arcana are the cards that show the routine events and day-to-day feelings we encounter in our lives. These events may be happening at the time of the reading or about to happen in the very near future. Like the royal Minor Arcana, these are free will cards, and so we have control over how things unfold.

Everyday Wands explore your daily work, as well as any new projects you may be considering, including travel. These cards stand for your creativity and enthusiasm as well as your ambition and competitive nature. Here's where you'll find the passion and the power to get what you want done.

Each card has its own energy and power. Wands represent how we get up in the morning and go about our day. This suit shows exactly what your energy is today and the next day.

Fools Rush In

You know how you feel full of energy and really motivated one week, and then just pooped out the next? When everyday Wands come up reversed, they're reflecting those times when you're just not that motivated. Wands, upright for energy and reversed for lack of energy, reflect the changeability of life that we all experience at times.

Wave Your Wands: An Exercise

Place the Ace through 10 of Wands in front of you on a table to see how the energy grows and develops as you make your way through this suit. It's fun to look at the whole suit in this way: You can see the green leaves popping out of each card, and the development from the Ace to the 10 of Wands.

Now, place the same ten cards upside down. Oh my! Laying them out this way on your table, you can see that all the green leaves are pointing down. There's not much growth, and their pointing downward can represent setbacks and lack of ambition and enthusiasm. Except for the 5 of Wands, which has more problems in its upright position (more on that a little later in this chapter), all the others have become slowed down, with their energy at a halt.

Try this exercise as you go through each suit and watch what happens as you make your way from the Ace through the 10 of Wands, Cups, Swords, and Pentacles. You can actually watch the story of each suit unfold!

Ace of Wands: Great Beginnings

Ace of Wands.

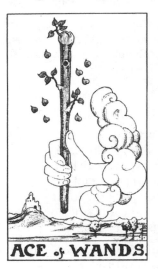 

Upright Imagery and Meanings: In the Ace of Wands, a Hand (and we capitalize that Hand of God intentionally!) comes out of the clouds holding a flowering wand. This represents the beginning of new energy, renewed courage, good self-esteem, and being ready to face a new day. The Ace of Wands shows a desire to initiate a new direction in life, as well as the energy to start a new project. You'll have plenty of ambition and motivation to get you started, too.

A fresh start in a new direction can represent anything—from a new job offer, to a new attitude toward something, or a condition in your life that you approach with renewed energy. There may be a new baby on the way, but even if that's not the case, a birth of some kind is definitely in the works.

Reversed Imagery and Meanings: How does this upside-down Ace of Wands look to you? For starters, the Wand pointed downward is a sure sign of false starts or low self-esteem. The fire in the wand is almost out when it's reversed. But remember, you have the matches to start that fire up again!

The Ace of Wands reversed lets you know you must look at something you're missing. Is it something you didn't do right? Are you not as motivated as you appear, or too tired to accomplish what you set out to do? This card suggests that you need to start over again, to regroup and see what you need more of. "It's time to go back to the drawing board," says the Ace of Wands reversed. "Do not pass Go. Do not collect $200."

Spinning the Wheel of Fortune

Aces always mean new starts or new conditions just entering your life. Aces show that you have the motivation, power, and enthusiasm to get on with your projects. So take those Aces by the horns, er, by the cards!

2 of Wands: Waiting

2 of Wands.

Upright Imagery and Meanings: The 2 of Wands shows a man holding one wand, and there's a second wand here as well. The man has a globe in his hand *("He's got the* *whole world in his hands…"*), and is looking toward the world he's already put some energy into. Maybe he's started a business or project and is now waiting for his ships to come in. In any event, he's looking out with anticipation.

The 2 of Wands indicates that you're waiting for results. Upright, this card shows the patience and focus of your intent. You've set things in motion, so they'll surely develop, and you can patiently wait for your rewards.

The 2 of Wands can also represent someone who'll give you help along the way. As your new enterprise grows and develops, things are starting to move along. It's beyond just an idea; now you get to see how things start to materialize.

Reversed Imagery and Meanings: When the 2 of Wands is reversed, the globe is falling away from the man, who's standing on his head, and there's only one wand he'll have control over in this position. Is he going back to square one? Reversed, the 2 of Wands *is* back—to the Ace of Wands. Because the man can't hold on to both wands at the same time, backwards action or motion is indicated.

The 2 of Wands reversed suggests that there's no movement toward your goal. There may be a lack of follow-through or harmony, but in any event, your venture will have many delays and frustrations. It could mean that help hasn't come, that the partnership isn't balanced, or that global conditions aren't helping at this time. It may be time to go back and regroup or change the plan, or you may have to start over entirely.

3 of Wands: Advice Through Partnership

3 of Wands.

 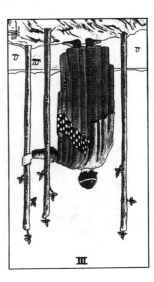

Upright Imagery and Meanings: Here we have the same man from the 2 of Wands, but now he's looking toward the future of his developments. Look with him toward the sea, and you'll see the boats of his labors coming back, just as he does. They're full of new resources to fulfill his next goal.

When he arrives at the 3 of Wands, the man feels more established in business and education. He can tell things are moving along much better and that the momentum has increased. He knows he'll benefit from his efforts so far and receive the rewards of the hard work he's put forth. He's also rightfully proud of his accomplishments.

The 3 of Wands often comes up when you're being offered help. It indicates good partnerships and solid cooperation with others. In business or education, there's support all around you, and everyone involved wants to either help out or support your efforts. Success can't be too far away when you have that kind of back-up and positive thoughts from others!

Reversed Imagery and Meanings: Reversed, the 3 of Wands can indicate the same desire for accomplishment and the same amount of focus as its upright position. But when it's upside down, the two wands slip away, so we're back to square one and the Ace of Wands (there's only one wand left in his hand) all over again. Reversed Wands are starting to sound a lot like "One step forward and two steps back," aren't they?

When we turn this card over, the sea and boats are hardly noticeable. The 3 of Wands reversed represents that your talents and skills aren't as fine-tuned as they should be. The competition or condition around you is stronger.

Sometimes, this card shows energy being wasted, or too much attention being given to details at the cost of the big picture. It could mean you're preoccupied with other conditions or have too many irons in the fire. The 3 of Wands reversed wants to remind you that pride or overconfidence isn't the right way to go. These can make the ships come back to you without the proper cargo or resources, leaving you high and dry, with inadequate resources or information.

4 of Wands: Celebrate the Good Life

4 of Wands.

Upright Imagery and Meanings: What a beautiful card this is! Students in Arlene's classes often say they'd love to find several 4 of Wands in the deck. This card shows a celebration after hard work, a gathering of family and friends to celebrate a joyful time in life, and garlands welcoming people into the peaceful setting of home and garden.

Harmony, peace, and fulfillment of your ideals are occurring at this time in your life. This card means a bountiful harvest for the farmer, a wedding celebration, a graduation, or a reunion with the ones you love. Here you'll find work well done and satisfaction to enjoy your rewards. Your home life is content, your garden is growing, and your children are developing their own talents. The foundation of a good life and stable conditions at home or work are evident here, so "Celebrate, celebrate…dance to the music!"

Reversed Imagery and Meanings: This is a good card either way! The 4 of Wands reversed represents that, while the celebration isn't as big or spectacular, nonetheless, congratulations are due. When the 4 of Wands is reversed, you're learning to appreciate the little joys of life, such as the first flower to blossom in spring, the first step a baby makes, a breath of fresh air, the final payment on the mortgage!

These are the blessings in life you often see but sometimes don't notice. The 4 of Wands reversed is thankful for the people and conditions around you and happy that the basics are secured. It's time to give a little thanks for what you *do* have, no matter how big or small.

5 of Wands: Struggles

5 of Wands.

Upright Imagery and Meanings: In the 5 of Wands, we see men fighting. They all have issues with each other, it seems, and the 5 of Wands, like all the other fives upright, indicates competitive action. In this card, the wands are all over the place. There's no organization and no particular focus, so the energy is scattered. The men look as if they just woke up to something they hadn't planned on. It's likely they were caught off-guard and are reacting defensively.

This card represents opposition or struggles. These fellows are not exactly sure what they're fighting against or about, but they feel the need to defend something. Maybe they're confused, overly agitated, under constant stress, or simply disorganized, but these men need to release or understand what threatens them.

When this card comes up in a reading, you should remember that something's gone awry. This is a difficult situation and more clarity must be found before you make any further movement. Legal issues can be represented by this card and the need for advice is very evident now. Don't let yourself get struck down!

Reversed Imagery and Meanings: Because the number five is positive in its reversed application, here we have the opposite of strife: Harmony will once again prevail. The men put down their wands and sit down to talk and discuss their problems. This card comes up a lot for problem-solving, rather than physical fighting about things.

In the Cards

Fives—the midway point of the numbered Minor Arcana cards—represent turning points. In their upright positions, they often show confusion or disunity. Reversed, though, fives are more positive, and represent more creative approaches to problem-solving and getting over those humps.

When the 5 of Wands is reversed, the men put down their wands. This indicates that your "fights" will be constructive and you'll find a way to work out your differences using good old common sense, resulting in a constructive outcome. Everyone involved will agree to sit down and talk about the problem, and, with good energy applied in the right way, there will be victory for your goals.

This card represents a win-win situation. Be prepared for exciting new opportunities coming your way, such as a new idea you never thought of to help you through a difficult situation. Compromise and negotiations are successful here.

6 of Wands: Coming Home to Success

6 of Wands.

Upright Imagery and Meanings: In the 6 of Wands, a horseman comes home to victory, wearing one laurel wreath on his head and carrying another on his wand. Five other wands surround him, as well as townspeople who applaud him on his return.

This card describes the recognition you receive when you come through a difficult time successfully; you've won a battle and become a good example for others. It can also represent good news coming and success just right around the corner. Relationships will improve when the 6 of Wands appears, and all problems, whether personal- or business-related, are in the process of being solved.

Guests or family may be coming soon, or there may be a group or organization reunion. This card also predicts the possibility of a safe journey out of town, with successful results for the reason you traveled in the first place. There's good news all around!

Reversed Imagery and Meanings: In a reversed 6 of Wands, the horseman and wands have turned upside down. This indicates delays, or that the opportunities are not available. You may be feeling like you just can't pull off the victory; you're tired, world-weary, and in need of some rest and relaxation.

Whichever way you try to go, you'll be met with frustration and obstacles. Stress and tension seem to be building

Spinning the Wheel of Fortune

The 6 of Wands reversed could indicate that someone or something is stronger or more victorious than you are at the moment. It's a time to be introspective and think about your next step. Time's on your side, and it's just what you need right now—time to reflect before you make your next move.

up, and you should try not to overreact to events that seem to be at a standstill. Here the need is to develop patience and ride out the storm.

A planned journey may be postponed or delayed for some reason, but further in the future anything delayed will be shown to have been for the best.

7 of Wands: Competing Interest

 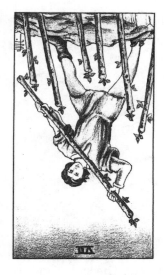

7 of Wands.

Upright Imagery and Meanings: In the 7 of Wands, we see a man in a defensive mode, holding his own against some enemy. Standing atop a hill, he looks as if he's not sure whether to strike or stand his ground. Notice he has the advantage of being just a little above the crowd, though.

When you get this card, you have inner strength and stamina, and the ability to stand your ground whatever the circumstances. Your courage is evident, and you can work through adversity and all sorts of pressure. Stiff competition in business or in personal issues may be indicated, or someone or something may feel like an enemy.

The man is protecting what he believes in and feels the need to fight for those ideals and beliefs. His courage is developed by maintaining his position.

Reversed Imagery and Meanings: The 7 of Wands reversed is actually better than its upright position. The man hangs on to the one wand he holds, but the threatening wands will fall away from him. This indicates that the threats have passed by. His enemy is gone, and the feelings of insecurity have passed. Whew!

With the 7 of Wands reversed, your position is upheld and you're stronger for it. You may have won a legal case or the acceptance of others, had some kind of near miss, or found the competition wasn't as strong as you thought. Your fears should leave you now and you'll realize that you've overcome a rough time in your life. You'll have patience and make slow progress toward your original goals because the storm has passed.

8 of Wands: Love and Enthusiasm

8 of Wands.

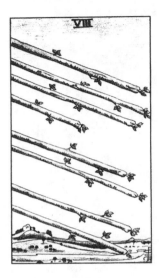 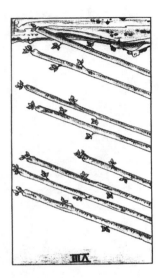

Upright Imagery and Meanings: The 8 of Wands is a simple scene of eight wands traveling through the air across an open countryside. Success on your travels! Success with your new love interest! Success for the goals you now have in mind!

With the 8 of Wands, everything will take flight and land in happiness and pleasure. The movement's in the right direction and you'll get what you've desired. There's progress toward a goal, a business idea, a new education, a new relationship, or possibly a positive change in the environment. This card indicates that your goals are within reach, so keep moving in the direction you've planned. This card encourages all your actions at this time.

Reversed Imagery and Meanings: With the 8 of Wands reversed, the arrows fall out of the sky. Your new love interest is waning, your journey is postponed, or arrows of conflict or jealousy may arise. You may need to control some unruly emotions or feel apprehensive or insecure.

Don't let your feelings get out of control; anger can develop with this card. Learn not to force an issue if the 8 of Wands reversed comes up as part of a spread. It's time to slow down like these slow-moving wands and take the time to reorganize your goal. Stand back and observe what's going on rather than jump in and force your hand.

9 of Wands: Prepared to Handle Adversity

9 of Wands.

Upright Imagery and Meanings: The 9 of Wands shows a man with a bandage on his head, leaning on his wand and waiting for someone or something that appears to be an enemy. Behind him are the eight wands we've seen before, now seeming to be protecting him from an enemy from behind. The bandage represents wounds from past conflict. You are wiser now from the experience and now know what it takes to keep your life in order.

The man is well prepared to handle adversity and hostility. He protects all that he's worked for, including his home, livelihood, and the friends and family who've been loyal. He has strength and stamina in reserve and is able to maintain control over his own interests.

"So far, so good," says the 9 of Wands. You're on your way to greater success. You've earned your standing in society and will fight to maintain the rights and livelihoods of others. Hold on to what you believe in and the philosophy you've developed through your experience. Perseverance, stamina, strength of character, and the ability to defend yourself or others are indicated here.

Reversed Imagery and Meanings: The 9 of Wands reversed still has the desire to protect and to be of help to others, but this man can barely take care of himself. Most of the time, the reversed 9 of Wands indicates the lack of stamina and physical strength to see things through. You've been beaten down either mentally or physically, and your health isn't good enough to follow through on the difficult tasks ahead.

You need to rest and recuperate, rather than go out and fight the battles again. You're not prepared, and need to check on things before you make your next move. You could be vulnerable, too weak to fight, or just plain exhausted. Sometimes this card comes up when you feel let down by others or are worried about something. The 9 of Wands reversed suggests it's best to regroup and calm yourself before taking another step.

10 of Wands: Shouldering the Burden

10 of Wands.

 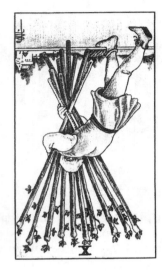

Fools Rush In

The 10 of Wands is the card of the codependent: Sometimes, it appears you like carrying this burden. Maybe you're such a good caretaker it seems as if you can handle anything. But remember, this card represents too much stress, which can ulti- mately affect your health. So don't overburden yourself with other's problems—*your* well-being or health can truly suffer.

Upright Imagery and Meanings: The 10 of Wands shows a man bent over from carrying ten flowering wands to the marketplace. Not only has he taken on many responsibilities from all areas of his life, he's chosen to take on others' responsibilities as well. Now he has too many wands to carry. The 10 of Wands indicates an oppressive burden, both physically and mentally.

The 10 of Wands indicates that you want to help others—but at what cost? Maybe you're taking on the burdens of your immediate or extended family, and you may shoulder these burdens well, but not for long. There's a need to look at how much you're carrying and to decide which wands are important to keep and which wands you should drop. The 10 of Wands reminds you to keep your priorities straight.

Reversed Imagery and Meanings: In a reversed 10 of Wands, we finally see someone letting the burden dissolve! The man is letting go of the guilt or pressure he once felt: "Whew! That was heavy! I didn't realize how much I was carrying around on my shoulders!" The burden was there for so long he didn't realize he could drop it. Or maybe he didn't know how he could or if he could be allowed to drop the extra things he was doing.

Sometimes this card represents someone who can abuse others into carrying a heavy responsibility; the reading will tell us which way this card should be read. This could be a clever person trying to unload his burden onto someone else or shifting responsibility to others—delegating, but with a hidden agenda.

The 10 of Wands reversed can indicate the burden is finally lifted and that you're free to go. But it also reminds you that the right approach would be to take responsibility for these burdens and then resolve them yourself, rather than shifting them to someone else.

The Least You Need to Know

➤ Wands represent your enterprise, growth, and development.

➤ Royal Wands are your strength and determination to begin something new.

➤ Everyday Wands give you the energy to work your way through your projects.

➤ Wands can be used to further your enterprise or to stall it.

Chapter 14

Cups: Life, Creativity, Emotions

In This Chapter

➤ Cups explore your emotional life and creativity

➤ Royal Cups: The nature of your heart and soul

➤ Everyday Cups: Your interaction with others

Where Wands were concerned with your growth and enterprise, Cups are the cards of your heart and soul. Here's where you'll find your emotional nature and the way you interact with others, and your creativity as well. From the strong-hearted faith of the King of Cups to the happily-ever-after of the 10 of Cups, these cards show the path to—and from—your heart.

The Royal Court

The watery Royal Cup cards reveal your emotional nature. And, as we all know, our emotions can be as changeable as the weather. That's why we have both the King of Cups and his fatherly love, and the Queen of Cups and her motherly, more maternal love. Then there's the romantic young Knight of Cups and the eager and gentle young Page of Cups, both harbingers of good things to come in your love life!

King of Cups: A Heart-Centered Leader

King of Cups.

Upright Imagery and Meanings: The King of Cups sits upon a turbulent ocean from which a dolphin jumps. Looking out, we can see a ship at anchor as well. The King looks peaceful as he feels the conditions around him. He holds the Cup of the Water of Life, knowing that he has to handle and deal with emotions and heart-centered issues. He also wears a golden fish on the chain around his neck, signifying his dominion over the sea.

The King of Cups is a man of devotion, introspection, and kindness in all that he does. When he speaks, it comes from the heart, and he has a quiet power. He can be a great leader in religion, at home, or as a counselor. Above all, he wishes to do humanitarian work or some kind of work with people. He can handle the rocky emotional side of humankind, and he does so with compassion.

The King of Cups is also very interested in the arts, music, or careers related to the ocean, fishing, nature, and the home/environment. The main concern of this king, though, is to understand and share human feelings and sensitivity. He covers his emotional nature with a calm exterior and enjoys watching progress from behind the scenes.

Reversed Imagery and Meanings: The reversed King of Cups has fallen into the ocean; his throne is tossed through these turbulent seas! Upside down, the King of Cups still has his feelings, but they're being tossed around, causing emotional upheaval or unsteady conditions.

When the King of Cups is reversed, there may be stormy weather for your affections, as there's no control over what's going on in your home or family. Because the environment is emotionally volatile, you may lose your sense of perspective. Maybe you're

186

suffering some loss and so are naturally reacting very moodily or seem detached. You are being asked to rise up and face an emotional issue with wisdom and maturity, but you don't feel up to it.

Sometimes, this card comes up reversed to tell us there's still deep-seated emotion and sensitivity, but the King can't express it or handle it at all. Instead, he'll stay detached, not tell the truth about an issue, or become reclusive, almost Hermit-like.

When the King of Cups is reversed, secrecy or shyness may be indicated, but the other cards around it can tell us more about him. Just remember, the King of Cups is emotional whether he's upright or reversed, but when those emotions are upside down, they can prove hard to handle.

Fools Rush In

When the King of Cups is reversed, emotions are turned inward, so you can easily be misunderstood. You're certainly not saying what you're *really* feeling. You need to express yourself better and express your true feelings—before it's too late!

Queen of Cups: Nurturing Intuition

Queen of Cups.

Upright Imagery and Meanings: The Queen of Cups sits on her beautiful throne, gazing into the cup of her imagination. Notice that this cup is closed, showing us that her thoughts are in the realm of the unconscious. The Queen is on the beach, with the quiet waters ebbing and flowing around her, showing that beauty and love surround her.

This sensitive Queen devotes herself to matters of the heart. Her attachment to others is strong and her desire to nourish and help others is evident as well. She's usually a good wife, a loving mother, and devoted to whatever she's committed herself to.

The Queen of Cups is willing to be of help and concerned with the welfare of others. Among the possible careers for her are caretaker, nurse, home-care worker, artist, or writer. Her imagination, in fact, can be one of her most powerful talents, and art, music, home, or family careers are most attractive to her.

Poetic and dreamy, the Queen of Cups is sensitive and relies on her intuition more than logic and reason. She feels everything, and wants to know what's going on at a deeper emotional level. Usually soft-spoken and good-natured, she wishes to please above all.

Reversed Imagery and Meanings: Reversed, the Queen has lost her cup, the ocean has become rough, and the tide is coming in too fast. This Queen has developed an overworked imagination. She's always worrying and concerned about things over which she has no control—maybe a lot like your mom!

The Queen of Cups reversed can exaggerate the conditions around her by her emotional outbursts. She means well and wants to be of help, but she's out of balance emotionally and can't see clearly through the turbulent conditions.

When the Queen of Cups comes up reversed in a spread, you need to take a deep breath and take a moment to think about what's going on instead of reacting. Just go within that cup and meditate on what's the best thing to do, without reacting at all. Sometimes this card comes up for a secretive nature or self-deceptive personality, but mostly, there's a need to harness the emotions. Remember: This, too, shall pass.

Knight of Cups: The Romantic Dreamer

Knight of Cups.

Upright Imagery and Meanings: The Knight of Cups is a handsome young man who sits on a gallant horse that's traveling across the countryside. This card reminds us of the white knight who's come to save the day. This white knight wears a winged helmet, the sign of the imagination, and he and his horse are about to cross over a river into a romantic adventure.

The Knight of Cups is a man of genuine character who's offering an invitation or proposal, and this card can represent the beginning of romance and falling in love. Skilled in the arts and music and with a good understanding of human needs, this is one knight who knows how to romance!

The horse is a symbol of bringing an issue or condition closer to you, and, for this young Knight, this means an issue of the heart, or learning to develop relationships of a heart-centered nature. Action in the heart and emotions are being brought to the fore when this Knight appears in a spread. Also considered a romantic dreamer, the Knight of Cups is full of ideas that can open your heart and make you look at your deepest feelings.

Reversed Imagery and Meanings: The reversed Knight of Cups has fallen off his horse, and that will postpone the offer or proposal. In romance, it means turbulent times, and that emotions aren't being shared equally between two people.

Upside down, the Knight of Cups doesn't relate well with others around him. The horse can't carry him across the water of his subconscious, and so there's a fear of getting involved with others or a fear of commitment.

All these fears and overworked emotions have left this Knight tired and weary of relationships. Sometimes the Knight of Cups reversed is a person who will hesitate or not tell the whole truth about what he or she feels.

Fools Rush In

Look before you leap into this situation, warns the Knight of Cups reversed. Caution is advised before committing to what's being offered when this Knight shows up. This could suggest that you need to look more deeply at the reality of what you're being offered—including a new romance that may not turn out as you'd like it to.

Page of Cups: Messenger of Love

Page of Cups.

Upright Imagery and Meanings: This little Page holds a cup outward to us, from which a mischievous fish, a symbol of the emotions and the imagination, peeks out. The Page of Cups brings attention to love and feelings in our lives. "Wake up and notice there's love in the air and in your heart," he reminds us.

The Page of Cups upright can indicate a message concerning romance, help from others, and devoted friends and family. This young Page wants to offer help and cooperation, and he has a gentle and good nature. When he appears in a spread, he brings joy, happiness, and a good omen that your life is changing for the better.

The Page of Cups offers gentleness, sweetness, kindness, and the desire to make you happy. There may be romantic or encouraging letters coming in the mail, and music, the arts, and poetry come with this young Page as well. He could also bring news of a birth of a child or happiness in family conditions, with a young person bringing the good news.

In the Cards

Congratulations are in order! The Page of Cups comes up quite often when young people are graduating from school, or receiving awards or some sort of recognition. The news is always happy and positive when he arrives in your reading—so accept your just rewards!

Reversed Imagery and Meanings: When the Page of Cups is upside down, the fish and water run to the ground. Messages either don't arrive or a happy message is delayed. Plans may be postponed, or the desire to plan ahead isn't there. Sometimes, this page is just too emotional to say much. He can be moody, brooding, or detached, because he's feeling sorry for him- (or her-) self.

When the Page of Cups is reversed, there's not much action. Instead, he withdraws from people, preferring to be alone. If this is a child in your life, try to get him to talk about his feelings so he won't overreact to conditions in the future. You know how difficult it can be for a child to sort through all those confusing emotions—but you can help.

So even though the Page is reversed and prefers not to communicate right now, the child needs to say something to relieve the built-up emotion that will eventually express itself, and it's up to you to encourage this. The Page of Cups reversed can represent an oversensitive child or a situation that calls for calm and introspection. Assert your free will and turn the Page upright again!

Everyday Cups

Everyday Cups take us on a sensual, emotional journey. We begin with the unfolding of the heart in the Ace of Cups, and continue through courtship, joy, dancing and dreams. Sometimes, there's the heartache of the 5 of Cups, but as we get older, the old loves of the 6 of Cups can find us. And in the end, we all can achieve the happily-ever-after the 10 of Cups promises.

Ace of Cups: New Love

Ace of Cups.

Upright Imagery and Meanings: Here we have the beginning of the opening up of the heart. Five streams of water, symbolic of the five senses, come out of a cup being held by the great Hand and fall into a pond. Water lilies, which symbolize psychic unfolding, float on top of the pond. Meanwhile, the dove of spirit descends, holding a wafer.

Spirit is manifest in soul, and you're in a cycle of opening up your heart to new emotions or beginning a new romance. It's the beginning of something wonderful! Joy surrounds the start of this new venture, and there's an openness of the heart and a desire for happiness. The Ace of Cups can promise new spiritual insight, a new awareness toward love, or a breakthrough in spiritual understanding.

Spinning the Wheel of Fortune

If the Ace of Cups reversed comes up for the beginning of your new relationship, it likely means the relationship will take a while to get off the ground. You may have a sense of feeling unwanted or uncared for, and so be moody and hesitant about putting yourself in the vulnerable position of giving away your heart. Remember though, reversal of this free will card is up to you.

In this card, we find blessings from above. It can also represent fertility and the conception of a child, for above all, this card stands for joy, happiness, and good health to come.

Reversed Imagery and Meanings: When the Ace of Cups is reversed, all the water is spilling out, so there's a rushing out of emotion. Soon, the cup will be empty, which can be symbolic of a heart that's not as open toward love as it should be, or the insecurity of a new relationship. This card may represent the fear of starting over in a relationship or insecurity concerning the new person who's arrived in your life. You may be preoccupied with yourself rather than others. Sometimes, out of low self-esteem, we act selfishly, and this card can describe just that.

The Ace of Cups reversed can also indicate that you're bored or tired of the same old conditions. You may have a desire for something or someone new, but a new relationship won't take shape at this time. In addition, there may be delays in attaining contact with someone, or frustration with a new start.

2 of Cups: Friendship

2 of Cups.

Upright Imagery and Meanings: The 2 of Cups heralds the beginning of a friendship, with two people pledging their devotion. The couple on this card has decided to make a commitment to friendship and to begin to share their feelings with each other. The serpents are twined around a staff, an emblem of life's male and female energies, and the lion has the wings of spirit and so shows a good balance between spiritual and earthly love.

Understanding and balanced friendships are developing here. Together, these two can achieve their plans. The 2 of Cups represents good partnerships, cooperation with each other, and the kind of sharing that can lead to bigger and better things. Here you'll find harmony and a sharing of good ideas between you, and there's kindness and thoughtfulness, bringing out the best in both of you. Sometimes the 2 of Cups predicts a letter, gift, or happy event on the horizon. This is a card about the best of relationships.

Reversed Imagery and Meanings: When the 2 of Cups is reversed, the couple still has the desire to connect and understand one another, but the water is running out, and the lion has no power to give help or protection. Upside down, there's no longer any balance, and disagreements with the one you love or respect, or misunderstandings with a good friend or loved one, may occur.

The 2 of Cups reversed represents that the problem can be solved but first, someone has to make the first move. Perhaps one of you is being stubborn or unwilling to give assistance. Emotions can run away with you when this card turns over, so try to stay balanced and aware that the need for communication is more important now than ever before.

This card can indicate a loss of balance in a close relationship, so you should try not to be possessive or jealous. There's a need for understanding or a new perspective to get

193

things back on an even keel. Sometimes this card comes up for people who are at the point of breaking off a relationship, or who are involved in a passionate situation that needs to be kept in check.

3 of Cups: Celebrate!

3 of Cups.

Upright Imagery and Meanings: In the 3 of Cups, three young maidens hold high their cups full of promise and celebration. Fruitful garlands and vines lie at their feet. Perhaps they offer us a look into what pleasure good friends and family bring us or a celebration of the harvest time of the year; fruition with success is worth celebrating, after all.

This card represents the happy conclusion of an undertaking and the success and recognition that follow. "Party time!" the girls seem to be saying. Their work has been done and the harvest has been brought in, so now they're ready to celebrate the bounty of their labors.

There's plenty to go around when the 3 of Cups appears: Good food, good friends, and the happiness to enjoy the good things in life are all present. This card can also indicate talent in the arts, music, design, beauty, or the hospitality business. In any event, you have that good combination of friends and family, and can look forward to great things coming into your life.

Reversed Imagery and Meanings: The 3 of Cups reversed shows the maidens tired or uninterested in what's around them. In this position, this card reflects that overindulgence or overdoing a good time can lead to arguments or poor decisions. Sorrow or pain can come from this card reversed, especially because gossip, or talk without thinking about what you're saying, can show here.

The 3 of Cups reversed suggests that it's time to take command of yourself and make new plans. You may need to apologize to friends, but it can all be worked out. Meanwhile, you recognize your excesses and bring them under control. It's important to try to communicate your feelings with the someone you're asking about in the reading, too.

4 of Cups: Reevaluating From a Distance

4 of Cups.

Upright Imagery and Meanings: Here we see a young man sitting under the ol' apple tree, being offered a fourth cup, which is coming toward him out of the blue. We recognize the three cups on the ground from before, but now an added cup gives us a different feeling. The man is being offered a fourth cup—and yet he refuses them all! He's so busy pondering the three cups, he wonders if he should go into *anything* that could bring out his emotions.

This guy looks a little leery—his arms and legs are crossed as if he were protecting himself (remember Body Language 101?). This card represents a person or situation that's detached from the world. For you, it could mean discontent or boredom as you reevaluate your life.

Sometimes it seems as if you don't care what happens when this card appears. You may have no motivation or a lack of concern for others at this time. You're feeling introverted and looking for a spiritual level to attach to. You may feel as if no one understands you right now, and that's because you have inner work to do.

Reversed Imagery and Meanings: The 4 of Cups reversed allows you to come out of your contemplation and go in a new direction. You're once again motivated to try something new, including new love or a new focus on something that truly moves you. You'll have a great desire to accomplish new work, new goals, and new ambitions.

Now's the time to turn to action and start to re-create your goals and dreams. It may appear as if nothing's happening, but be prepared for an exciting change of events when the 4 of Cups reversed appears: Movement is in the right direction, and there will be renewed activity with the hope of a good cycle starting.

5 of Cups: An Emotional Loss

5 of Cups.

Upright Imagery and Meanings: The 5 of Cups shows a man in a dark cloak looking down at three cups that have tipped over and spilled the wine of life. He has such sorrow as he looks and concentrates on those three cups that he doesn't look at the two cups behind him.

The 5 of Cups always represents loss of some kind, usually something or someone you've been attached to. When this happens, you can find it difficult to explain how you feel inside; you're experiencing grief, loss, or heartache, and it's hard to express those painful emotions.

The 5 of Cups knows that sorrow takes a while to heal. It's okay to cry or grieve over a loss, and sometimes, it's good to get emotions out and release pent-up feelings of sadness. The distant bridge reminds us there's a time when this loss will pass, and the two upright cups behind the man show that tomorrow will bring a renewed interest in love, as hard as that may be to believe right now. For now, though, you're engrossed in your loss, whether it's the end of a relationship, someone who's left, or disillusionment, regrets, and broken dreams. Not all matters of the heart are happy ones, after all.

Reversed Imagery and Meanings: When this five is reversed, it brings a positive message, as do all fives in the Tarot. The 5 of Cups reversed indicates the reversal of negative energy. Loss is replaced by improvements. Hope and happiness return, and your energy is increasing daily.

You may make new friends when the 5 of Cups reversed appears, or old friends or acquaintances may call on you. It's time for the return of good memories, new hope, renewed confidence, and just feeling back to your old self. You've summoned the courage to rise above your loss. Don't be afraid to start to develop new ideas or make new plans.

You've learned from your past; now remember that tomorrow is a new day. This card can indicate a new job on the horizon or a change in plans that will turn out for the better. "All is not lost," says the 5 of Cups reversed. "So cheer up! New things will replace the old ones." The 5 of Cups reversed reminds us that as one chapter closes, another opens.

6 of Cups: Happy Childhood Memories

6 of Cups.

Upright Imagery and Meanings: The 6 of Cups is a good indication that friends and family have generated happy memories for you. A little boy is giving a cup of flowers to a little girl in a nice hometown atmosphere. Nearby, five more cups hold flowers, which are, as we all know instinctively, gifts of the heart. The cottages in the background can bring us back to good memories of our childhood, past, or hometown.

This card represents meeting with someone from your past, such as a childhood friend or old love, or a reunion with family members. You will find the happiness and enjoyment that come from the past, and good thoughts about your past as well. If you're presented with an opportunity to grow into a new relationship or new job, it will have some connection to the past, too.

This card comes up often to refer to siblings and family values. It could mean a gift from an admirer or old friend, or that something from the past will resurface or be returned to you. At the same time, new people for whom you feel an affinity may enter your life. Maybe they'll be from your hometown or have graduated from the same high school or college as you. And, if a gift or inheritance is represented by the 6 of Cups, it will be more than you expected!

Reversed Imagery and Meanings: The 6 of Cups reversed represents the past turned upside down. This translates to rewards being delayed, a memory of the past that's not as happy, or news from the past that could be disruptive to you. Maybe you're clinging to outworn ideas or experiencing feelings of nostalgia, or living in the past instead of the present.

The 6 of Cups reversed can indicate that you wish the past would return, although sometimes people get this card to reflect on the past but not to live in it. Perhaps you need to get out of a condition that's harmful or hurtful to your future—to put it in the past, in other words.

This card can represent disappointment having to do with family or your expectations of family. Maybe you expected your family to be there for you and they weren't. It's time to let go of outworn ideas and obsolete conditions in your life when the 6 of Cups reversed appears. "The times they are a changin'," and you can grow into a new future that will once again create new memories.

7 of Cups: Fantastic Visions

7 of Cups.

Upright Imagery and Meanings: The 7 of Cups shows a man trying to make a choice. Should he take the castle or the jewels? The wreath of victory or the red dragon? The woman or the ideal of himself? Too many choices! And then, in the center of the card, is a draped individual ready to be revealed. What's under that draped cup?

All these questions are part of the interpretation of the 7 of Cups. Maybe your imagination's working overtime and you're having difficulty making a decision. Chances are you can't see the forest for the trees.

With your dissipated forces, you're meeting confusion at every juncture. Which way should you go? What should you do? Which do you choose? This card can indicate a selfish indulgence in dreams instead of action, or being stuck in a condition due to wishful thinking, daydreaming, or choosing illusion over reality.

Reversed Imagery and Meanings: When the 7 of Cups is reversed, there will finally be a decision. The man can choose his direction through good use of his will and determination. Now that he's made up his mind and chosen one direction to go, he's on the right track and will continue on this course.

When the 7 of Cups is reversed, it always means you've made a choice you'll follow through on. You'll select a project and have the commitment to see it to its end. Don't give up your ideas, because your plan is starting to work when this card appears. The choice you made was right for you. Persist with that choice, and soon, you'll be reaping what you sowed.

8 of Cups: Leaving an Attachment

8 of Cups.

Upright Imagery and Meanings: The 8 of Cups focuses toward the spiritual side of the heart. Here we see a man with a staff walking toward the barren mountains. He's walking away from what was once near and dear to him, because now he has a need for spiritual insight.

In the Cards

Why do we climb mountains? Why do we search the world (or the universe) for new adventures or new land? The 8 of Cups is a spiritual quest, a search for something you can't see but can only feel. When this card appears, your higher self will proceed with an inner search. It's time to get in touch with your own heart.

When the 8 of Cups appears, you're totally dissatisfied with your present mode of life and want something higher. Is the grass greener on the other side of the mountain or does it just seem that way? You may abandon your present daily routine in order to find out.

Note that in this card, the man has stacked his cups neatly before moving on. He appears to be finished with those past concerns and worries of the material world. Now he seeks something different, and even though he's not sure what he'll find on the other side of those mountains, he's setting off to seek it.

Reversed Imagery and Meanings: When the 8 of Cups is reversed, the man turns back around to the material world and his search for pleasure and success of a material nature, with joy and feasting on the horizon. With a flip of the card, he's back in the physical world, which isn't always a bad place to be.

When this card appears reversed, you have renewed interest in people and connections to the earthly plane. This can mean that a new love interest is in view, whether a person or a condition. You'll get your passion for the physical world back again with the 8 of Cups reversed. It comes up for people wanting to enjoy life, whether through friends, travels, or new adventures. It indicates a need for love, passion, and adventure, all of which add up to bliss, a time for reentering the world after a period of retreat.

9 of Cups: Wishes Fulfilled!

9 of Cups.

Upright Imagery and Meanings: The wish card! Naturally, a lot of Arlene's students want this card in every spread they have! The well-satisfied man sits content, with his nine cups on the arched shelf behind him. As if he's rubbed a magic lantern, he will get his wish!

In the Cards

The 9 of Cups was called the wish card by the Gypsies of Europe, and you, too, can depend on an answer of "Yes!" when this card appears. When the 9 of Cups comes upright in your spread, you will get your wish. It's like a genie!

This card assures material success and a secure future. "Your wish is my command," said the genie. "What you desire will come to you!" You'll have much happiness in attaining your wish, whether it's a new car, a new relationship, a new job, extra money, or simply happiness coming your way. Other cards in the reading will tell us how and when the wish may take place. With your love of luxury and the physical pleasures in life, it's nice to have those wishes come true.

Reversed Imagery and Meanings: The wish card reversed is cause for pause. What do you mean it won't happen the way I want or not happen today!? Most people who get readings want to have a positive outcome with every question they ask, but the wish card reversed indicates that the wish won't be fulfilled as asked or that the wish won't be fulfilled at this time.

Sometimes, the 9 of Cups reversed can come up to represent a lack of money or resources, or overindulgence or overdoing a good thing. Are you pushing for this wish to happen? Are you anxious about not getting what you want? Are you trying too hard to have it happen NOW? Your wish can come another day, but for today, you'll just have to wait.

10 of Cups: Success in Family, Marriage, and Love

10 of Cups.

Upright Imagery and Meanings: Here's the ultimate the suit of Cups can bring. It's the "happily-ever-after" card, where a young couple stretches out their arms in happiness and gratitude for home, love, and family ties, which are joyful and happy. Their modest home is in the background, and two children are playing next to them.

When the 10 of Cups appears in your spread, you're experiencing the happiness you've always wanted. You've realized your personal hopes, dreams, and desires, have a happy family life, and enjoy true friendships.

Here's lasting happiness inspired from above. This can be an indication of a marriage or having a family, or there may be a family reunion, a celebration, or an anniversary. With the 10 of Cups, things happen in a way that makes all of us shed tears of joy. This card may also come up to predict buying a new home, bringing home a new baby, or moving into a cycle of your life where everything just flows like magic. With the 10 of Cups, you really do live happily ever after!

Reversed Imagery and Meanings: When the 10 of Cups is reversed, there's still the desire for family contentment, but it hasn't completely arrived yet. The present situation may be bothersome: Perhaps the house deal isn't going through correctly, the children are turning against their parents, the wedding's being put off, or the new job's being put on hold.

Some delays and difficult times are ahead before anything goes well. For certain, patience is needed, because your wonderful venture is not going to happen right now. Perhaps a family upset or disagreement is causing problems, or your reunions are unhappy ones. This card can indicate the loss of a friendship or fighting among siblings or relatives.

There could be a loss of reputation or damage done to the home or family. This card sometimes comes up for physical damage done to the home because of flooding, bad weather conditions, or what those insurance policies call "acts of God." It can also relate to thoughtless or painful action from those close to you.

It's important to remember with the 10 of Cups reversed, as with any card with a negative message, that time will bring healing. And, as with all the Minor Arcana, this is a free will card that *you* can turn upright with effort and determination.

The Least You Need to Know

➤ Cups represent your emotional life and creativity.

➤ Royal Cups explore the nature of your heart and soul.

➤ Everyday Cups indicate the ways you interact emotionally with others.

➤ You control your emotional nature.

Chapter 15

Swords: Action, Power, Obstacles

In This Chapter

➤ Swords represent conflict, obstacles, and aggression

➤ Royal Swords: Logic and thoughtful attention to all sides of issues

➤ Everyday Swords: Struggles and difficulties

Swords represent strife and aggression, and the process of developing courage and mental strength. These are the cards of everyday conflict and problems, the obstacles you encounter, and the way you deal with those obstacles. No life is entirely a primrose path, and Swords are the first to remind us of that!

In medieval times, the way someone held his sword next to him would tell those of other tribes what his tribe was thinking. Imagine sending messages via a sword's position—it sounds like something our politicians might use today. Anyway, if the sword pointed up, it meant victory; pointed down, it meant retreat or submission. If it was held to the side of the body facing downward, the tribe was ready to speak or negotiate, while pointed down with both hands on the sword meant the tribe was ready to listen or debate with an open mind. Lastly, if the sword was held across the front of the body horizontally, it meant the tribe was prepared to hand over a victory or power to another.

The Royal Court

Royal Swords are logical, analytical folk, well-educated, reasonable, and always looking at issues from a balanced perspective. This is the suit where the term "Royal Court" can be taken quite literally to mean those who sit in judgment. When we look at these cards, we see William Rehnquist and Sandra Day O'Connor!

Royal Swords bring messages about how to deal with the problems facing you. The message may be one of using rational analysis to get to the core of the issue; this is the way the King of Swords approaches things. Or the Swords may be saying that you should look at the issue from every side, which is the message the Page of Swords is quick to remind you of. But when Royal Swords talk, people should listen.

King of Swords: Logical Counsel

King of Swords.

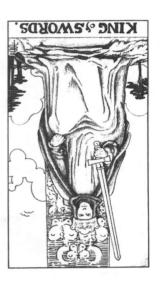

Upright Imagery and Meanings: Behind the King of Swords, who holds a sword in his hand, are storm clouds, as well as the cypress trees we'll see in all of the royal Sword cards. The air movement and the clouds represent some turbulence and stormy weather. This is a stern king who sits on a throne decorated with butterflies and sylphs, and he's looking right at you, as if he's studying or analyzing you. He can make you feel rather uncomfortable!

The King of Swords is well educated, understands the human mind, and deals well with logic and reason. He has the right authority for his ability to counsel, and he can give good logical advice. He can also represent a judge in government or law.

The King of Swords has the power to command because he always knows what's at the crux of a situation. Good counsel and good advice help him come to a fair and rational decision. He's just and honorable in all that he does, making him a firm friend. And he desires fairness is all his dealings.

The King of Swords has a good memory and can be sharp as a tack when it comes to statistics, analysis, and recall of an event. He's direct in all that he does, but because he's upright, he's also flexible—as long as the argument's logical.

In the Cards

The King of Swords can appear cautious, and that's because he needs time to come to a conclusion. He's a good debater and a master of intellectual pursuits. As a father he can appear stern, serious, and thoughtful—the better to hone his children's mental abilities.

Reversed Imagery and Meanings: This King isn't too happy when he's reversed. His sword is pointed down, like he's fought too many battles, or that someone else has won the battle. Upside down, the storm clouds have become dominant, and the wind has blown through and made the King of Swords retreat from his throne.

He certainly has a bad attitude now. He feels mentally exhausted, unable to handle the stress of the situation. Possibly there's been bad news that he's not handling well. He's critical, cool, and aloof, as well as obstinate, and he can be cruel, especially in his words.

The King of Swords reversed won't be sensitive to the needs of others. He's preoccupied with his own thoughts and ideas and can become obsessed with his own intentions and actions. Because of his lack of concern for others and his lack of diplomacy now, he can upset others. In addition, he can be severe in his judgment, make unfair assessments, and just be downright opinionated about everything.

Queen of Swords: Analytical Thinker and Advisor

Queen of Swords.

Upright Imagery and Meanings: The Queen of Swords is seated on a high throne that looks out into a clouded sky. She's resting her sword on her throne and holds out her hand to us, maybe to call our attention to something. Note, as in the King of Swords, the presence of the cypress trees, the sky with clouds, and the throne of butterflies: All of these focus our attention on our thoughts and our mental state. In this card, a bird hovers above, symbolizing messages coming through.

The Queen's upright sword represents spirit penetrating matter and informing us with knowledge, and like the King of Swords, this Queen can be an excellent teacher, lawyer, or counselor. She has a sharp mind, is a keen observer of people, and a good listener who, with her sound logic and reasoning, will analyze all conditions.

The Queen of Swords is a good public speaker and organizer. She's got great leadership qualities and can handle a crowd quite well. She's also thoughtful and able to keep her emotions in check.

This card indicates a woman of strong character, but also one who's seen many hardships. Because of her character, she bears her sorrow well; she's adept at handling loss, too, and knows how to deal with the most difficult of human conditions. And, with her clear and direct way of speaking and addressing issues, the Queen of Swords is a good psychologist.

Reversed Imagery and Meanings: The Queen has lost her sword! Oh my! She won't like that—it indicates she's been through some kind of loss. Upside down, she can barely keep her calm exterior and is easily angered, unable to discipline herself as when she was upright.

This reversed Queen still has keen observations, but can use them in a narrow-minded way. She's not so open to listening, but will instead tell us what to do. Often when she's reversed, she'll be misunderstood, which is why she'll have difficulty with others. But she can also cause her own downfall by being too judgmental or dogmatic.

The Queen of Swords reversed is, as in her upright position, both strong and stern, but she needs to use more self-control when she's reversed. Her perception of a situation will now be colored by her one-sided view, and she may have a tendency to gossip and embellish matters to force others to share her opinion.

Knight of Swords: A Quick Cut to the Core

Knight of Swords.

Upright Imagery and Meanings: The young Knight of Swords is off on a journey on his beautiful thoroughbred racehorse. With his speed, this Knight brings messages of caution and the need to stay alert. When he comes up in your reading, he's telling you to pay attention to coming events. This Knight can also represent a person or event coming into your life. Either way, he cuts to the chase and tells the truth—even if it hurts!

The Knight of Swords has a great need to inform us of something important. He represents urgency to get things moving in your life—now! He doesn't dilly-dally along; he's a mover and a shaker. While this Knight's courteous and kind and has good intentions, he's also quick-witted and sharp, and, as he expects the same of others, he can seem a little pushy at times. Still, his focus never wavers.

This is a courageous, skillful Knight, who with his good mind can be a helpful advisor. He'll always defend the underdog and is concerned with getting the truth of the matter out in the open. His desire to warn us makes us alert and ready for action. "Forewarned is forearmed," says the Knight of Swords.

Reversed Imagery and Meanings: Reversed, the Knight of Swords' mighty horse is upside down and can no longer move in the direction he was going. This can mean delays, apprehension, conflicts, or battles yet to be won. There may be difficulty maintaining stamina, strength, or mental attitude, and he's not able to cope with conditions because he's just mentally worn out. This Knight may also be unable to help or warn others of an impending trauma.

Sometimes the Knight of Swords reversed can be argumentative or a troublemaker, or—you know the type—always ready to start a fight or a war. This can also be someone who's opposed to your thoughts and actions right now.

This card reversed signals constant delays and struggles that can seem never-ending. If there is a young man around you, make sure you understand his lack of concern for others, and try to steer clear of this guy when he's reversed. Something's wrong around him and he may not be saying what; because he can't carry his sword well, he may not be communicating very well either. This card can also represent dishonesty and deception, so in any event, caution is advised.

Page of Swords: Messenger of Vigilance

Page of Swords.

Upright Imagery and Meanings: This Page holds his sword with both hands, ever vigilant and intent on the message he's carrying. If this is a young person, he or she is very intelligent, a quick thinker able to handle any emergency situation well.

The Page of Swords is a messenger who urges us to look deeper into the meaning of a situation. "Pay attention!" he keeps saying. "Take a closer look. There's more to this than meets the eye!"

The Page of Swords has the qualities of grace, dexterity, and inquisitiveness. There's a desire to communicate and help others by giving added information. At the same time, there could be a delay in your plans or some disappointing news. Courage may be needed to deal with the problem at hand.

Reversed Imagery and Meanings: When the Page of Swords is reversed, he's got a lot to do with information

Spinning the Wheel of Fortune

Sometimes, the Page of Swords upright means spying or receiving information through a third party. This can be the card of secret agents and secret information, or of hiring a private detective!

that will reveal the whole truth and nothing but the truth. This card is actually better reversed than it is upright; now the Page of Swords shows unpredictable behavior or sudden events, or those with a strange twist coming into your life. But whatever these changes are, they usually turn out for the best.

Remember, all changes the Page ushers in eventually come out for the better, like the proverbial silver lining around the dark cloud. If the Page of Swords reversed represents a young person or dealings you're having or will have with teenagers, it can suggest that they'll be unpredictable—but you will be able to get to the source of the frustration and talk about it. Great communication comes with the Page of Swords whether he's upright or reversed, because truth eventually comes forth. The desire to speak is too great with this card to be kept silent.

Everyday Swords

Life can't always come up Cups and Wands, and everyday Swords are the cards that help us face and deal with some of life's more difficult aspects. It's important to remember that the force of Swords can be used for good as well as for harm, and with this positive aspect, you can force difficult situations to resolve themselves. Remember, too, that like all Minor Arcana cards, everyday Swords are free will cards. How you use their force is up to you.

Ace of Swords: Conquest and Victory Begin

Ace of Swords.

Upright Imagery and Meanings: The Ace of Swords is double-edged and so can cut both ways: constructively, to cut away the dead wood; or destructively, to harm or force a situation. This card shows a Hand coming out of the clouds (which you should by now recognize from the other Aces we've seen) firmly holding an upright sword encircled by a crown with the olive branch of peace and the palm of victory. Six *yods*—the life force or drops of light from heaven—protect the sword.

The Ace of Swords signals the beginning of an undertaking that will prove successful. Forward thinking and focused action assure that victory is near and that conquest and success for the goal are at hand. This card can signify the birth of a child who could become a courageous leader, or people who champion the underdog. The Ace of Swords assures new ideas and swift action will win the day.

When this card appears in your spread, you feel powerful and in control. The situation you're in may have risen out of a more difficult one, but now you hold the cards, so to speak. You've got focus and logic on your side and the strength to see your project past difficulties to its conclusion.

Card Catalog

Yods are actually representations of the Hebrew letter *yod*. This letter represents the name of God and is also symbolic of the life force, or the light from heaven that protects us all.

Reversed Imagery and Meanings: The reversed Ace of Swords has a negative focus: It cuts to harm or inflict pain. Remember, the sword both penetrates matter and informs it, so this sword reversed is too forceful and can hurt others. Beware of trying to use too much force to gain an end. Do your work gently and try not to push the river.

The Ace of Swords reversed wants to remind you not to apply pressure to the situation because it will just make it worse. You can attract opposition at this time so you should be cautious and diplomatic. You can try to avoid arguments by using good common sense and reasoning ability.

2 of Swords: Stalemate, Indecision

 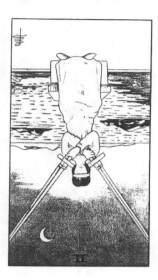

2 of Swords.

Upright Imagery and Meanings: In the 2 of Swords, we find a blindfolded young woman sitting on a bench holding two large swords. Because she's blindfolded, she can't see her way through these difficult times. In addition, she's turned her back on the water (her feelings), and therefore can't see or sense anything to help her out of the stalemate she's in. The jagged rocks and new moon symbolize the instability around her.

This card shows the need for a well-balanced life. The woman is at a point of indecision: Which way should she turn? Which way should you turn in life? When you get this card, not only will it be hard to make a decision, it will be difficult to even think of moving on it. This card also can indicate a temporary truce, stalled negotiations, or inadequate information.

You'll feel completely on hold, and delayed and confused about your direction. The 2 of Swords suggests a need for guidance and direction, but note that the woman can still hold those swords upright! She can sit in contemplation instead of action for now—and this may be the best course when this card appears.

Reversed Imagery and Meanings: The reversed 2 of Swords indicates a decision has been made. The woman will now take action and things will occur quickly. When you get this card in a spread, you'll be free to make your own decisions with the faith that action is now taking place.

This card indicates release and forward movement in your affairs. The rocks are still in the water and therefore you need to deal with the right people and be careful not to share any confidences, but you should follow through and keep to your own path. What the 2 of Swords has reversed and that it doesn't have upright now is confidence—the confidence to get going on your goal.

3 of Swords: Heartache and Disappointments

3 of Swords.

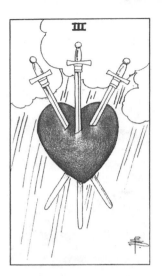 

Upright Imagery and Meanings: The 3 of Swords' symbol of a red heart pierced by three swords is a universal symbol of loss of a loved one, grief, and sorrow in life. Rain clouds fill the air and a storm has developed. When this card appears, sorrow is evident, and it's the other cards around it that will tell us in more detail where the sorrow comes from.

Fools Rush In

There are times when life just doesn't seem to go well at all, and we need cards to reflect the human condition in these negative aspects, too. The 3 of Swords is one of the sadder cards of the Tarot, but remember, crying or grief are normal human emotions and should be accepted as part of life. The entire suit of Swords reflects that part of ourselves which can—and which we allow to—feel uncomfortable.

This card comes up to indicate that an argument can lead to a separation or that a quarrel can lead to the breakup of a friendship or partnership. Pain and sorrow are expressed when this card appears, and disorder or upheaval may cause distress. Due to some kind of misfortune, loved ones may be separated by war or political strife. The 3 of Swords indicates that you need to express the sorrow you're feeling in your heart.

Reversed Imagery and Meanings: When the 3 of Swords is reversed, its intensity has lessened. The situation isn't as severe as when this card is in the upright position. You may be dissatisfied with the present outcome or situation, and there may be upsets and tears, but when the 3 of Swords is reversed, they'll be of a passing nature.

The 3 of Swords reversed means that you'll work through this difficult time more quickly than you thought you would. There may be an apology in the works, and so a peacemaker is at hand. As when it's upright, its surrounding cards will tell us where the sadness is coming from, as well as whether the sorrow is in the past or future.

4 of Swords: Convalescence

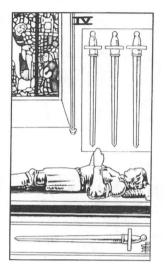 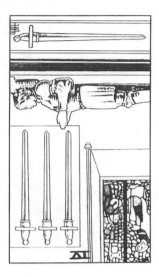

4 of Swords.

Upright Imagery and Meanings: This can be a frightening card to those unfamiliar with the Tarot's imagery. "Am I going to die?" more than one Querent has asked. In this card, a knight is resting upon a tomb, but he's resting after war and strife. This is not a card of death, but of convalescence and repose. The three swords we've just seen in the previous card hang over him, while the fourth rests alongside him.

This card actually means that the knight is now at peace with all that's happened. He's finished his work and can rest and take time out to think about his future. What shall he do now? Where shall he go? What if he has to fight the same battle again? The 4 of Swords represents a break in his life, a rest to contemplate and evaluate what he's accomplished.

Sometimes this card represents someone on vacation or on a retreat. It can mean convalescence after surgery or coming home from the hospital and resting comfortably there. The 4 of Swords represents a time to renew your energies, both physical and mental. This should be a calming period in your life. Enjoy the peace and quiet before the next storm rolls in!

Reversed Imagery and Meanings: The reversed 4 of Swords signals that the knight's now ready to get back into action. The three swords come alive off the wall, so the knight will get up from his tomb and focus on future plans with renewed energy.

Good opportunities lie ahead, this card suggests, but be thoughtful in how you handle them. Sometimes it can indicate that there's political upheaval or unrest in the work force. The place of work may have labor problems, employee discontent, or unions or political parties that want to take action to change existing laws or practices. This card suggests upheaval, in both its positive and negative aspects.

5 of Swords: Fall from Grace

5 of Swords.

Upright Imagery and Meanings: The young men in the 5 of Swords are just spoiling for a fight, and three of them have difficulty even dealing with each other. Storm clouds gather and the wind howls as one rebel looks at the others, whose swords he has captured.

This card shows a lack of sensitivity or concern for others. The young man's tenacious grip on the sword indicates both selfishness and the breakup or severing of ties. This card can represent an unfair application of power, degradation, or worse—disgrace.

Legal complications often come up with this card, and the cards surrounding this one tell exactly how things will turn out. The 5 of Swords can represent taking what's not really yours, stealing away energy, power, or literally the swords of the other men. It can come up to represent slyness and cunning, or the ability to coerce others out of something.

The 5 of Swords can also represent deceptive actions or the ability to manipulate either people or a condition to suit one's own needs. It can indicate developing a bad reputation, an unethical victory, or just plain destructive behavior.

Reversed Imagery and Meanings: The 5 of Swords reversed isn't as difficult as it is upright. The men are on more equal footing, so there's no deception going on here. Instead, all three know exactly what each is thinking or planning.

This card can indicate sneaky behavior or a desire to create conflict. When it appears upside down, you're aware of the difficult lawsuit ahead of you or of a certain situation that can cause all kinds of emotional problems. There's still a chance of loss, but to a lesser degree—small claims court, say. Or perhaps you win, but it's not the victory you wanted.

Gossip comes up with the 5 of Swords reversed. When you hear about it, you try to clear it up and get to the truth of the matter. This isn't the easiest card to have, so when it comes up, it's important to study the surrounding cards to accurately describe the question's outcome.

6 of Swords: Leaving Sorrows Behind

 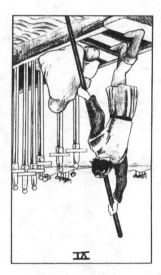

6 of Swords.

Upright Imagery and Meanings: The picture in this card shows a ferryman rowing a sorrowful woman and child to the farther shore. When we focus on the rough water on the right side of the boat and the calm water on the left side, though, we see that they're moving away from difficulty.

The 6 of Swords indicates that a difficult cycle is now starting to come to an end. You can set your vision on the future, which is certainly brighter than the recent past. This card can also represent a journey taken over water or a trip away from a sad condition.

Once you leave the old conditions behind, harmony will once again prevail. The woman and child in this card are recovering from problems, and a family may have had much loss. Now, though, the healing process will begin. This can indicate that an unpleasant work situation or difficulty or sorrow in your family life will give way to peace once more.

This journey to tranquility can be done in the mind. No matter how it comes about, though, you'll journey to a higher state of consciousness and be at peace with yourself on the opposite shore.

Reversed Imagery and Meanings: In the 6 of Swords reversed, the boat is no longer afloat and the people have had to abandon ship. This indicates that the journey to a better environment has been postponed. You'll feel as if you're stuck in a negative situation with no way out.

Nothing will be accomplished at this time and you'll need to wait for a better opportunity. You may need to go within yourself to find an answer, or to rethink a situation. Plans will be kept on the shelf, and it's advisable to shift to a different frame of mind in order to proceed.

There may be a postponement of the freedom to do what you wish. A legal issue could be holding up your life, or a loss or grief may be slowing you down, creating stagnation at the present time. The 6 of Swords reversed indicates delay.

7 of Swords: Sneaky!

7 of Swords.

Upright Imagery and Meanings: This is a pretty literal card! It shows a man sneaking away with five of the seven swords, unseen by those in the encampment behind him. Two swords remain in the ground, left behind as evidence that something has been taken.

When the 7 of Swords appears, things may not work out the way you've planned. It's possible that someone's being deceptive or stealing away with something that's important to you. Unreliability can be indicated, or perhaps someone's not telling you the truth or is hiding it from you.

Reversed Imagery and Meanings: This card is actually good reversed. The swords will be returned or the person who's been keeping a secret will reveal the deception. You'll find out what's really been going on now.

An apology may be forthcoming, and the people involved will accept it. "Sorry for causing so much trouble. It was an innocent mistake, honest!" Good advice and counsel will be given if you're involved in a lawsuit or in need of legal advice. A thief will return what was stolen, or what was lost will be found. In short, the truth will come out. The other cards around this one can help you interpret it more specifically.

Fools Rush In

The 7 of Swords isn't a traumatic card, but rather one of the mind. It represents an attitude, and a sneaky one at that. This card is kind of like, "Don't tell Mom, but..." There's flight away from a dishonorable act when this card appears. So if *you're* not sneaking around, maybe you need to take a good look around you and see who is!

8 of Swords: Fear, Fear, and More Fear

8 of Swords.

Upright Imagery and Meanings: A woman stands alone in a marshy place, with eight swords surrounding her—but notice that they don't pierce her. The woman is bound and blindfolded, and a castle in the distance may be either home or a place of future refuge.

The 8 of Swords reminds us that our fears can certainly render us helpless and put us in the very position in which the woman in the card finds herself. This can be the fear of moving out of a situation or of leaving something because we don't know what will replace it. The bondage of fear is a strong one, and when it's got you in its claws, you don't feel secure with anything new.

The 8 of Swords represents restricted action because of indecision and an inability to cope with the changes going on around you. Sometimes, this card makes you feel like you've created your own prison, or that your fears have kept you from attaining your personal goals.

The woman could be too weak to fight for her rights, or continuous worry may be causing her still more stress, initiating a vicious cycle of self-imposed restrictions. Unable to think clearly, the woman needs good, sensible advice.

Reversed Imagery and Meanings: When the 8 of Swords is reversed, the woman can let go of those swords that surround her and relax from her fears. She's now able to see through her difficulties, make a decision, and feel back in control again.

New beginnings are now possible. Hope and inspiration have returned, and you're free from the restrictions brought on by your own fears. The pressures that were once there are now leaving you. The 8 of Swords reversed gives you some breathing room.

Spinning the Wheel of Fortune

Sometimes, the 8 of Swords can actually mean someone you know is in prison. Like all the Tarot cards, the card has its literal meanings as well! Remember, too, that fear can keep you from accomplishing some wonderful ideas, putting you in a prison of your own devising.

9 of Swords: Depression and Desperation

9 of Swords.

Upright Imagery and Meanings: Of all the Sword cards, the 9 of Swords is the most difficult. The woman crying in her bed represents the loss of hope, bad dreams, and nightmares. Despair and anxiety are causing misery and pain, and the woman can't seem to get out of bed, as if too much trauma has occurred. Maybe she needs medical or legal help, but in any event it's clear that truly unfortunate conditions and sad circumstances surround her.

When the 9 of Swords appears, analyze the cards around it to see if the other cards reflect more of the same or a turnaround for the better. Each card in a spread either magnifies the turmoil or decreases it. Sadness, loss of a loved one, or just plain depression are here in this card—but whether it's coming or going depends on the surrounding cards.

In the Cards

For obvious reasons, the 9 of Swords is called "the Nightmare Card." When it appears in a reading, the Querent is often not surprised and tells the reader exactly what the nightmare is. Like dreams, nightmares can represent many things: fears, worries, or difficult times.

Reversed Imagery and Meanings: In its reversed meaning, the 9 of Swords shows the woman getting through the traumatic events or conditions in her life. Time will bring healing, as all things heal with time. Tomorrow is a new day.

Patience and prayer can help you pass through the long journey. This card can indicate that the goodness of a loved one is coming, or that the life-threatening surgery was a great success. The dark cloud of trauma will pass and you'll have developed strength of character because of it, along with the awareness that you can surmount a major tragedy.

10 of Swords: The End of a Cycle

10 of Swords.

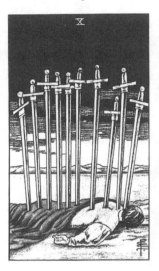
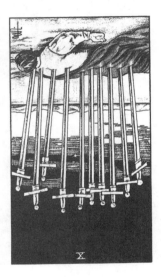

Upright Imagery and Meanings: The 10 of Swords shows a graphic picture of a man lying in a desolate wasteland with ten swords piercing his back. He represents what war, strife, and major trauma can do to all of us: They can break us down so that we give up our will and fortitude.

This card represents the end of a cycle. This could be getting a divorce or quitting a job, but the final conclusion is at hand because there's no life left in the situation anymore. The conditions are obsolete and could lead to sudden misfortune if they don't reach their natural conclusion.

This card can indicate a deep sense of loss, which could be about a legal, work, or social situation. This card signals the end of a karmic cycle and the end of a lifestyle the way it has been. Past obligations are now concluded so that the old lifestyle comes to a close, and the karmic debt is completed.

Reversed Imagery and Meanings: The reversed 10 of Swords indicates that the cycle of change has finished. Now we can see the sunrise in the background of this card; the light is at the end of the tunnel.

The 10 of Swords reversed indicates a steady improvement in health, and that any losses are now in your past. If you went through a divorce, for example, it's now final and you're ready to move on. Usually, by the time you get this card, you don't have deep feelings about the loss anymore. It was something important that you experienced, but you've detached yourself from it emotionally; the trauma is now truly in your past. This card comes up a lot when people have gone into rehab of some kind and are ready to come out, start clean, and renew their lives. New horizons and a positive cycle will begin when you receive the 10 of Swords reversed, because you've been released from a long and difficult struggle.

The Least You Need to Know

➤ Swords represent mental activity, often leading to conflict, obstacles, and aggression.

➤ Royal Swords represent a logical and balanced approach to issues.

➤ Everyday Swords indicate daily struggles and difficulties.

➤ The way you wield the power of Swords is in your hands. You have the strength to overcome your obstacles!

Chapter 16

Pentacles: Possessions, Wealth, Security

In This Chapter

➤ Pentacles explore your material and financial world

➤ Royal Pentacles: Matters of money and success

➤ Everyday Pentacles: Your path to financial success

Pentacles are the suit of wealth, possessions, and security. They are the cards we look to for our security in the material world. Here's where you'll find the things you own: your money and investments, your home and the things in it. As you look at the cards, you'll notice all the yellow; this is the color of success and optimism, the color of the sun.

The Royal Court

The Royal Pentacles have the qualities required for material comfort and security. Here's where we'll find the steadfast prosperity of the King of Pentacles, the Earth Mother Queen, the hardworking Knight, and the studious Page who brings the good news we've been waiting for.

King of Pentacles: Steadfast, Prosperous, Benevolent

King of Pentacles.

Upright Imagery and Meanings: This is a king of regal robes; his are embroidered with bunches of grapes and vine leaves. Bulls' heads are on the back and arms of his throne, and his home and vineyard are behind him. In his lap, he holds a pentacle and a scepter, which shows his power.

The King of Pentacles has an easygoing exterior and is friendly, kind, generous, thoughtful, and industrious. He can represent a father of kind disposition, a business-man of prosperity, or a reliable married man with his main focus on the security of his family. This king has tremendous ability to make decisions about financial issues, and he's logical, thoughtful, methodical, responsible, and very solid and steady with everyone he meets.

The King of Pentacles truly believes that everyone can have security on the material plane, and he wants his family and friends to attain material success to ensure their future security. He's also accomplished at math, science, and business, and so deals well with investments, banking, and real estate. If you ever need any financial advice, this is your king!

Fools Rush In

Though slow to anger, the King of Pentacles reversed can react quite harshly if threatened. He reminds us of a bull in the field—make sure you don't wave a red flag at him!

Reversed Imagery and Meanings: The King of Pentacles reversed will lose the pentacle he holds and his scepter will fall away. He stills desires financial security and prosperity, but upside down, he has an ulterior motive: He doesn't want to work too hard for it!

The reversed King of Pentacles wants all the good things in life, but isn't able or willing to do what it takes to get them. He's stubborn, materialistic, slow to move on things, unaware of his spending habits, and makes unwise choices about money matters. This card may come up for a person easy to bribe or to coerce, or a situation where deceptions about money or finances are evident.

Queen of Pentacles: Brings Home the Bacon

Queen of Pentacles.

Upright Imagery and Meanings: This queen holds a pentacle in her lap as she sits on a beautiful throne covered with nature and animal symbols. A bower of roses is above her and a cupid and goats form part of the throne's arm. This scene of abundance is in the midst of a fertile field, and indeed, the Queen of Pentacles is the queen of fertility and abundance.

This queen is a creative woman who knows how to raise a family and take care of the financial conditions in life. She's good at business careers, taking care of children and gardens, and is not afraid of hard work. The Queen of Pentacles is a productive individual and enjoys seeing things or people grow. She's charitable and generous with what she has and wishes to share it with others.

The Queen of Pentacles has a quiet personality, is responsive to others, easygoing, and kind of the Earth Mother type. Because she's responsible, she always fulfills her duties well.

Reversed Imagery and Meanings: When reversed, the Queen of Pentacles has a lot of insecurity about finances and her ability to make ends meet. She can appear moody and melancholy, and that's because she's having a hard time with the material world.

The Queen of Pentacles reversed can become too dependent on others for her well-being, or she might neglect her duties or responsibilities because of insecurity or fear. She can show a mistrust of others as well, and is suspicious by nature.

Fear of failing makes the Queen of Pentacles quite vulnerable to changeable moods. She can appear needy and can manipulate funds to acquire things other than life's basic needs. She's seen some hard financial times in her life—and she may see more.

Knight of Pentacles: Depend on Nurturing Prosperity

Knight of Pentacles.

Upright Imagery and Meanings: The Knight of Pentacles holds a pentacle out to us to show us the way to prosperity. His horse is a dark draft horse that plods along the fields of life, cultivating and developing new horizons. This young Knight is thorough and will take his time in doing a good job. Trustworthy and honest, he'll get the job done the way you'd like, too.

The Knight of Pentacles has an easygoing nature, is compassionate, loves animals, enjoys children, and loves the gifts he can give others. His focus is one of helping others get ahead, and he can represent the coming of an event to go with a sale, business deal, or investing in something solid and stable.

Solid and stable himself, the Knight of Pentacles can bring good news concerning a pay increase, new job offer, an investment that will increase in value, or a loan that's been approved. He could be a good broker, financial investor, veterinarian, or farmer.

Reversed Imagery and Meanings: The reversed Knight of Pentacles can be irresponsible, because he's scattered and can't focus on the job at hand. He can't follow through on things and is slow and laborious in his action. In fact, his upside-down horse means progress is impeded.

When the Knight of Pentacles appears reversed, money, new work, and important matters in his life are at a standstill. He needs lots of encouragement to get through this difficult time. He seems to wish to avoid any confrontation and is moody and withdrawn, wishing to be far from the crowds.

The Knight of Pentacles reversed could be called the loner of the Tarot, or worse, the malcontent. He's probably received his share of hard knocks and can't seem to get his life going on track the way he'd like. He neglects his duties and is unable to follow through on the commitments he originally made.

Page of Pentacles: A Studious Messenger of Hope

Page of Pentacles.

Upright Imagery and Meanings: The Page of Pentacles brings to the forefront the need to study the pentacle before him. He loves to study and learn practical things, and is diligent about his life. The messenger of the Pentacle suit, the Page brings to us hope and the promise of good luck in the material world.

The Page of Pentacles can be a young, persevering scholar, generous and kind with all he meets. He's enthusiastic about education, progress, and the material rewards that come with them. Careful and cautious, he studies everything before making a decision.

Reversed Imagery and Meanings: The Page of Pentacles reversed comes up a lot when there are delays in receiving good messages about finances, job offers, or scholarships.

This Page reversed is someone who can't follow through on directions. He'll be the one to follow his young peer group, refusing to listen to good, logical counsel from adults. Rebelliousness and frustration are hallmarks of this Page reversed.

When his card is upside down, the Page of Pentacles is quiet and moody and can withdraw from or sabotage events. He has a love of luxury and material goods, but not much desire to work for them. We could call him lazy, with his procrastination and lack of motivation.

Spinning the Wheel of Fortune

What a guy! The Page of Pentacles' messages include things like: "You got the job!" "You got a raise!" "You got the grant for college!" "You won something for your efforts!" We hope he'll show up in your spreads often.

Everyday Pentacles

We all want to know if the money's coming—and what to do with it when we've got it. Everyday Pentacles are the cards of your material resources: how you work to earn your money, whether to take that gamble or play it safe, and how your efforts will pay off over time. Here is also where you'll find the comfort of your home and the security of your family.

Ace of Pentacles: You're the Top!

Ace of Pentacles.

Upright Imagery and Meanings: The Ace of Pentacles' Hand coming out of the clouds offers you a shiny bright pentacle, while below is a well-tended garden with an archway entrance.

This card heralds the beginning of prosperity, wealth, and new business. You'll find it come up when you're seeking a new direction in career or work, and also when you're curious about matters concerning money, investments, and loans. There could be a gift of money or material goods coming.

A good foundation is developing when the Ace of Pentacles appears in a spread. You're slowly making headway with your finances, and extra money and/or an inheritance could help. The Ace of Pentacles can also signal awards, as it represents a gift given, not necessarily just money or something of material worth.

Reversed Imagery and Meanings: The Ace of Pentacles reversed represents a lack of prosperity. You've taken the wrong road for the new beginning, or the new beginning may not be prosperous. When this card appears, you need to look at what you're lacking before jumping into this new venture. Are you really prepared? Are you sure this is the right way to go with your money?

You may have a false sense of security, and great plans may not materialize. Take caution against greed or being preoccupied with money at the cost of the heart: Comfortable material conditions may not be what you need right now. Take a closer look at your checkbook and make sure everything is in order. Have you overextended yourself financially? The Ace of Pentacles reversed advises you to take a closer look at your financial management.

2 of Pentacles: Small Profit

2 of Pentacles.

Upright Imagery and Meanings: In the 2 of Pentacles, we find a juggler balancing two pentacles, with the ribbon of life connecting them. This juggler is literally juggling funds, trying to balance his decisions about money matters. Fortunately, he's lighthearted about this; he knows he can handle the situation at hand.

The 2 of Pentacles indicates the ability to handle several conditions or proposals at once. You're able to maintain balance in the midst of change and decision-making. New projects may be difficult to get started, but you have the stamina and strength to get through. It's important that harmony is maintained and that you don't let disturbing news set you back. Helpful advice is on its way.

Reversed Imagery and Meanings: The ships in the background of this card reversed show that the ideas and conditions around you are having a hard time staying afloat. The juggler now has too many irons in the fire and can't handle all the problems at once.

Fools Rush In

The 2 of Pentacles reversed can represent discouraging news or indicate negative information that could make your venture stop. It can also indicate too much money being spent on small things or frivolous goods. It could be time to double-check your numbers.

When the 2 of Pentacles appears reversed, disorganization may be causing difficulty, and you should think ahead to prevent total failure of your plans. You may be handling more than necessary and need to let go of one of those pentacles—they may not be so hard to handle one at a time!

3 of Pentacles: Recognition for Skill at Work

3 of Pentacles.

Upright Imagery and Meanings: In the 3 of Pentacles, we see a man receiving approval from a nun and a monk. He's finishing a masonry piece in the church, and his skill and ability will be rewarded.

This card promises recognition of your skill and ability. For example, your boss will approve of your work and a pay raise may be in the works because of it. It could indicate a good review at work, or acceptance for your education and skill.

Congratulations are due you. Material gain and success are yours through your hard work and effort. The 3 of Pentacles can also represent being accepted in a group, club, or other organization.

Reversed Imagery and Meanings: When this card is reversed, the rewards are not coming and approval of your work and skill is delayed. The man on the bench has had all his tools fallen away from him, so he can't do his work the way he had intended.

Sometimes, the 3 of Pentacles comes up reversed to mean loss at the workplace because of a lack of goods or equipment to do a good job. This card can also represent union or contract disagreements. Negotiations are possible when it appears, but they may not have the outcome you desire. The card can also indicate mediocre work or that workplace conditions are not safe.

4 of Pentacles: A Firm Foundation

4 of Pentacles.

Upright Imagery and Meanings: In the 4 of Pentacles, we find a man holding tightly to the gold he's worked so hard for, and in the background we can see the city where he lives and works. This card expresses both the solidity and sound foundation of the number four and the security pentacles can bring.

This man has a strong attachment to the money and possessions he's worked so hard for and earned over time. He has a love of earthly possessions and feels comfortable when he has all his earthly goods around him. In firm command of his money and possessions, he'll work very hard to gain even more in the future.

The 4 of Pentacles indicates good judgment in business matters as well as many talents that could bring you and your family prosperity. Sometimes this card comes up when you're a little too tight with your money or if you have a somewhat ungenerous character. But this comes from the reality that it took a long time to get your money, and you're not likely to give it out so quickly. It also indicates conservative spending.

Reversed Imagery and Meanings: Upside down, the man's no longer in control of the four pentacles he's trying to hold and balance, and one of these pentacles will fall away from him. The reversed 4 of Pentacles shows a person letting go of money or having to spend more than anticipated, as well as the chance of losing some money or earthly possessions.

This card can indicate an opposition toward financial security at this time. There may be a delay in attaining the paycheck you thought was coming, or extra money you were anticipating doesn't arrive in time to pay off something. In business matters, there will be opposition or extra cost you hadn't counted on. Or, if it's about you, you may be overextending yourself financially and need to be cautious not to go overboard.

5 of Pentacles: Financial or Spiritual Difficulty

5 of Pentacles.

Upright Imagery and Meanings: The picture on the 5 of Pentacles shows two homeless people out in the snow in front of a church window; it's frightening. But are they willing to go in from the cold? Or do they even see they're being offered help? Maybe they'd rather take care of themselves? These are just some of the questions that come up when we study this card.

The 5 of Pentacles upright describes a condition of some kind of impoverishment. Is it spiritual loss? A financial one? Or is it just that you don't feel connected to your community? Do you feel lost or abandoned? All of these descriptions can be found in the 5 of Pentacles upright.

It's possible you've neglected your health or spiritual needs and feel at a loss as to how to handle those areas of your life. Sometimes, depending on what question you asked, it can mean loss of a job or unemployment, but this depends on the other cards around it. Clearly, though, this is a card of feeling left out in the cold.

Reversed Imagery and Meanings: The 5 of Pentacles is better in its reversed position. This is a reversal of bad luck, and you may now find new work so that your unemployed days are over. You may feel that your courage has come back to you and that you're able to get back into the action of your community or home life.

When the 5 of Pentacles appears reversed, you've accepted the conditions of loss and have moved on to a higher level of understanding. You've develop compassion for those homeless folks and understand that life has its highs and lows. You have a new interest in spiritual matters and feel more hopeful with the 5 of Pentacles in this position. Courage and hope return now.

6 of Pentacles: A Bonus!

6 of Pentacles.

Upright Imagery and Meanings: Here we see the two people being offered help and extra money. The man handing out the pentacles or gold is distributing a bonus or gift, or sharing what he has with the two people. The 6 of Pentacles represents sharing alms. Gifts are given and monies are shared with everyone involved.

This card can indicate a happy union with fellow employees, a raise in pay, a possible promotion, or profit-sharing opportunities. "You will receive what is rightfully yours," it says. Inheritance can be another description of this card, and it's a good one.

In the Cards

The 6 of Pentacles represents charity, philanthropy, and the sharing of wealth. What you do will come back three-fold, the ancient wisdom goes, and in this case, it's a happy return of fortune!

Reversed Imagery and Meanings: When the 6 of Pentacles comes up reversed, the man handing out money is upside down and the scales are no longer balanced. This card indicates that the gifts may be small, the bonus not as large as hoped for, or that a gift is coming, but with strings attached.

There could be unfairness in the distribution of an estate or bonuses when the 6 of Pentacles comes up reversed. Business practices may be unfair or unethical, or your present prosperity may be threatened in some way. It's possible you're not being recognized for all the hard work and time you put into the situation. There's also a possibility of a 401(k) plan not being managed very profitably after all, or that your investments have lost value.

7 of Pentacles: Investment and Profit

7 of Pentacles.

Upright Imagery and Meanings: The 7 of Pentacles shows a farmer leaning on his hoe, contemplating how much his crop will bring this year. This card suggests that we've put our time and labor into something and will now reap the rewards.

Spinning the Wheel of Fortune

If the 7 of Pentacles comes up reversed when you've asked about whether you should invest or not, it's best not to take any chances: Money is slipping away in this card!

This can mean the investment you made will have a good return, or that the garden you planted will reap a harvest plentiful enough to feed your family. The 7 of Pentacles indicates all your hard work and effort will pay off, and you'll make a good profit for your time and work.

This card doesn't predict wealth, but rather good solid accomplishments in your investments and workplace as well as satisfactory rewards. Notice that one pentacle is not yet in the pile; there are still a few finishing touches needed to bring your project to completion. With the 7 of Pentacles, though, good work and satisfaction are guaranteed.

Reversed Imagery and Meanings: The 7 of Pentacles reversed shows the farmer upside down, so that his hoe will slip away from him, and the pentacles will fall away as well. Hard work and a goodly amount of labor have been put into this venture, but there seems to be little or no profit. This card can indicate that your crop failed because of bad weather or that your investment showed no profit because of low economic times. Perhaps you didn't get a bonus because of circumstances beyond your control. Poor speculation may be indicated, and in fact this card comes up a lot when people are gambling on what they mistakenly think is a sure thing.

8 of Pentacles: Focus on Productivity

8 of Pentacles.

Upright Imagery and Meanings: The 8 of Pentacles shows a craftsman who's worked hard on the previous seven pentacles, and is now focused on an eighth one. He's hammering away, producing more of his talent. He's good at what he does and is skillful in the process. Quick and sharp, he can produce his wares at an amazing speed (kind of like us, if we do say so ourselves!).

Here you have the ability to move ahead quickly because your talents and capabilities are well-rounded. Your past expertise has culminated as profit and recognition. The 8 of Pentacles predicts that you'll do well in your career or job, or profit because of your keen awareness of the need to continue and develop the skills you have. You can only get better at what you do by keep on keepin' on! That's the 8 of Pentacles.

Reversed Imagery and Meanings: When the 8 of Pentacles is reversed, a slowdown in production is evident. Now the craftsman has trouble finding his tools and can't produce as quickly as he would like. Mediocre work or a mediocre workplace add up to slower or delayed production, and therefore a loss in attaining the desired results of good and steady profit.

Work conditions with this card can lead employees into a labor dispute with the company, or employees may not be happy with the results of a contract. Investments will show little or no profit this year, and it's possible you should be thinking about either finding a different place of work or training for a new career. Now's the time to think about how you spend your time and what you can do to change this non-productive situation.

9 of Pentacles: Stable Finances

9 of Pentacles.

Upright Imagery and Meanings: Here we find a woman in her garden with rich surroundings, looking very calm and peaceful. She's reached a secure position in her life and can spend time with family and friends or by herself. She's content in all she does.

The 9 of Pentacles indicates self-sufficiency, independence, and self-mastery of your financial/material world. This card can come up for anyone who's working toward any type of financial independence, and it assures success in those ventures.

Your past investments are coming to sound fruition with the 9 of Pentacles, and you've mastered the road to prosperity. Now, you're able to share what you have with others and still have enough for yourself.

The 9 of Pentacles also represents a strong connection to the environment. It can mean a lover of wildlife and wide open spaces, someone who appreciates the beauty of Mother Earth. The woman in this card has her feet planted firmly on the ground, so if there's ever a problem (especially if it's of a financial nature), she can handle it with sound judgment. This is a card of personal security.

Reversed Imagery and Meanings: The 9 of Pentacles reversed shows the woman's security slipping away. The bird will fly away, the garden hasn't been tended, and the pentacles will lose their luster. Upside down, the woman is no longer secure about her present situation.

This card could suggest that you're upset with your present home environment. Maybe the money's not available for what you want to do, or your growth is restricted in some way. It's possible low income is causing concern or there's anxiety over a business deal or investment, but whatever the case, you're not happy with your present financial condition.

There may be a fear of losing all you've worked for when the 9 of Pentacles comes up reversed. As with all cards, the cards around this one will tell how well or poorly it all will go. Perhaps there's too much dependence on others in a rough time, or there are inadequate sums of money. The freedom to do what you want just hasn't come, so move with caution on any speculation and don't let others take advantage of you.

Spinning the Wheel of Fortune

It's wise not to be too generous when the 9 of Pentacles shows up reversed. You may need that money for yourself in the near future! Generosity is wonderful—but not at the cost of your own personal security.

10 of Pentacles: Success!

10 of Pentacles.

Upright Imagery and Meanings: If we could wish for any of the Pentacle cards this would be the one! The 10 of Pentacles represents all the wonderful conditions and material things we can accomplish in this lifetime.

This card shows a stable family with the riches we all dream of. This family has worked hard for long periods of time, maybe even generations, to accomplish this type of security: The grandparents, parents, and children represent several generations of acquiring this financial stability.

This card comes up often when the purchase of a large item, such as a house or car, is in your future. You have the money or the financing to be able to attain your dream with the 10 of Pentacles. If it seems out of your reach, your family may be able to help or a bank loan is on the horizon.

Everything is simply wonderful in the world now. Not only do you have money, you have security as well. Your wise investments will last a long time, providing a strong stable foundation for future generations as well as for yourself. Great wealth or great security! We'll take both!

In the Cards

The 10 of Pentacles also comes for large corporations that have done well in the world and are able to employ many people. A corporation is solid financially if the 10 of Pentacles shows up in its cards.

Reversed Imagery and Meanings: The 10 of Pentacles reversed shows an inharmonious family. This card can signal family fights and feuds over an inheritance, estate, or stocks in a corporation. Whatever it is, the established wealth is now in question.

Did the group jeopardize its company? Its investments? Did it take too many chances that are now proving unstable? Values go up and values go down—that's the story on this card.

Sometimes, the 10 of Pentacles reversed represents family misfortune, poor investing, or squandering of finances. Corporations may have a hard time making ends meet when the 10 of Pentacles reversed shows up, and the investors/shareholders may be up in arms about their stock prices going down.

This card can indicate financial loss due to either weak economic conditions or because of poor business management. As always, what it is depends on what other cards appear around this one. Sometimes, with a 10 of Pentacles reversed, financial loss can lead to a legal battle, or it may be one connected to a will, pension, or investment property.

The Least You Need to Know

➤ Pentacles are where you'll find your material and financial world.

➤ Royal Pentacles are your financial advisors.

➤ Everyday Pentacles show you the path to financial success.

➤ You hold the cards when it comes to Pentacles. You can create your own wealth—both financial and spiritual!

Part 5
Tarot Readings Any Fool Can Do

Getting the cards to tell a story involves a Tarot reading, which in turn requires a reader, a Querent (or questioner), a question, and a spread. Quite possibly, there are as many Tarot spreads as there are Tarot readers. To help you decide which spread works best for you in a given situation, we're providing you with lots of choices and samples from which to choose. Happy reading!

Getting or Giving a Good Tarot Reading

Now that you've gotten to know the cards, it's time to take advantage of what they can do for you. A Tarot reading brings together a Tarot reader and a Querent, who is a seeker with a question. The reader uses a Tarot spread, or card layout, to explore the Querent's question.

There are as many different Tarot spreads as there are Tarot readers, and as you get to know the cards better and better, you may develop some spreads of your own as well. But first, let's talk about the things (and people) involved in a good reading.

Getting a Good Reading

The first essential for a good reading is for the Querent to feel comfortable with the idea of having a reading! You've got to want to have a reading, be willing to talk with others who've had readings, and be ready to trust both the reader's instincts and your own.

When we Tarot readers know it's your "first time," we like to make sure the reading's a good one, as well as an introduction to what the Tarot (or any metaphysical tool) is. And we don't want to overwhelm you. When you're a first-timer, we think it's nice to do a reading that gives a basic overview of your life now, beginning in the present tense, in other words. Then we like to move on to either future conditions or things that could possibly happen.

After we've gone over the present and the future, we like to talk a little about the past, which helps you know we're good at what we do. "Hey," you may ask. "How'd you know that?" "Hey," we'll answer. "It's in the cards."

A good reading leaves you both enlightened and personally empowered. You come away feeling that things you know have been validated, while at the same time, you've become aware of future possibilities and conditions. A good reading should make you feel "whole," or complete at some level.

How to Choose a Tarot Reader

Most people find their Tarot readers through word of mouth, going on the recommendation of a close friend or family member. Because a Tarot reader can and will get to the heart of what's going on around you, most people are understandably a little cautious about whom they trust—and so turn to those they *do* trust to find the right reader for them.

While collectively we humans may seem interested in the gory details provided by the mass media, when we consult someone privately about the future, what we really want to know is the truth—and how to handle that truth. When it comes to a Tarot reader, then, we all want someone who will help us make progress in our lives.

So ask around. Check out the bulletin boards in your local metaphysical bookstore—and then ask the people working there about the readers who've posted their notices. Tarot's an instinctive art—and you'll instinctively know when you've found the right Tarot reader.

What About 900 Numbers?

Those who've called 900 numbers have had mixed results, because, like any reading, these depend on who the reader is. With 900 numbers, there may be the additional factor of the reader being pressed for time, because he or she has to do so many readings an hour. You'll hear the rush in the reader's voice immediately, and if that's the case, you can just say, "Sorry, no thanks."

But we've also heard that readers get paid based on how long they keep Querents on the line. If a 900 number reader seems to be playing on your fears, hang up fast—he's in it for the money, not your best interests.

We recommend that for an in-depth reading you go to someone who can sit down with you for a good hour or so and "pick up vibes" from you.

Can You Get a Good Reading over the Internet?

We think it's always nicer if the reader and Querent can be in the same room, but when necessary, phone readings can be just as enlightening and helpful. It really depends on who the reader is.

As with all readings, when it comes to those on the Internet, it's a matter of how the cards are interpreted. Tarot is unique in that it needs a *person* to interpret the cards. That person can be someone who knows little about Tarot, because the pictures themselves can give a good straightforward answer to a question, using the language of universal symbols, but the best Internet reading, like any reading, will include both a Tarot reader and a Querent.

In the Cards

In our newer, faster, 21st century, cyberspace world, there's actually a software program that can "shuffle" the cards. You decide when the shuffling stops with a push of a key, and then the cards that come up are the cards for your reading. Arlene's tried this, and it's not too bad!

Here's an example of an Internet reading. Arlene in Washington state sends a Three-Card Spread answering a question for a friend in Atlanta, Georgia, via the Internet. The friend (let's call her Sally) gets the info instantaneously (well, let's say soon, depending on her net server).

Arlene begins the reading by concentrating on Sally's question, shuffling the deck without her presence (but feeling it nonetheless), and then dealing the cards, one at a time. When the spread is complete, Arlene looks at the cards and reads and interprets them, then sends her reading to Sally via electronic mail (e-mail).

Later that day, or the next day, Sally e-mails Arlene back about that day. Sometimes, the reading may not seem very accurate: The Tarot may have answered a question that's farther out in the future than a day or two.

Ultimately, the Tarot reader and the Querent will determine whether a reading is accurate or not. If Arlene and Sally both focus on the question at hand, this method can work very well. The only thing that's really different with an Internet reading is the method of sending the answers, and how they're sent doesn't really matter if the Tarot reader and Querent are concentrating. Whether by fax, e-mail, or mental telepathy, a good message gets where it's going!

Whether You're Getting or Giving, Keep an Open Mind

Lisa went to the chiropractor this morning. "Relax," he kept saying. "I am relaxed," Lisa kept answering. But of course, she wasn't. And until she did relax the chiropractor couldn't do his best work on her computer-weary neck and shoulders.

In a similar way, you need to relax and keep your thoughts and heart open during your reading. When you're relaxed, you're helping the reader get and give more information rather than blocking her ability to "pick up" what's going on with you.

Your thoughts are powerful things; look at how they kept Lisa from relaxing while the chiropractor tried to help her relax. In the same way, your thoughts can get in the way of your reading.

Sometimes, when Arlene knows her client, she'll actually stop and say, "Hey, knock it off! Stop thinking that way and listen for a minute, would ya?!" (Needless to say, this might not be so effective with new clients.)

Before you even shuffle the deck, you need to concentrate on what you want to know now. Don't worry about the small details of life. Think about the big picture and sweat the small stuff later on in the reading. Stay open and the reader will be able to help you even more.

Is There a Specific Question to Answer?

Many times, a student or client is surprised by the fact that he can ask a specific question. Many think they can only ask a general question such as, "How are things at work?"

Instead, you can (and should) ask far more specific questions. Here are some examples:

➤ "How will I get along with my boss in the next six months?" (Notice we put timing into the question.)

➤ "How will the company (include its name in the question, too) I work for do financially this year?"

➤ "Will I stay in my present work group for the next six months?"

➤ "Can I pay off my Visa card within the next three to six months?"

You can ask any type of question—but make sure you want to know the answer! If you don't want to hear that you need to start saving money, maybe you'd better ask about your love life instead.

As for including timing in the question, when a reading says you'll get a new job, wouldn't you like to know when or where, or even what? The cards can answer those questions—if you phrase your question right.

Spinning the Wheel of Fortune

Be sure to phrase your question so that you get the answer in the form you want. Many people ask when their next "romance" will come along. When the cards say soon, the next person who comes along may indeed be "romantic"—but not the Mr. or Ms. Right they want. Be as specific as you can, and you'll get the answer you're looking for.

Understanding Tarot Spreads

There are many different kinds of Tarot spreads, each specific to the type of reading you wish to do. Variety is the spice of life, we always say, so here's some Tarot spice:

➤ If you just want to know a little bit about something, use a Three-Card Spread. (Lisa loves this one and uses it for her daily readings.)

➤ If you want an overall picture of the events in your life, use the Horoscope Spread.

➤ If you just want a "yes" or "no," use the Wish Spread.

➤ More universal is the Celtic Cross, which many readers use as a general, all-purpose spread. We use it often in this book as well.

You can also make up your own spreads. Some people like the Three-Card, while others prefer to use a Four-Card Spread. Whatever feels right to you is fine.

The Most Commonly Used Spread

The Celtic, or Keltic, Cross is the most commonly used spread. Ten cards are laid out in the form of a cross and a staff. The cross represents the earth plane and the staff represents a connection to heaven; in other words, heaven and earth in communion.

The Celtic Cross Spread.

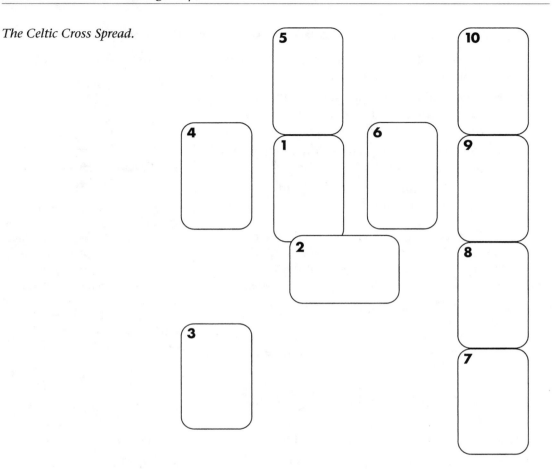

This spread can be used for any question when you want to know not just an outcome in the mundane sense but also the spiritual applications. Some of the things related to a question that a Celtic Cross covers include:

➤ The question's background

➤ How you're standing in your own way regarding the question

➤ How others feel about the question

➤ How the question can be affected by others

➤ What kind of free will and karma are present

➤ The question's ultimate outcome

The Celtic Cross Spread was created so you can see all of a question's ins and outs. Now you can see why it's the tried-and-true favorite most Tarot readers use for others' readings.

Shuffling and Dealing the Cards

Shuffling the deck is one of the most important aspects of the reading. How the deck is shuffled helps put the energy of the Querent, or seeker, into the reading. The Querent should always be the one to shuffle the deck, and should do so as many times as he wants. Whether it's five times or ten, the Querent should feel comfortable with his shuffling.

Having the Querent do the shuffling accomplishes two things. First, it gets him to concentrate on this big deck, and second, it focuses his energy and subconscious thoughts on the Tarot. Readings shuffled by the Querent tend to be more accurate because the reader gets the feel of that person very quickly and accurately.

Separating the deck into three stacks is equally important, and you should make this part of the seeker's job as well. According to ancient wisdom, this separating is considered "blessing the deck": As the deck is cut into three piles, the Querent's giving permission to be read with good blessings from above. We think a little ancient wisdom, not to mention a blessing, never hurt anyone.

Pick a Card, Any Card...

For certain spreads, such as the Horoscope Spread (we'll show you one in Chapter 19), we like to have the Querent pick out a court card which she feels represents herself. But how do Querents know which court card represents them?

The answer is to ask the Querent to pick a card that feels like herself. To do this, have her separate the royal court cards (Pages, Knights, Queens, and Kings) from the rest of the deck, and then lay them out by suit: Wands, Cups, Swords, and Pentacles. As the Querent looks at the cards, she should consider the following:

1. Which one of the suits do you gravitate toward?
2. After you've picked a suit, which one of the court cards in that suit do you think represents you?

In many Tarot books, you can find physical descriptions of each of the suits. Wands represent light- or reddish-haired people, with light or ruddy complexions and blue or hazel eyes. Cups are considered fair types, with sandy-colored hair and blue or green eyes. Swords represent brown-haired people with brown or hazel eyes and medium to fair complexions. And Pentacles are people with dark or even black hair and brown or black eyes.

But what if a Querent picked a card that doesn't "look" like her? Not to worry—the card is an emotional representation, not a physical one. That's why we stuck all those descriptions in one little paragraph; we think they're too limiting.

At the same time, though, royal court cards can represent people in a reading. If a Querent's asked a question that involves someone in his future, we can sometimes tell what that person looks like (in general) before she even shows up.

251

The Querent has to ask a specific question to get a specific answer like this. For example, he might ask the Tarot, "Show me what my next relationship appears or looks like," or, "Give me a physical description of the person who's coming into my life." If a court card appears in the spread, it will be that person!

Fools Rush In

If there's a Doubting Thomas in the room, the reading will be adversely affected. The cards pick up that negative energy and may turn it into a garbled or nonsense reading, which is, of course, what the person was expecting. The same goes for people who laugh at the cards—their negative energy is what the cards pick up, and they in turn will laugh at them.

When You're Reading Someone Else's Cards

Atmosphere is important in a good reading. You don't have to light candles and talk softly—but both can add to the creation of a comfortable atmosphere for both reader and Querent. The Querent should feel comfortable in the room and in the chair, and with you the reader.

If you sense the Querent is feeling uncomfortable, it's up to you as the reader to voice it. "Are you feeling uncomfortable?" or "What can I do to make you feel more comfortable with this?" are some of the ways you can phrase this. Offering tea or water can help put a person at ease; sometimes, just moving to a different room can help, too.

Staying Focused

Staying focused is important when you're doing a reading, and it's easy if your surroundings are quiet, comfortable, and relaxing. Take the time to create a space where you and the Querent feel relaxed so you can focus on the job at hand.

When everybody's comfortable, shuffle the deck before the question is even asked. Then focus the question itself into the deck as the shuffling continues. You can do this by either thinking about the question or asking it aloud.

How the question is asked will also keep you focused. Before the shuffling starts, you should ask the Querent, "What do you *really* want to know about this subject?" Gently insist that the Querent phrase the question to get precisely the answer he desires.

A Querent may answer, "I really want to know how I should handle my boss when she seems like she's not listening to me." Or he may say, "Is my girlfriend as committed as she says she is? I think she's seeing someone else."

A Querent can ask the Tarot for advice as well as just a plain "yes" or "no" answer. The Tarot can give as much information as a Querent's willing to ask for. You should encourage Querents to ask what they want to know, then have them shuffle the deck several times and divide it into three stacks, as described a little earlier in this chapter.

A spread put out according to this method will give information on what the Querent wants to know. "How should I handle my husband's temper?" "What can I do to communicate better with my child?" "What's the best way to go on this investment that everyone is so enthusiastic about?" Questions like this come up often—and, if they're phrased right, the Querent will receive the advice she's seeking.

Let the Cards Do the Talking

The Tarot will communicate what the Querent *needs to know* about the question—but this may not always be what the Querent wants or expects to hear. Sometimes the cards confirm the Querent's suspicions, but just as often, they throw a surprise answer the Querent wasn't expecting, or suggest an aspect the Querent hadn't considered before.

When you let the cards do the talking, the Tarot is a great tool for working with others on problem-solving. With its open perspective on the subject at hand, a Tarot spread reveals the truth about a given situation while saying it in a subtle way that allows the Querent to think about her life constructively.

You can think of the Tarot as a philosophical tool. Allow yourself and your Querent to muse over a layout of cards and think and meditate about what they just said to you. Thinking about a spread in this way can force us to pause in our busy lives to actually think about an issue. Introspection allows us to become aware, once again, that we always have choices, and that there are always alternatives to choose from, no matter what the circumstances.

Creating a Positive Context

No matter what cards come up, it's your responsibility as a reader to put them in a positive context. If a reading seems filled with "negative" cards, you should spend the time with the Querent exploring what those cards might be trying to tell him.

Remember, Minor Arcana cards in particular are free will cards, but the Querent always has the power to turn any reversed card upright, including the Major Arcana. Reversed cards in a Tarot reading can signal that the Querent, or someone near the Querent, is standing in his or her way, blocking the energy required to get something done. By understanding the energy of a reversed card the Querent receives in a reading, the Querent learns how to turn that energy in a positive direction by making good life decisions. The Querent's next reading may deal that reversed card in an upright position—a reversal of fortune, indeed!

You can create a positive context by asking the Querent questions about the cards. "Is this someone you know?" "Does this represent something that's already happened?"

In one reading Lisa did, the skeptical Querent became convinced of the reading's validity when the King of Swords reversed appeared. "That's my boss!" he said. "It looks as if he's trying to keep me where I am, instead of promoting me, because he wants me to keep doing the work I do." The rest of the reading indicated that the Querent would soon be moving on to something new. A company man, he hadn't seen his boss in this negative way, and this new point of view encouraged him to strike out on his own.

One More Time: Practice, Practice, Practice

We can't say it enough, so we'll say it again: practice, practice, practice. You can't play the violin if you don't practice every day, and you can't master the Tarot if you don't stay in touch with the cards on a daily basis.

This can be as simple as taking a card from the deck every day and just noting what the card is. Or you can select a different card from the deck each day and spend some time meditating on its meaning.

No matter how you choose to get to know your Tarot deck, the key word is "know." By working with the cards on a daily basis, the messages they've got to tell will become second nature.

The Least You Need to Know

➤ Your Tarot reader should be someone you trust.

➤ You should ask questions phrased as specifically as possible.

➤ Different spreads are used for different questions.

➤ Reading someone else's cards requires an open mind and a positive attitude.

Ask the Cards a Question

In this chapter, we're going to look at three of the most common Tarot spreads: the Three-Card Spread for a quick answer; the Seven-Card Spread for "higher knowledge" about a question; and the classic ten-card Celtic Cross, which provides all the information you need to know about a question—and maybe some you wish you didn't!

Three Cards for a Quick Answer

Sometimes you just need to know something *now*. When this happens, a Three-Card Spread can give you a quick answer to your question. Just remember—it may not always be the answer you want to hear.

The Three-Card Spread.

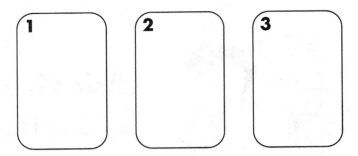

A Sample Reading

Background: Debby's father had recently passed away, and Debby was left to deal with all the legal details. Naturally she was a little overwhelmed and needed some guidance and direction to help her jump the legal hurdles.

One of the major things facing Debby was selling her father's condo quickly. As you already know, a reader can't "make" a sale go faster, but we *can* give a Querent an idea about *if* something will sell and how long it might take. That's the approach Arlene suggested to Debby. It took two Three-Card Spreads to get both her questions answered.

What the Cards Mean

Debby's first Three-Card Spread: "When will Dad's condo sell?"

Debby's first question: "When will Dad's condo sell?"

Card 1: The Sun. This is a good beginning. The Sun suggests that the answer will conclude in success, so the condo should sell. Besides, it's a good, clean condo in a good neighborhood!

Card 2: 9 of Cups. Whenever the 9 of Cups (the wish card!) appears, the answer to the question is YES! YES! YES! This is especially true in a Three-Card reading, and therefore Debby will get her wish—getting the condo sold.

Card 3: Ace of Wands. This card indicates that positive energy is being put in the direction of the question, so again we have a positive result on the horizon. Arlene concluded that Debby will be able to sell the condo—but when?

We can find the timing in this reading by looking at the seasonal representations of the Minor Arcana. Remember, Cups are summertime and Wands are spring. Because Debby put the condo up for sale in the spring, it should sell by the suit of Cups' time, summer.

Note that in this spread all three cards are upright and all read in a positive direction, pointing toward a "yes" rather than a "no." This is an easy spread to read (which is why we chose it to include here!).

Debby's second Three-Card Spread: "Will the sale of the condo go smoothly?"

Debby's second question: "Will the sale of the condo go smoothly?"

Card 1: Strength. In this Major Arcana card, a lady's taming a lion, which indicates that Debby needs to be patient and positive about selling the condo. The Strength card means Debby needs to have faith and confidence that everything will work out the way it's supposed to. Fortunately, Debby does have patience and kindness, which will enable her to wait for the right offer.

Card 2: The Wheel of Fortune. This is the second Major Arcana card in this reading—that's two out of the three cards here. Remember, Major Arcana mean that Debby herself can't speed up (or slow down) this process; how quickly it will go is in other peoples' hands. But whose?

From this card Arlene felt that the person or people who will want to buy the condo are destined to

Spinning the Wheel of Fortune

When you do a similar reading for yourself, be sure to put timing in the question. For instance, ask, "Will my car sell within the next month?" If you ask, "Will I sell my car?" you'll get a "yes" or a "no," but won't find out just how long that yes or no might take. So, the more specific you are, the more info you'll get in your answer.

have it. That means there won't be any confusion about who's supposed to get the condo. The Wheel of Fortune indicates that good things are coming. Debby will sell the condo in a timely fashion.

Card 3: 2 of Pentacles. This last card shows that Debby may have two proposals at once and so may have to dicker on the offer, weigh the price, or start high and go down in price to sell. This is not a bad card that indicates anything will go wrong with the deal, but negotiation may be required to make the sale go smoothly.

Again, these are not bad cards, and when we look at the two different readings for the two questions together, we find similar outcomes. There may be some difficulty in the deal, but the overall feeling is that the condo will sell and that negotiations will proceed fairly smoothly.

P.S. Since we did this reading, Debby's Dad's condo has been sold. At the last minute, the buyer wanted two windows fixed and they had to renegotiate the price in order to close the sale.

Your Tarot Journal Worksheet: Do a Reading

Now it's time for you to try a Three-Card reading of your own. Go ahead, ask the cards a question.

Your Three-Card Spread Question:

_____

_____

Now shuffle the cards as you think about this question. When you're ready, place the cards as shown and write them in the spaces that follow.

Your Three-Card Spread.

Interpretation:

Card 1:

_____

_____

Card 2:

_____

_____

Card 3:

_____

_____

The Seven-Card Spread

The Seven-Card Spread is also used to get a "yes" or "no" answer, but it adds some extra spice to your answer. This spread was originally called the "Magic Seven" Spread, because the last (seventh) card is the one that gives the resolution to the question— and the number 7 is the number of wisdom, higher knowledge, and introspection. So with a Seven-Card Spread, you get some higher wisdom thrown in to help you on your way. Lucky 7, yes?

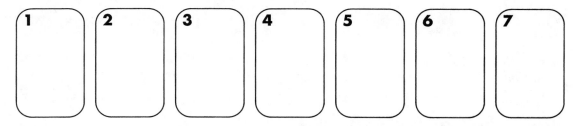

The Seven-Card Spread.

In the Cards

Numbers have all kinds of associations, both mystical and practical. In Chapter 26, you'll be taking a numerological look at the Tarot, but if you'd like to peek ahead now, we do understand!

A Sample Seven-Card Spread

Background: Mary and John are starting to run a nursery and landscaping business together. Mary wants to know if their relationship will grow into more than just a business one.

Mary's question: "Will John and I develop a romantic relationship or will it be a strictly business one?"

Mary shuffles and divides the deck by three and picks one of the three stacks. She picks the middle stack because she says she's conservative and sticks to the middle of the road! Let the Querent pick the stack she wishes: The Querent is in control of the reading, we always say. Not only does this help the cards "feel" the question, it helps the Querent focus and calm down.

Mary's Seven-Card Spread:
"Will John and I develop a romantic relationship or will it be a strictly business one?"

What the Cards Mean

Card 1: 6 of Wands. Victory after hard work and effort, says the 6 of Wands. This card refers to work and business ideas, and shows where Mary and John are right now. Not bad for business—but no love message here.

Card 2: The Hermit. This card comes up to ask the Querent to look within and focus on the truth of the matter. Maybe at some level Mary already knows what the relationship could or will be; she needs to listen to her inner voice as she works with John. She needs to listen to what John says, too, because he'll tell her later on which way he'd like to go with the relationship.

Card 3: 3 of Cups. This card indicates good energy between the two people in the question. They bring joy to each other, and a good emotional connection has already been made. The message in the 3 of Cups is to keep the relationship light, happy, joyful, and pleasant.

During this reading, Arlene suggested that Mary and John seem to enjoy each other's company already, and maybe something deeper could grow from that. But the 3 of Cups is reminding them to enjoy their good friendship now and not worry about what the future might bring.

Card 4: 6 of Cups R. Someone is clinging to an outworn idea about this relationship. But is it Mary or is it John? It could be either one of them, but because Mary's the one asking, Arlene talks with her about it. Could she be living in the past, being too nostalgic, or hoping for something that may not develop?

Arlene thinks Mary's wishing for the romance to develop, but it's not wise to wait for this or expect this now because it can cause difficulty with the basic friendship Mary and John already have.

Card 5: 3 of Wands. This is another good card for business dealings. It indicates cooperation in business affairs and trade, as well as profit coming into the business, with the business partners (Mary and John) working well together. The 3 of Wands represents that good partnership brings success. That says it all! This one card almost answers Mary's entire question: There's good partnership for business here—but nothing about love.

Card 6: Queen of Swords. Well, this is surely Mary: brown-haired lady, focused, concentrating on the business—and on John. Mary's highly intelligent and more than capable of running a business with her good logic and sharp, keen mind. She doesn't miss a beat and is very perceptive in her work and her personal life.

Mary agreed this was her card in regard to this question. Swords people often have been through rough times in either a relationship or a situation in the past, and Swords person Mary knows difficulty and adversity but has the strength and courage to face the truth of any matter. Arlene told her that no matter what happens with this relationship, she'll accept the way it goes because she's strong and has good logic and common sense.

Card 7: Knight of Pentacles. This last card can represent John because of his business acumen, public relations skills, and desire to develop this business enterprise so that it makes a good profit. But notice it's not an emotional card (Cups) but rather a business and productivity one (Pentacles).

Arlene told Mary that the answer at this point in the relationship is that it's better to keep it as a good sound business relationship. That should be grown first, and then Mary can take a wait-and-see approach to the romantic part. "Don't push the river," Arlene told Mary. "John may not want to move quickly into a romance but rather move methodically into the business relationship you have."

Overall, the cards were positive, but they were clearly more focused on the business angle rather than the romantic one. "Cool your jets," Arlene

Fools Rush In

So you want to rush into a romance and the cards say, "Cool your jets"? If you've been paying attention, you should know to listen to the cards. Maybe this isn't the right guy or gal—or maybe it is, but the time's not right yet. The cards pick up on the energy of everyone involved, and if they say, "Hey! Hold on a minute!", it's in your best interests to listen.

said (this is really how Arlene talks!). "You have a good man here. Allow the relationship to grow and see where it can go. Take your time, and things can turn out exactly as you hope. But don't push it!"

Your Tarot Journal Worksheet: Do a Reading

Now it's time for you to try a Seven-Card reading of your own. First, ask the cards a question.

Your Seven-Card Spread Question:

_____

_____

Now shuffle the cards as you think about this question. When you're ready, divide the cards into three stacks. Pick one of the stacks and deal the top seven cards, placing them as shown here. Write the cards down in the spaces that follow. Then look up what the cards mean.

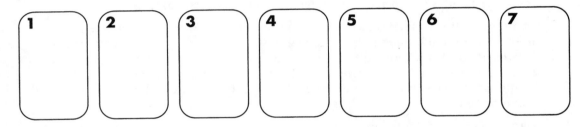

Your Seven-Card Spread.

Interpretation:

Card 1:

_____

Card 2:

_____

Card 3:

_____

Card 4:

_____

_____

Card 5:

_____

_____

Card 6:

_____

_____

Card 7:

_____

_____

Put Your Cards on the Table: The Celtic Cross

The *Celtic Cross Spread* is far and away the most commonly used Tarot spread. There are a lot of reasons for this, not the least of which is how much this spread can show about a particular situation.

Let's look at these cards one at a time.

Card 1: This card represents the Querent, and should be selected by the Querent for that purpose. Many readers insist that this must always be a royal court card, but (and you know us by now) we think this is too limiting. What if you're feeling pretty 3 of Swords about the question? Or a bit like the Fool? Whether you're doing a reading for yourself or for someone else, take the time to find the card that feels right for this particular question.

Card 2: This is the cover card. It is always upright and represents opposing forces. When it's a good card, it's supporting the Querent's energies—always good news. Yes, cards can be dealt reversed, but if that happens, the Querent will physically position card 2 upright for the reading. That's the ancient wisdom on the energies of card 2 in the Celtic Cross Spread.

Card 3: This card represents the Querent's energy and shows the foundation of the matter and where the question came from. In other words, this card answers the question of why you asked the question in the first place!

Card Catalog

A *Celtic*, or *Keltic*, *Cross* represents everything there is to know about a question. Using the cross as its basis, it shows how a question (and its Querent) move through time.

Card 4: Here's your past experience regarding the question. This is the immediate background and it's passing away or has already gone. Especially when it's a negative card, we like to say, "So long, sucker!"

The Celtic Cross Spread.

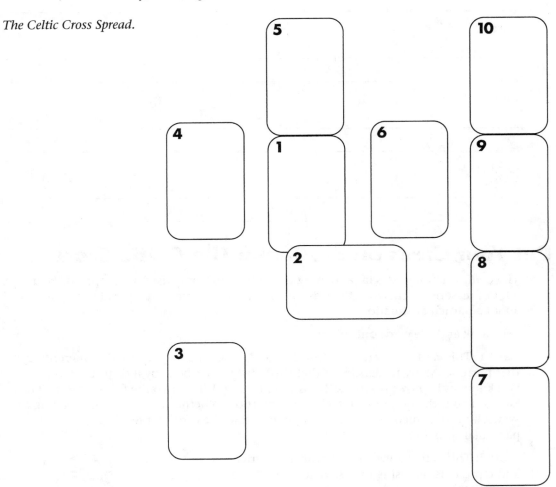

Card 5: Here's the energy around you now. This energy may manifest itself in the future, but it's free will energy, so its manifestation is up to you.

Card 6: This is what's before you. Whatever the sixth card shows will *always* happen in the future regarding the question. The energies here are already at work but have not yet manifested themselves. They will. The sixth and the tenth cards in this spread also indicate timing.

Card 7: Here are your fears regarding the question. If you're afraid of others' opinions, you'll find it here. Afraid of rejection? This is your card. Afraid of change? Of stagnation? Whether you recognize your fears or not, they'll show their faces here in the seventh Celtic Cross card.

Card 8: The eighth card shows how others feel about the matter you've asked about. These can be others directly involved, or they may be tangential others who don't know diddly. This card really depends on the question and how others may or may not affect its outcome.

Card 9: Here are the positive feelings about the question. You've got to get through whatever the ninth card represents to get to the tenth, and sometimes it won't feel quite so positive. If you've got to jump through hoops of fire, this is the card that will show how high up those hoops are—and if you've got a net.

Card 10: This card represents the final outcome of the question. It will be modified and influenced by what the other nine cards have divined, but this is it, folks. Like the sixth card, the tenth card also indicates timing.

To us, a Celtic Cross is like a story about a question. What's its history? How did you get to where you are now? Where do you go from here? Who's involved? What's scary and what's not? When you want to know a question from every angle, a Celtic Cross is the spread to use.

A Sample Celtic Cross Spread

Background: In July of 1991, a woman named Bea came to Arlene. Bea was going through a divorce and wanted to know if she'd ever have a nice relationship in her life again.

At the time, Bea was 55 years old. Dark-haired with dark eyes, Bea's a good business-woman and good at developing career abilities. Bea knew she'd be okay with her work, career, and kids, but she wanted to know if she'd have a good, committed relationship in the near future.

*Bea's Celtic Cross Spread:
"Will I have a good,
committed relationship in
the near future?"*

Card 1   *Queen of Swords*

Card 2   *9 of Pentacles*

Card 3   *5 of Wands*

Card 4   *King of Cups R*

Card 5   *6 of Cups*

Card 6   *Ace of Cups*

Card 7   *8 of Swords R*

Card 8   *The Tower*

Card 9   *Ace of Wands*

Card 10   *King of Wands*

What the Cards Mean

Bea's question: "Will I have a good, committed relationship in the near future?"

Card 1: The Querent.

Queen of Swords. Arlene and Bea chose this card, with its dark hair and dark eyes, to represent Bea. She was feeling losses from her previous husband and their time in court, too, and this card just felt right to her.

Card 2: Crosses.

9 of Pentacles. This card represents a self-sufficient woman, someone who's able to take care of business and who has the money, property, and/or resources to take care of herself.

Card 3: Foundation.

5 of Wands. This card indicates obstacles, oppression, and feeling as if one is always struggling. Bea was struggling, and the struggle with her ex-husband continued for $2^1/_2$ years after this reading. They were in court about both business and personal property, fighting all the time.

Card 4: Past.

King of Cups R. Bea's ex-husband was a Cancer, but, as Arlene told her, "At least he'll become part of your past now!" This position indicates that he'll be leaving Bea's life, either gone completely or no longer as disturbing to her as he had been.

Card 5: What may or may not happen.

6 of Cups. This card indicates a meeting with a childhood friend or loved one. "Maybe," Arlene said, thinking out loud, "the new guy is around you through your friends or social groups? Maybe the new relationship will start out as a friendship and grow into something more." (This is a good example of why you want your Tarot reader to really "know" the cards.)

Card 6: What will happen.

Ace of Cups!! This card represents the beginning of a new relationship that will fulfill the heart! Arlene (and Bea) was very happy to see this card, but Bea immediately wanted to know, "When is he going to get here!?" Naturally, she loved the card, too, but he hadn't come into her life yet when this reading was done, so of course she wanted to know more. Arlene just told her the Ace of Cups was definitely a good omen.

Card 7: Fears or attitude toward the question.

8 of Swords R. The 8 of Swords reversed reminded Bea of the need to release the old in order to have the new. Bea was learning to release her fears about herself and being alone. Soon, Arlene told her, she'd have nothing to fear!

Card 8: Others.

The Tower. SURPRISE! cried the Tower. "He will come out of left field," Arlene told Bea. "You don't know him yet, but through your friends or social connections (6 of Cups), you'll have him appear in your life when you least expect it."

Card 9: What you go through to get there.

Ace of Wands. This card indicates the beginning of a new job, career, or work situation. Bea would have to pass through this first, before "he" would arrive. She actually was starting a new real estate course soon...

Card 10: Ta da! Outcome.

King of Wands! When Arlene saw this card, she said, "He's got sandy hair, light eyes, and a fair complexion. He's enthusiastic about his work/career, is ambitious, self-motivated, encouraging, funny, and candid." (Hey—where do *we* order one of these?)

And now, the rest of the story...Bea took that real estate class to help her career along—which it did. Then she took another class. The person who was giving that class was Doug...you know, The Guy!

Doug and Bea began by talking. Then they became friends, and then they started going out. And, in December 1997, Bea and Doug got married!

Your Tarot Journal Worksheet: Do a Reading

Are you ready to try a Celtic Cross reading of your own? (But we can't guarantee Doug will show up for you, of course.) To begin, ask the cards a question.

Your Celtic Cross Question:

_____

_____

Next, pick out a card that you feel represents you at this moment. People most often pick royal court cards, but if there's another card you feel better represents you for this question, by all means use it. This is your number 1 card, sometimes called the significator.

Now, shuffle the rest of the cards as you think about your question. When you're ready, place the remaining cards as shown in positions 2 through 10, and write them in the spaces that follow. Then look up what the cards mean.

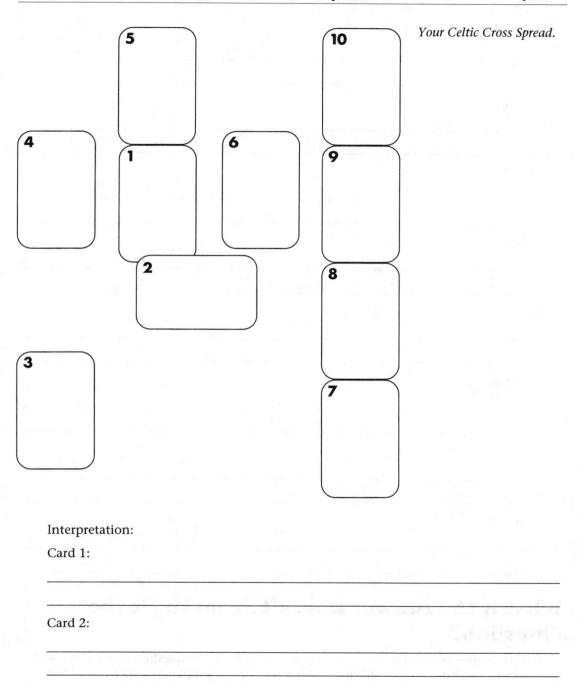

Your Celtic Cross Spread.

Interpretation:

Card 1:

_____

_____

Card 2:

_____

_____

Card 3:

_____

_____

Card 4:

_____

_____

Card 5:

_____

_____

Card 6:

_____

_____

Card 7:

_____

_____

Card 8:

_____

_____

Card 9:

_____

_____

Card 10:

_____

_____

What If the Answer Doesn't Seem to Fit the Question?

It happens—sometimes the answer doesn't seem to fit the question at all. You asked about love and the cards talked about money. Or you asked about money and the cards talked about sex (things could be worse...). But what gives? Why aren't the cards addressing the question?

There are a couple possible reasons for this:

➤ *You may have been thinking about another question when you were shuffling.* Maybe you were doing so subconsciously, but the cards know. The cards are going to answer the question closest to your heart—whether it's the question you voice or not.

➤ *The cards ARE answering your question.* Maybe you asked about a relationship, but you've got to work to get there. Or the relationship you're in isn't the right one, no matter how much you want it to be. You and the reader should examine each card's meanings carefully to see just what the cards are trying to tell you. You may not want to hear it, but you may *need* to.

With time, an answer will prove to be the right one, even if it doesn't seem to fit the question at the moment. Sometimes, at the time of the reading, there are situations that haven't happened yet, or we don't think could ever happen. Six months later, the situation we thought wouldn't happen (or were a little foggy about) did happen.

For this reason, it's very important to either record the reading or to write it down. You'll want to recall everything that was said. Most readings do take time to play out. While the Tarot may be telling you things you already know, it may also be providing additional information about things to come. In fact, the events in readings can take from two to ten months to actually happen!

There's one more answer to consider, too, though you may not like it. Many years ago, Lisa went to see a Gypsy who read her cards. The Gypsy told her many things that made her laugh: "What, me marry a lawyer?" "What, me lose something?" But everything the Gypsy told her came to pass (including the lawyer).

Lisa took her mother to see the Gypsy, and the Gypsy told her that her marriage would end. Her mother laughed. "We're happily married," she said.

Then Lisa took her father to see the Gypsy, and the Gypsy told him lots of lies. "See?" her father told her, laughing. "You can't believe what Gypsies tell you."

Six months later, Lisa's father was dead of cancer. Within a year, Lisa had met that lawyer (they're not still married, but that's another story). We leave you to think about what the Gypsy said.

The Least You Need to Know

➤ A Three-Card Spread is a good way to get a quick answer to a question.

➤ A Seven-Card Spread adds divine wisdom to the mix.

➤ The Celtic Cross, the most commonly used spread, takes a question from its roots to its outcome.

➤ With time, an answer will prove to be the right one—even when it doesn't seem to fit the question at the moment.

Chapter 19

Laying Out Your Future

In This Chapter

➤ The Horoscope Spread: Your year in cards

➤ Past/Present/Future: The connection's in the cards

➤ Covering your Celtic: Double your info

➤ A map to help you on your way

Now that you know how to phrase your question and the basic Tarot spreads, it's time to take a peek into the future. The three spreads in this chapter give you three different methods of seeing things that have yet to occur: the Horoscope method; the Past/Present/Future method; and a method we call covering your Celtic, which doubles the information you receive from a Celtic Cross Spread.

Your Year in Cards: The Horoscope Spread

This method of reading the Tarot is called the Horoscope, or Zodiac, Spread. Your *horoscope,* or *birth chart,* is divided into twelve pie sections called *houses,* each for a specific area of your life. When you place a card in each house, the cards will show a general cycle of what will be happening in the Querent's life for the next twelve months.

Card Catalog

Your *horoscope,* or *birth chart,* is an astrological map for the moment of your birth. It's divided into twelve pie sections called *houses,* each for a specific area of your life.

Think of this spread as a yearly overview, which shows both what cycles the Querent's currently in, and a general glimpse of what's coming up for him. This type of spread is a good one for folks who want to know a little something rather than specific details, and it's the spread Arlene uses for anyone who tells her, "There sure isn't much going on in my life right now. Can I see if something's coming—maybe something exciting or different?"

See how the twelve pie sections here are marked "1" through "12"? If you know astrology, you know that this is what a horoscope looks like. Each of these twelve sections represents a specific area of your life.

The Horoscope Spread.

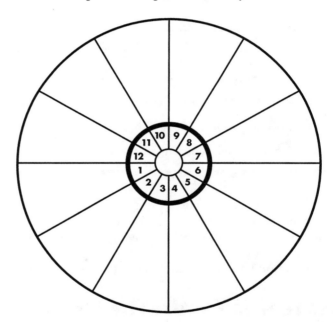

What's in Those Houses?

Each of the twelve houses represents a specific area of your life. You'll find everything from self-esteem to sex here. But look for yourself:

➤ *First House.* The first house is the area where you'll find your physical self, your personality, and your early childhood.

➤ *Second House.* Here's where your possessions, earning abilities, and self-esteem are located.

➤ *Third House.* The third house holds your knowledge, siblings, and environment.

➤ *Fourth House.* In the fourth house are your home and family, and the literal foundation of your life.

➤ *Fifth House.* The fifth house contains your creativity. Here's where you'll find fun, romance, risks—and children.

➤ *Sixth House.* The sixth house is your house of personal responsibilities, your health, and how you serve others.

➤ *Seventh House.* This house is where your primary relationships and partnerships are located.

➤ *Eighth House.* Here's where your joint resources can be found. It's also the house of sex, death, and rebirth.

➤ *Ninth House.* The ninth house is where you'll find your social areas: higher education, philosophy, law, religion, and travel.

➤ *Tenth House.* In the tenth house reside your reputation, career, and social responsibilities.

➤ *Eleventh House.* This is the house of your goals, groups, and friends.

➤ *Twelfth House.* This house contains your subconscious. It's the house of privacy, past karma, secrets, and hidden knowledge.

As with any other reading, the cards will be shuffled as the Querent focuses her energy on the cards. The difference with this spread is that instead of thinking of a specific question, we look at a general overview of the life of the Querent for the next twelve months or less, and so the Querent isn't thinking of a specific question. But if you're thinking, "Ah-ha! Twelve months...twelve sections..." We say, "Verrry good."

After the Querent shuffles, she divides the deck into three stacks. Then she selects one stack, whichever feels right (it's up to the Querent, as always). The reader will then use the top twelve cards, one for each month of the up and coming year, to lay out the spread.

Spinning the Wheel of Fortune

When a client's being introduced to the Tarot, or when there's no "burning question," the Horoscope Spread's a great way to see how the year will go in general. Also, it's a good way for the reader to become acquainted with someone new to the Tarot. This spread gives the novice a good feeling for the Tarot, calmly and gradually showing what the Tarot can do and how helpful it can be, rather than hitting him with one prediction after another.

A Sample Horoscope Spread

It was "Sue's" birthday when she came to Arlene and asked, "How will my year be? What can I expect?" Arlene had Sue shuffle and then divide the deck into three stacks. Sue gave Arlene the one stack she felt moved her, and Arlene laid out the cards in a Horoscope Spread.

Sue's Horoscope Spread: "How will my year be? What can I expect?"

What the Cards Mean

Card 1: 8 of Swords. The card starting the circle of twelve cards was the 8 of Swords. Sue looked at the card and said, "It looks like I'm all bound up!" Arlene explained that the 8 of Swords means that in that next month (one card for each month of the year ahead), Sue would feel restricted or be dealing with her personal fears about something. "You're fearful of moving out of a situation," Arlene said.

"I'm afraid to leave my boyfriend," Sue confessed. "There just isn't that zest anymore, but I'm afraid to hurt him."

When a Querent confirms a card in this way, it gives the reader the go-ahead to continue because both reader and Querent have confidence in the reading.

Card 2: Temperance R. This card suggested that Sue needed to be patient with business/financial issues, or to adapt to some conditions around her that she wasn't expecting. She might feel restless and impatient for something new to come, but in the next two months (remember, this is Card 2), she wouldn't handle some area of her life well because of her impatience.

Card 3: 7 of Pentacles. Sue would be speculating on money matters, learning to handle her money, and evaluating what to do with either savings or something she might want to invest in or purchase. There's nothing negative with the 7 of Pentacles when it's upright; it's just a matter of thinking about the issues of finance and savings.

Card 4: Queen of Cups. Sue's first royal court card showed up in the fourth position. The Queen of Cups is a woman who's kind and considerate, a good mom or nurturing type, with light hair and blue or hazel eyes. A woman such as this would be of help to Sue in the next several months, bringing good advice and excellent support, including the emotional kind.

Card 5: 2 of Cups. "Well, look what's coming," Arlene said. "Here's the beginning of a new friendship or romance! Maybe you don't have to worry about that old boyfriend now!" The 2 of Cups is a great card, predicting new friends or a new romance getting started within the year for Sue. It can also predict a good support group of friends, both old and new.

Card 6: 5 of Cups. While she'd have the support of the Queen and 2 of Cups, Sue would have to deal with an emotional loss in the coming year. The 5 of Cups upright indicates a loss over a loved one, the loss of a valued friend, or some sort of sadness because of a relationship gone awry. Arlene tried to prepare Sue for this event by reminding her that life has its up and downs. "This year," she told Sue, "it looks like you'll have a great relationship, but you may also suffer a loss over a former relationship."

Card 7: 8 of Cups R. This card relates the idea that Sue would once again regain her optimism and joy toward life. The 5 of Cups would be a loss, yes, but Sue would rebound, and good energy would come after. The old translation of the 8 of Cups R is joy and feasting, or a new love interest, on the horizon.

Card 8: 6 of Wands. This card predicted that Sue would have several victories during the year. She'd overcome any kind of adversity and, in the end, be victorious. This card could also predict a journey during the next year, perhaps out of state, that would benefit her greatly. Lastly, it indicated that Sue might win an award or get some kind of recognition during the year to come.

Card 9: Page of Swords. Sue had to be prepared for the unexpected, according to this card. Sometimes Pages represent messages coming in, and the Sword message can be something upsetting, such as news of a loss or not accomplishing a goal. Maybe, Arlene suggested, Sue would be wanting to hear from someone, but it would be delayed or difficult to communicate with this individual.

Card 10: The Devil R. This card indicated that Sue would be learning to release her fears and the difficulties around her. This would mean letting go of either someone or something that was restricting her. Perhaps she'd let go of an obsession, or learn how to get control back into her life. At the same time, she'd develop a sense of self-worth, so that no temptation would affect her.

Card 11: 7 of Swords R. In the up and coming year Sue would receive wise advice from others she respected, according to the 7 of Swords R. It could be from her teachers, her boss, her peer group, or her family. This card was reminding her to pay attention to good advice and counsel when it arrived, or that she'd need advice or counsel this year. Whichever it was, Arlene told Sue to listen, because the 7 of Swords R predicts good counsel *will* be given.

Card 12: King of Cups R. This light-haired, blue- or hazel-eyed man would be difficult for Sue during the upcoming year. The King of Cups R is quiet but deceptive about his intentions. He could be someone not supportive of her, so Sue needed to avoid all entanglements with him. This man is not always what he appears to be or says he is.

Sue had a feeling this card represented an old boyfriend from ten years before, for whom she still had feelings. Thinking about him always made her feel sad or depressed. Arlene reminded her that this wasn't the present boyfriend, or the future new guy they'd seen (2 of Cups in the fifth position), but someone far back in the past. Sue might still be affected by this past relationship and still be dealing with it, even if the fellow isn't really in her life anymore, because this, after all, was her 12th house card. Remember that the 12th house is the astrological house of privacy, karma, past secrets, and hidden knowledge.

In the year that followed, all of Sue's cards except the Page of Swords came to pass. Of course, Pages are messages, and maybe the message all year long was to handle the difficulty of the past. Sue ended up doing quite well. She met a new guy, and her old relationship faded into the sunset within a year and half after this reading.

Your Tarot Journal Worksheet: Do a Reading

If, like Sue, you're curious about the future but just want an overview, a Horoscope Spread is the reading for you. And it works! If you're ready to try such a spread of your own, get out your cards and start shuffling.

When you're ready, divide the cards into three stacks, and then select whichever stack feels right. Place the top twelve cards from that stack in the pattern shown here.

Your Horoscope Spread.

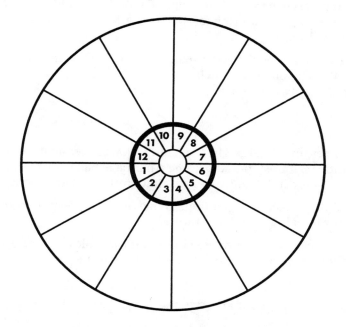

Write the names of the Tarot cards you've dealt in the appropriate slice of the Horoscope form, and then write your interpretations of the cards in the spaces that follow.

"How will your year be? What can you expect?"

Card 1: _____

Card 2: _____

Card 3: _____

Card 4: _____

Card 5: _____

Card 6: _____

Card 7: _____

Card 8: _____

Card 9: _____

Card 10: _____

Card 11: _____

Card 12: _____

Past/Present/Future: Taking Stock

This type of spread relates our past experiences to the present and then shows a future outcome. It's used to show the inter-relationship between experiences and lessons you have learned and those you will learn.

This is quite an interesting spread. Arlene's tried it many times when clients really wanted to know why something happened in their past, how they're affected presently, and what will come of that past experience in the future.

A Sample Spread

"Sarah" was bothered by something she thought she hadn't properly brought to a close in her past. A strong romantic relationship that became a marriage had ended abruptly seven years later. Since that time, Sarah had had a hard time trusting any relationship.

Sarah shuffled the deck and then asked this question: "What am I supposed to learn from my past marriage that will help me with my future?"

For the Past/Present/Future Spread, seven cards are put out on the table after the deck has been shuffled and divided by three. The Querent again chooses the stack from which the cards are dealt.

Sarah's Past/Present/Future Spread: "What am I supposed to learn from my past marriage that will help me with my future?"

What the Cards Mean

The first two cards of this spread represent past conditions.

Card 1: 6 of Wands. In the past, Sarah's marriage had been developing well and seemed solid and stable. The partnership appeared to be harmonious.

Card 2: 2 of Cups. The marriage brought luck and harmony to both, and both worked well together and offered help and understanding to each other. Not bad! Sarah said yes, that was how it was at the start of the marriage; all looked well—in the beginning.

The next three cards represent the present conditions:

Card 3: Ace of Swords R. Here we find argument or frustration over the relationship. The marriage began to turn on itself, as the Sword represents the development of argument or mistrust. In addition, remember, Sarah said she now mistrusts others and is afraid to go into anything new.

Card 4: The Tower. Here's the surprise of the separation! Sarah didn't know what happened to break up her marriage and said that after two years she was still confused and unclear about the real reasons for her marriage's undoing.

This card was a reminder of how Sarah's divorce and loss still affected her, almost as if it had just happened. Sarah kept saying she still had a hard time letting go but knew she had to. But while the Tower represents how shock forces us to deal with a surprise, we have to remember the question Sarah asked: "What am I supposed to learn about the past that will help me with my future?"

In this regard, the Tower indicates that Sarah was learning about the element of surprise in her life. Sometimes things just happen without apparent warning, and those unexpected events are represented by the Tower. There are times in our lives when we're forced into situations where we have no control. When this happens, if things have to go in a different direction than planned, we have to allow it.

It turns out that Sarah's ex-husband just didn't want to be married anymore; he wanted to be free. There was no other woman, no real motivation. He just fell out of love, he said to her. Sad, but true. Naturally, Sarah still has that little tug at the heart that asks, "But why?"

Card 5: 5 of Wands R. Eventually Sarah would learn that the shock of the divorce would end and peace would once again come into her life. Sarah agreed she'd been feeling better already. "So," Arlene said, "maybe it's best that he spoke the truth, so you two can get on with your lives. Maybe you'll find someone else who's as committed as you." Sarah thought about that, then Arlene said, "It's better to know early in your life, rather than having to hear he's not into marriage anymore when you're 60 or 70, huh?" Of course, Sarah agreed.

The last two cards speak to the future. The sixth card is the future, and the seventh, future resolution or outcome.

Card 6: The Chariot. Sarah will learn to maintain stamina, have perseverance, develop a strong character and outlook, and understand that all is not lost. The end of one marriage can lead into

Fools Rush In

If you don't want to know what the future holds, don't ask! The Tarot is a powerful tool for getting you in touch with your subconscious and the energies all around you. Sometimes, you may want to walk toward your future cheerfully ignorant of what may happen next. We understand the impulse—but don't ask the Tarot, or you may find out what you don't want to know.

another, one with more awareness and maturity, Arlene reminded her. The Chariot meant that she'd learned a major lesson in devotion, loyalty, and stamina, and would remain that way for her next relationship. Through the challenge of her marriage's break-up, Sarah developed courage because her love never changed and she always maintained her values.

Card 7: 8 of Swords R. This card indicates that Sarah's learning to release her fears about loss and the lack of trust. She'll soon get back to herself and open up once again to new relationships. She'll begin to slowly get her trust back.

The 8 of Swords R is a woman who'll release herself from her self-imposed prison, Arlene told Sarah. Because of her divorce, she learned to develop courage and strength for the next relationship, and to let go of her fear of putting herself into relationships.

Arlene told Sarah she'd get out of her fearful state of mind in the next year and move on in her life. She just needed to work on her fears and free herself from her own restrictions. "Freedom is coming," Arlene assured her. "So you can go on and feel like yourself again!" Sarah was naturally happy to hear this, and agreed that she was becoming more and more like what Arlene was describing.

Your Tarot Journal Worksheet: Do a Reading

Now it's your turn to try a Past/Present/Future reading. First, shuffle the cards. When you're ready, divide the cards into three stacks, pick one stack, and then deal the cards out as shown here.

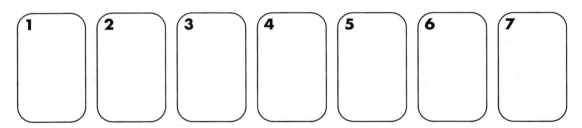

Your Past/Present/Future Spread.

Write your cards in the diagram above. Then write your interpretations in the spaces that follow.

Past:

Card 1: _____

Card 2: _____

Present:

Card 3: _____

Card 4: _____

Card 5: _____

Future:

Card 6: _____

Card 7: _____

Cover Your Celtic: Double Your Info

The Celtic Cross, which we last encountered in Chapter 18, is one of the most ancient methods of reading the Tarot. In the olden days, the reader would ask the Querent to write his wish or specific question on a piece of paper, then fold the paper and place it on the table where the reading would take place. The reader would then shuffle the deck and meditate on the Querent—without asking the Querent anything, nor reading the paper! The deck would be divided and dealt in a Celtic Cross, with the cards placed over the folded paper with the question on it. In this way, both Querent and reader concentrated together on the reading—and the Querent never questioned the reader's psychic powers!

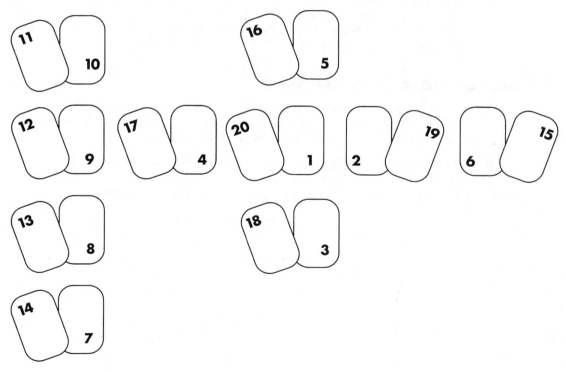

The Celtic Cover Spread.

Adding a second ten cards to the Celtic Cross enhances the meaning of the original spread. Let's review the meanings of the first ten cards, showing you how the second ten cards connect to them. (Cards from the first and second spreads are separated here with a slash.)

➤ Cards 1/20. The Querent (what surrounds the question)

➤ Cards 2/19. Favorable or unfavorable conditions

➤ Cards 3/18. Foundation of the matter

➤ Cards 4/17. Conditions passing away

➤ Cards 5/16. Might materialize

➤ Cards 6/15. What will occur

➤ Cards 7/14. Negative feelings/fears

➤ Cards 8/13. Others and the question

➤ Cards 9/12. What you have to go through

➤ Cards 10/11. Final outcome

As you've probably guessed, each of the second ten cards amplifies the card that it covers. The 11th card reveals more about the outcome; the 14th, more about your fears; the 17th, more about the past; and the 20th, more about you! But rather than try to explain it any more, we've got a sample Celtic Cover Spread to show you.

A Sample Celtic Cover Spread

Debbie (not the same Debby as in Chapter 18) had a two-fold question for Arlene, so Arlene decided to use the Celtic Cover Spread to get more details and information out of the cards to tell Debbie specifically what she wanted to know.

Debbie concentrated and shuffled as she asked: "When will my new job occur and where?" Difficult two-fold questions like this are challenging but we like to take such challenges on: We know as readers that the more you challenge yourself, the better you become.

Positive forces   (8 cups)
   - Leaving old attachments

Foundation of Matter - Justice
   I feel its not balanced or
fair that I'm alone

Past - 10 of Cups
         Dark

...ccur and where?"

f Pentacles R. Arlene's interpretation of
...rk, Debbie had undergone discrimina-
...Someone else was chosen under unfair
...oss was sorry that she (the boss) had
...Debbie, but by then it was too late.

...ard 19): 8 of Cups/8 of Swords R. Because this position is
what Debbie had in opposition to her, Debbie had to give up on the job for which she
was turned down. And she had decided at the time not to fight the situation, to leave
it alone (or, as the picture in the 8 of Cups shows, walk away).

Card 3 and its cover (card 18): 3 of Cups/The World R. At the foundation of
Debbie's question was a good card; it suggested that an offer was coming. The World R
simply indicated it (the new job) would be a little delayed. Arlene told Debbie, "Never
fear. Something good will come out of what's happened to you."

Card 4 and its cover (card 17): 5 of Cups/3 of Pentacles. The 5 of Cups showed Debbie's sadness from the recent past, either not having a job she enjoyed or the fact that she didn't get the one she'd applied for. The good news was that the worst card of the spread (5 of Cups) regarding her job was in the process of leaving her life!

Card 5 and its cover (card 16): Queen of Wands R/Judgement. The Queen of Wands R represented the woman who got the job Debbie was promised. Now the Queen of Wands R is Debbie's new boss! Debbie told Arlene she'd had a very hard time with this woman, and she was the reason Debbie wanted to move to another place or situation. So even though the fifth position is what may or may not happen, the Queen of Wands R surely had been encouraging Debbie to get out and look for another job. The Judgement card on top of the Queen of Wands R meant the Queen wouldn't be able to manage her new position and would be "judged" by her higher-ups later, or that the Queen would have a personal awakening about her new position.

Then, news flash! Five days after this reading, Debbie called and told Arlene the position that Debbie didn't get (the one that the Queen of Wands R got), would be terminated at the beginning of the new year! The Queen of Wands R would be transferred to a nice job, still in the same government section, but not the same position at all. Obviously, Debbie had been protected, if in a roundabout way.

Card 6 and its cover (card 15): 6 of Pentacles/Ace of Wands. Because the sixth position card predicts what always will happen, it was clear there *was* a new job coming. The 6 of Pentacles represented that a job offer would bring both financial and personal success. And the Ace of Wands! This card indicated the beginning of a new job or career offer. Debbie smiled when Arlene told her this; she was happy to hear this news, of course, even though she didn't know what the new offer would be.

Card 7 and its cover (card 14): 9 of Wands R/4 of Swords R. Here were Debbie's fears and/or attitude toward her own question: anxiety and stress over the work conditions, and fear that they would never get any better. The 4 of Swords R enhanced her fear that the whole situation would either stay the same or that something new would continue her anxiety. Remember, the seventh card (and its cover card, card 14) is what you feel or fear. It's an attitude you have, not a prediction of the future at all.

Card 8 and its cover (card 13): 10 of Wands/10 of Pentacles. Now this was different. Arlene told Debbie that the burden (10 of Wands) she was carrying would eventually pay off in the 10 of Pentacles. She might have to struggle a bit longer, but she would come out okay in the end. Others—her friends and family—saw her exactly this way. They didn't like what she was going through and were hoping that she'd get out of it soon. At the same time, they knew all about the difficulties Debbie had been having about her job.

Card 9 and its cover (card 12): The Tower R/4 of Wands. This position was what Debbie still had to pass through or process and integrate about her question. The Tower R indicated a surprise job or new direction coming suddenly, while the 4 of Wands cover card represented a good offer that she'd be happy about. It would come out of the blue, yes, but no matter when and where, it would end up well.

These two cards are a good example of why the Celtic Cover Spread is so helpful. In the original ten-card spread, Debbie would only have seen the Tower R; she wouldn't know what direction the Tower was going to lead her. With its cover card, it was clear that this be a positive, pleasant surprise.

Card 10 and its cover (card 11): The Hierophant/Knight of Pentacles. The Hierophant represented Debbie's conventional job situation (remember, she worked for the government). Arlene told her she'd probably continue to work for the government (she wanted to get her full retirement eventually), but the Knight of Pentacles was offering good income and movement in the direction of a new job and possible change of residence because of a job. Debbie had said she'd really like to have a job within the system but in another district. It clearly sounded as if in time, Debbie would get exactly what she wanted!

Now for the second part of the reading. Remember, Debbie also asked, "And where?" The sixth and tenth positions of any Celtic Spread give us a sense of timing and possible direction:

Card 6 and its cover (card 15): 6 of Pentacles/Ace of Wands.

Card 10 and its cover (card 11): The Hierophant/Knight of Pentacles.

Major Arcana cards don't give physical directions, but Minor Arcana can. What directions? Here's the suits and the directions they represent:

Suit	Direction
Wands	South
Cups	West
Swords	North
Pentacles	East

From this, we can predict where Debbie's job would be. Starting from her original place of work, the direction was east or southeast. Since Pentacles = east and Wands = south, two Pentacles and one Wand = south, southeast.

Debbie had said she wanted to move closer to her parents, (exactly east-southeast of her present home and workplace), or to another location, which would have ended up about forty miles southeast of her present workplace!

As we go to press, Debbie is moving into her new home and all her job interviews have been in that area as well. Where? Exactly 10 miles southeast of where she started!

Your Tarot Journal Worksheet: Do a Reading

Now that you've seen a Celtic Cover Spread in action, it's time to try one of your own. Shuffle the cards as many times as you like, and then lay them out as shown here.

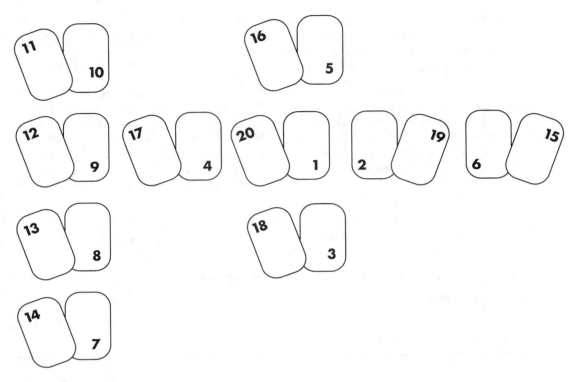

Your Celtic Cover Spread.

Write each card in its space on the diagram above. Then record your interpretation for each card in the spaces that follow.

Card 1: _____/Card 20: _____

Card 2: _____/Card 19: _____

Card 3: _____/Card 18: _____

Card 4: _____/Card 17: _____

Card 5: _____/Card 16: _____

Card 6: _____/Card 15: _____

Card 7: _____/Card 14: _____

Card 8: _____/Card 13: _____

Card 9: _____/Card 12: _____

Card 10:_____/Card 11: _____

Helping to Find Your Way

Now that you've done your spread, the key to reading it is to synthesize the messages of the two cards. Reading out of the book is always good, but you should use your own intuition as well. Write down what you feel the two cards mean together and then take a wait-and-see approach.

The more time that passes, the more you'll be amazed at the reading's accuracy. Return to it every month or so to check on the results. Not only is it fun to go back over a reading that was done four or six months ago and see how things have transpired, it's also how a good reader learns.

So do a reading, get it down on paper or record it, and then go back over it once a month. Over time, things that were foggy when you were doing the reading will become clear. And the more you go back, the more you'll relate to the cards you shuffled several months ago.

The Least You Need to Know

➤ You can look ahead to your next year using a Horoscope Spread.

➤ The connection between the past, present, and future of a question can be explored with a Past/Present/Future Spread.

➤ You can double your info by covering your Celtic Cross with ten more cards.

➤ Knowing in advance what might happen can help you prepare yourself for what's to come.

Chapter 20

Making a Decision or Finding a Solution

In This Chapter

➤ A spread to help you make a decision

➤ A spread to help your dreams come true

➤ A spread to find your karmic lessons

➤ Getting to the answers you want

It's natural to want to have some control over your future, and the three spreads in this chapter help you do just that. The first spread is called the Decision Spread, and gives you a tool for looking at your options regarding a question. The second, the Gypsy Wish Spread, is the one to use if you really want to know if you're going to win the lottery or get a date with that cutie in the next cubicle.

The last spread is a bit different—its four cards show you your karmic lessons, which can in turn help you understand why you're going through what you're going through at the moment.

What Should You Do? The Decision Spread

The Decision Spread can help you make a decision by showing both past information and present conditions about the subject, as well as the future direction(s) you can make wise choices from.

To begin your Decision Spread, lay out three cards in a row. Then, go back over the original three cards with three more cards, and then place one more layer over the first two sets of three cards, as shown below.

The Decision Spread.

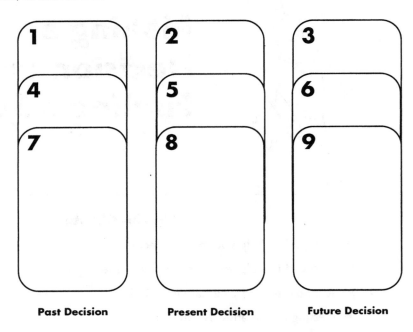

Past Decision   Present Decision   Future Decision

Fools Rush In

It's important to remember that the reader wants to give as much information as possible to the Querent. But it's the *Querent* who makes the ultimate decision on any question. It's the reader's duty and responsibility to help empower and support the Querent to his or her highest good—and let the Querent do the rest.

A Sample Spread

For our sample spread, "Nancy" asked a question that she's probably not the only one wondering about these days: "Should I become a single parent at either 39 or 40 years old?"

Here are Nancy's cards after the deck was shuffled and divided into three stacks:

*Nancy's Decision Spread:
"Should I become a single
parent at either 39 or 40
years old?"*

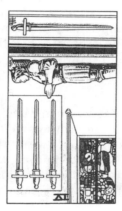

Past Decision   *Present Decision*   *Future Decision*

What the Cards Mean

Here's our interpretation of Nancy's question.

The Past: King of Swords, 5 of Swords, the Magician

These first three cards are a man of authority (King of Swords), possibly a doctor or advisor about pregnancy; the 5 of Swords, which represents a loss to do with children or a health problem that might have prevented a child from being born in the past; and lastly, a good card, the Magician, which says that there might have been help given to Nancy in the past from medicine or hope through a past relationship.

The Present: Temperance, Four of Swords R, the Tower

The second three cards in Nancy's spread are Temperance, which indicates Nancy has had to either have patience or has been waiting for the right moment to have children in her life. As this is the present, it looks as if she wants a child but still either has to, or should, wait. This is because what follows Temperance is the 4 of Swords R, which indicates renewed activity toward her goal. The last card here is the Tower, a surprise condition that will arise soon to allow Nancy to know exactly when and how things will come about.

Our advice is to be patient, especially at this time in her life. Something new or unusual will be coming into her life to tell her how, what, when, and with whom this could happen. The Tower in its upright position always indicates this. (As a great teacher of Arlene's put it, "If you think you know what the surprise is, you'll be wrong. The Tower is always the element of surprise. Only God knows exactly how it will come down.") It's the absolutely unexpected. This is a card that's telling Nancy the unexpected will come along before she'll have to make a decision. What will it be? Stay tuned...

The Future: 10 of Swords, 6 of Pentacles, King of Cups

The third set of three cards can be interpreted as a man of kindly disposition (King of Cups) who will share his knowledge or be helpful to the seeker (Nancy) regarding her question. This could be a new doctor who advises her or a new relationship in her life. Generosity and sharing of resources are indicated by the 6 of Pentacles, and the 10 of Swords means the end of the old cycle of wondering.

It seems this decision will be one of free will, because there are only three Major Arcana out of the nine cards. Still, it will be wise to wait for the Tower card to show itself first. Because the Tower is in the present, Nancy will know quite soon whether this will happen when she's 39 or 40. The best advice we can give is to wait until the end of this year to make a final decision. Too many things are developing around Nancy, either through science, a new relationship, or perhaps an adoption.

We do know that the King of Cups has light brown hair and light eyes. Possibly, he's a water sign type: emotional, sensitive, connected to the emotion of the question. Patience is a virtue and will be helpful to Nancy in making her decision.

When you read a Decision Spread, always bear in mind that the Querent wants to make a decision. Make her aware of the choices the cards show and try to predict timing that seems appropriate for the question. But remember: The decision is still up to the Querent!

Your Tarot Journal Worksheet: Do a Reading

It's your turn to try a Decision Spread. First shuffle the cards. When you're ready, divide the deck into three stacks and select one stack. Then deal out nine cards in the configuration shown here. Use the space under each card to write down what it is and its interpretation. Happy deciding!

Your Decision Spread

Card 1	Card 2	Card 3
_____	_____	_____
_____	_____	_____
Card 4	Card 5	Card 6
_____	_____	_____
_____	_____	_____
Card 7	Card 8	Card 9
_____	_____	_____
_____	_____	_____
Past decision	**Present decision**	**Future decision**

When You Wish Upon a Card: The Gypsy Wish Spread

This spread is a fun one. It used to be used for predicting the outcome of a personal wish, and the Gypsy's fortune-telling ability was strongly evident when it was read. The type of question that works best with this spread is of a mundane variety—one with a wish or desire attached to it. Some possible questions for this spread:

➤ "Will I win the lottery?"

➤ "I wish to make good money before I'm 35; will I?"

➤ "Will I get a new boyfriend soon—real soon?"

➤ "I wish I could go to Europe this summer. Will I get to go?"

The key to this reading is called the 9 of Cups, also known as the wish card. This spread is simple: If the 9 of Cups comes up in the reading, the wish will be granted!

To do a Gypsy Wish Spread, the Querent should first select a card to represent herself. This card goes at the "W" on the following diagram. Next have the seeker shuffle the deck while making a wish.

Then, instead of dividing the deck, have the seeker fan the cards on the table so that all of the remaining 77 cards have their backs facing you—you don't want the face sides to show! From the fanned-out deck, pick one card at a time, until there are 15 cards set aside.

These are the cards you'll use for the spread. These cards should then be shuffled by the Querent until she feels they're ready to be placed in the following spread.

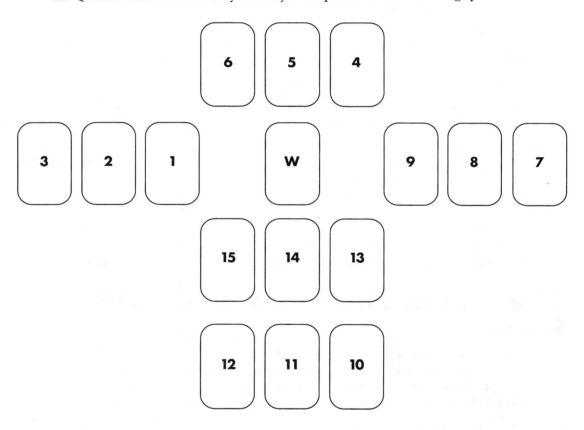

The Gypsy Wish Spread.

A Sample Gypsy Wish Spread

"Dave" had recently put earnest money down on a house. He wanted to know if he'd be able to buy the house, now that he'd made that first big step.

Dave's Gypsy Wish Spread:
"I wish to be able to buy the house I've put earnest money down on. Will I?"

What the Cards Mean

Card 1: Knight of Cups

Card 2: 2 of Swords

Card 3: Page of Swords

The first three cards concern the conditions around the wish. The offer was made (the Knight of Cups is here because Dave was already emotionally attached to the house), but hesitation or a slowdown was indicated by the 2 of Swords.

Dave said that when the mortgage company first began reviewing his file, they noticed a few glitches with his credit and bank statements. That would be the negative message from the Page of Swords.

Card 4: The Moon

Card 5: Death

Card 6: The Lovers

The next three cards represent the Querent's wish or the goal of the wish. The Moon here indicated that a change was going on in Dave's life—including a possible change of residence! Death, in the fifth position, is also a card about change, but change was what Dave wanted—he wanted to move out of his parents' house and into his own. The sixth card, the Lovers, was a good omen, indicating the right choice had been made about the house.

Card 7: The Chariot

Card 8: 9 of Wands

Card 9: The Hanged Man

These three cards represent opposition to the wish, but if they're all positive, then there is no opposition. Here we find the Chariot, the 9 of Wands, and the Hanged Man—all upright. These cards indicate Dave could fight this one through and get his wish—even if it meant he'd have to make a sacrifice.

Dave needed to be strong, stable, and have perseverance. He said he was really focused on this wish, and Arlene could really feel that he was: Dave was focused like the picture on the 9 of Wands, and so, well prepared to deal with any opposing conditions.

Card 10: 9 of Cups

Card 11: Ace of Cups

Card 12: The Emperor

The 9 of Cups! Yes! The Ace of Cups! Yes again! And the Emperor! Triple play! Here, with the three cards that show what Dave would realize, it clearly looked like he would get his wish, with the Emperor, or the decision-makers, approving his loan and the home! And any time the 9 of Cups shows up in a Gypsy Wish Spread, your wish will come true.

Card 13: The World

Card 14: Ace of Wands

Card 15: 9 of Pentacles

These last three cards show what will come into your life, and for Dave, the pretty amazing conclusion to this reading was that Dave himself was clearly the 9 of Pentacles—self-reliant, doing this on his own, focused on his intended wish. The outcome cards gave his wish a resounding "yes!" There might be a few more slow-downs, but it looked like Dave's wish was going to come true just as he wanted.

This reading was done June 10, 1998. The outcome and final "yes" happened on June 15, 1998! That was a quick turnaround—but Dave wasn't really surprised after his terrific Gypsy Wish Spread.

In the Cards

The key card in any Gypsy Wish Spread is the 9 of Cups. If it appears upright, you'll get your wish. If it appears reversed, the wish that you're asking about won't occur in the manner you're thinking or want. It may delay it, but it's possible you're not really sure you want what you're asking for in the first place. If it doesn't come up in the spread at all, you can look at any other favorable cards to see if will come about. You don't need the 9 of Cups to get an ultimate yes; other positive cards can do the same.

Your Tarot Journal Worksheet: Do a Reading

Do you have a wish you'd like to see granted? Find out if it's possible by doing a Gypsy Wish Spread of your own. Be sure to pick out a card to represent you, the Querent, before you begin.

Shuffle the deck and concentrate on your wish until you're ready to fan out the cards, face down. Then pick out fifteen cards, leaving them face down as well. Put the rest of the deck aside and shuffle the fifteen cards you've selected until you feel you're ready to place them in the Gypsy Wish Spread.

Is the 9 of Cups there? Lucky you! If not, you still can find out how your wish will turn out by noting what cards you have and writing their interpretations in the spaces that follow.

Spinning the Wheel of Fortune

Remember, pick the fifteen cards by fanning the whole deck face down and then picking the cards one at time. Keep them face down, put aside the rest of the deck, and then shuffle the fifteen you have until you're ready to put them down in their positions.

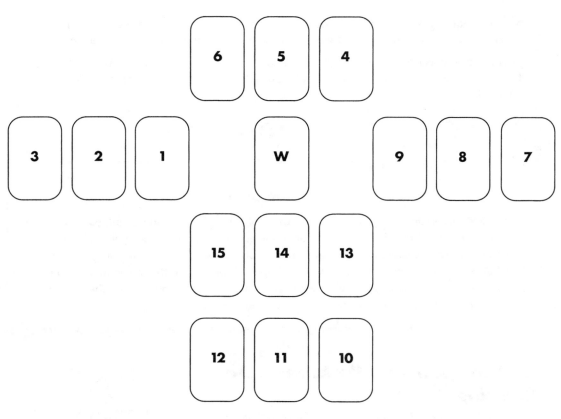

Your Gypsy Wish Spread.

What surrounds you

Card 1: _____

Card 2: _____

Card 3: _____

Your wish

Card 4: _____

Card 5: _____

Card 6: _____

What opposes you

Card 7: _____

Card 8: _____

Card 9: _____

What you will realize

Card 10: _____

Card 11: _____

Card 12: _____

What will come into your life

Card 13: _____

Card 14: _____

Card 15: _____

Your Lesson's in the Cards: The Karmic Spread

The Karmic Spread is a deceptively simple four-card spread. It can help you understand why you seem to go through the same sorts of situations again and again. Oftentimes, these are karmic lessons (see Chapter 7), which you're fated to practice over and over until you get them right.

A Karmic Spread always answers the same question: "What are the karmic lessons I'm learning now?"

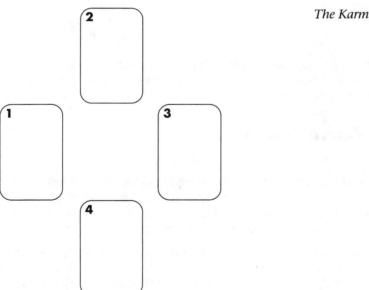

The Karmic Spread.

A Sample Karmic Spread

It seemed to Lisa that she'd been learning the same lessons waaaay too long, so she asked to be the subject of this reading. Here are the cards she came up with:

Lisa's Karmic Spread:
"What are the karmic lessons I'm learning now?"

Lisa's reading can help her decide which way she needs to go in her present conditions. Her cards indicate what she's learning presently and what's important *now* that she should pay attention to.

What the Cards Mean

Lisa's Four Cards

Card 1: The Devil. Lisa might be learning to deal with pressures of some kind and can become obsessed about them. Sometimes she may feel as if she's out of (or not in) control, or working in a direction that she gets too wrapped up in. This obsessive behavior can feel like an emotional roller coaster.

Lisa's learning to deal with overindulging in worry and stress. She needs to learn to relax! But when she does calm down, up pops that Devil card again, indicating she has to struggle with those feelings of pressure and the accompanying over-intense energy. This could also represent worry over the material world or too much concern over the physical conditions around her. Does she feel she's over-obligated herself?

Card 2: 3 of Cups R. This card indicates a need to concentrate Lisa's efforts in constructive areas now. She shouldn't try to overdo a good time and should beware of overreacting to things outside her control. Lisa needs to remember that she's basically balanced, but she just needs to slow down on the emotional issues she faces. If she centers herself more often, peace will once again prevail.

Sometimes, this card comes up when you thought you were going to have fun but it turned out instead to be a lot of work, or more work than expected! Maybe Lisa's supposed to take charge of things now but feels a little too overwhelmed to take on more. She needs to learn to say, "No. I can only do this now, and that later." One thing at a time!

Card 3: Page of Swords R. This card indicates a lesson about listening to what's coming. Something new or unexpected is coming Lisa's way, bringing with it a new cycle or direction that will turn out to be beneficial. Lisa shouldn't react to the first thing she hears from people—especially if it's trouble.

The Page of Swords R means there will be a reversal of a negative message and that things will start to lighten up. Lisa needs to have faith that things that feel difficult now will ease up in the next three to six months. (Hooray!)

The other interpretation of the Page of Swords R is that a child or young person will be part of her responsibility in the near future, or that she will have to focus her work and lessons on a young person (child or sibling).

Card 4: 6 of Swords. This card has several meanings, all of which could apply to Lisa's present life lessons. These include a journey to a high state of consciousness. Or she'll be getting out of a difficult cycle and entering a more pleasant one, with the rocky waters of life left behind as she heads for calmer and more peaceful waters.

There's a good indication that Lisa will have completed a karmic debt or lesson in the near future and can then get on with other goals she has. She might have felt stifled or frustrated recently, but this shall pass as well. The ebbs and flows of life will continue, and she'll get into a better state of mind and have a feeling of accomplishment.

The possibility of travel over water is strong as well, with a journey for a vacation or to see a loved one or family member (Dear reader: As we write this, Lisa's husband's in Guam...).

In the Cards

The four-card Karmic Spread shows what you need to work on presently—the "now"—and so can help you make decisions about how to respond to present conditions (both good and bad). This spread can help you remember that the cycle you're in has a beginning as well as an end.

Lisa's reading starts out showing difficulties that she has to deal with now, but the two cards that have numbers on them (the 3 of Cups and the 6 of Swords) indicate the timing of the cards. In this case, in three to six months Lisa will have learned a lot. She'll be able to cope far better with the conditions that exist around her and make decisions clearly. This reading is good for personal introspection, soul-searching, and an awareness that leads to self-empowerment.

Your Tarot Journal Worksheet: Do a Reading

One of the great things about a four-card Karmic reading is that it helps you acknowledge feelings, ideas, or concerns that you have and may never have shared with anyone up until now. The spread is not only good for showing you how you're feeling, it's also useful for helping you decide if you should act on those feelings or just accept the lessons as they come. The answer to that question is entirely up to you, the seeker.

So now, are you ready to find your karmic lessons? (Lisa highly recommends it!)

Your Karmic Spread.

Card 1:_____

Card 2:_____

Card 3:_____

Card 4:_____

Shuffle the deck until you feel you're ready to deal out the four cards into the Karmic Spread shown here. After you have, you're ready to interpret the cards and find what karmic lessons you're learning now.

The Karmic Spread.

Are You Satisfied with the Cards' Message?

When you're not satisfied with what the cards tell you, you always have the option of reshuffling the deck and asking again for your lessons to come through. Ask: "Show me what is essential to know right now in my life."

This question can help you focus as you reshuffle. When you're ready, divide the deck again, concentrate again on the question, then pick the four cards any way you want and place them in the diagram of the Karmic Spread. Interestingly, though, when you do this, the cards' message will be quite close to the original one. You may not always be satisfied with what the cards tell you, but the cards don't lie. Then again, you know that by now!

The Least You Need to Know

➤ Use a Decision Spread when you need to know your options.

➤ A Gypsy Wish Spread can let you know if your dreams will come true.

➤ A Karmic Spread can help you find out what karmic lessons you're learning now.

➤ You can always reshuffle the cards if you don't like the way they came up the first time.

Chapter 21

The Bigger Picture: Tarot, Humankind, and the Future of the World

In This Chapter

➤ A spread to find your life's purpose and challenge

➤ Our Tarot reading for the year 2000

➤ Two VIP readings!

➤ The world is at your fingertips

Every life has a purpose, and yours is no exception. Finding your life's purpose and challenge is what's behind the *Mission Spread*—a 21-card spread that enables you to look at your past, present, and future life mission and purpose. But why stop there? We thought you'd like to see a reading Arlene's students did for Bill Clinton—in 1992! See for yourself how this reading has panned out.

Lastly, our curious minds wanted to know what Oprah would ask, if she'd only return our calls—so we asked a question for her. Our last reading is for Oprah, a woman who to our minds embodies precisely what the World card represents.

What's Your Life's Purpose and Challenge? The Mission Spread

The Mission Spread begins with three rows of seven cards. The first row of seven represents what you've accomplished so far as a part of your mission; the second row, what you're presently doing about your mission; and the third row what you'll accomplish and contribute to this world, what mark you might make on the world, or how you'll touch the world and how it will touch you.

The Mission Spread.

Spinning the Wheel of Fortune

When you read a Mission Spread, do it as if you were telling a story. The story will include what you've done regarding your mission in life, what you're working on now (the present), and then the outcome of what you are and how the world sees your mission and accomplishment or how you accomplish your mission. Or, as Arlene's students would say, how you left your mark in the world!

A Sample Mission Spread

We know you're curious about Arlene, our Tarot expert bar none, so we thought we'd use a Mission Spread she had done at the beginning of 1997. After her divorce was finalized in May 1996, it seemed that other problems cropped up and many friends around her had left the scene, too. These were all big changes, so Arlene was a little confused (yes, Tarot readers are human, too!) because she thought she would stay in that marriage forever.

Basically, she wasn't all that disappointed with life—but she *was* confused. Her divorce threw her for a loop, and Arlene was both shocked and able to handle the situation at the same time. She still had (and has!) a good bunch of friends, and family members helped, too. Arlene picked a reader she trusted to do this reading. Here are the cards that came up:

Arlene's Mission Spread, February 1997: "What is my mission in life NOW?"

Arlene's Past Mission and Purpose

The first seven cards looked at Arlene's past mission and purpose. The reader was a good teacher of Arlene's. This is important to Arlene because she knew she couldn't read her own Mission Spread at that time of great emotional change.

The reading showed that the recent divorce was the termination of a good relationship at heart (10 of Swords, the Empress). Arlene had been working on developing the marriage and trying to get it to grow (Ace of Wands). She'd learned to be strong and determined, and to have compassion for situations out of her control (Strength).

Arlene was trying to hold onto a young man she felt was her life's work and purpose (Knight of Swords). They did business things together, which developed well. They were able to hold on to a good income and, either through the marriage or in her past, Arlene had developed a good business ability and acumen.

Arlene told the reader this was very true. Just before she got married, and continuing when she was married, she really learned about working with money, including saving toward a home and property. Arlene and her reader identified the Knight of Swords as an air sign young man (her ex-husband) and they interpreted the 4 of Pentacles as the lesson of learning to hold on to money—to save it and handle it better than before (which Arlene said was very true).

The last card of the past, the 10 of Wands, was carrying a heavy burden. "Difficulties are many," the reader said. This was also true. The end of that time wasn't pleasant, and the money and business ideas that Arlene had didn't go in the directions she'd thought they would. In the end, she had to let go and drop all the plans she'd had with her ex-husband.

Being in that situation was a lesson that Arlene had needed to learn. It was part of her mission in life to learn to work through such things. You can't stop someone from going in any direction they choose, though, so when her ex-husband decided he wanted out, she had to let go of their future plans and focus on her present challenges instead. Her goals had to be put on hold, the reader told her.

Arlene's Present Mission and Purpose

The second row of seven cards showed what Arlene was dealing with in the present—her present mission in her life.

Looking at this second row of cards, the reader told Arlene that she was now able to create her life and renew what she'd wanted to do (the Magician and the 8 of Cups R). Arlene now felt more confident about her ability and talents (and Arlene said that yes, she'd just come around to that feeling in the last ten months).

The Moon and the 2 of Cups suggested that Arlene would be working on re-evaluating all relationships, both personal and business, and that her emotional nature would change in a way that would surprise even her. Arlene didn't know how to take that. She knew she was still in pain about the end of her marriage. Still, she figured she'd at least listen to the reader.

While that's what Arlene thought then, now she knows the reader was absolutely right! She's grown out of any expectations she had about relationships and instead now takes them with an entirely new approach and a more relaxed attitude.

The Queen of Cups could be Arlene, the reader went on, changing from dealing with business to dealing with emotions (true). Then she looked at the Page of Pentacles and asked if Arlene had a child or children. "My great friend, my cat," Arlene answered. The reader said the cat was great, but she thought the Queen of Cups (guess who?!) would start to receive messages from her clients or work environment that would spur her on to do more work and be more productive.

In other words, she said, Arlene would develop a good sense of security and stability on her own, and would no longer worry so much about money (boy, did she pick up on Arlene's worry!). The Knight of Pentacles upright is a good omen for new business or improvement in business and career ventures, the reader explained.

It was hard to believe after her difficulties that this is what would happen, but Arlene knows now that after you get all the trauma and shock out of your system and psyche, you *can* do better! She even thought maybe it's best to have relationships that are enhancing and freeing instead of ones that fit traditional expectations. This was quite a change!

Arlene's Future Mission and Purpose

The third row of cards showed what Arlene would realize as her purpose or mission in the future. The reader studied the cards and then told this story of Arlene's future:

"You are and will continue to become and grow into a self-sufficient, self-reliant woman (9 of Pentacles)," the reader told Arlene. "Oh boy!" said Arlene. "You mean I can go live on my own!?" "Yes," said the reader, "with other people of like minds or like beliefs."

The reader continued: "Lots of Wands here indicate that your energy and life's goals will come to pass and that your enthusiasm and personal drive and ambition will be what make things happen for you. So, keep your energy up and don't let others drag you down. Allow people to be who they are, but if they try to control or need you too much, slow down and back up. There's prosperity and good fortune coming through your career, thanks to helpful advisors (two Kings), future travel is destined (6 of Wands), and the 5 of Wands R as the final card assures that harmony will once again be yours. You'll never again want to attract negative situations."

"Lastly," the reader said, "Anyone or anything that distracts you from the course you're on will not affect you or move you away from what's intended. Your work and life will come together as one, and you'll find happiness with others who believe the same way."

Way to go, Arlene!

Your Tarot Journal Worksheet: Do a Reading

Do you want to know your life's mission and purpose? Of course you do! Begin by shuffling the deck and asking the question, "What is my life's mission and purpose NOW?"

When you're ready, deal the cards into the spread shown here.

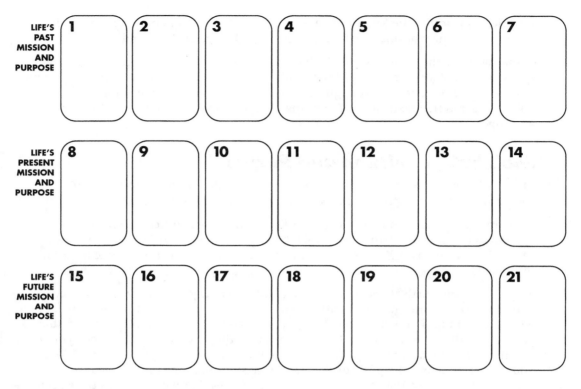

Your Mission Spread.

Write your interpretations of the cards in the spread form above, or on another page, if you'd like. Take your time—this is *your* story!

Our Reading for the Year 2000

Everybody's talking about the year 2000. Will the world come to a grinding halt as computers mistakenly turn their clocks back to 1900? Or will it be just another New Year's Eve, with the ball dropping down on Times Square at midnight?

For our reading for the year 2000, we were more interested in what we as a society need to do to prepare. So, without further ado, here it is.

The Spread...

Arlene began by shuffling the deck while meditating on the question: "What do we as a society need to do to prepare for the year 2000?" Here are the cards she came up with:

The Year 2000 Spread:
*"What do we as a society
need to do to prepare for
the year 2000?"*

Card 1   6 of Swords
Card 2   The Hierophant
Card 3   Justice
Card 4   10 of Cups
Card 5   5 of Wands
Card 6   5 of Pentacles
Card 7   Death
Cover of
card 7   Wheel of Fortune

You'll notice that when Arlene finished dealing the first seven cards, she decided the seventh, Death, needed enhancement, so she added a cover card, which came up as the Wheel of Fortune. Clearly, fate's an important aspect of this question!

Try Your Hand at Interpreting the Cards!

Before you look ahead to our thoughts on this reading, we'd like you to use this reading to practice your own ever-improving card-reading skills. First, you should be aware that when you look at a reading like this all the cards have equal weight.

But don't look ahead now! Instead, use this spread to write your own interpretations of the cards. After you've done this, see if you have the same take on the cards that we do. We'll bet you'll be surprised at how much you know already!

Card 1: _____

Card 2: _____

Card 3: _____

Card 4: _____

Card 5: _____

Card 6: _____

Card 7: _____

Cover of Card 7: _____

The Year 2000 Interpreted

It looks to us as if difficult times are ahead, but there's also a sense of getting on to better things for the highest good of all of us (6 of Swords). World regeneration and transformation or political revolution (the Hierophant R) may be exactly what we might need or want by the year 2000!

The cards reflect both what we need to prepare for and what we (the people of the world) are actually creating now and in the recent past that will lead up to this. With this in mind, we see some economic difficulties (5 of Pentacles), and some people who may deal with impoverishment of the financial or spiritual self (5 of Wands).

The 10 of Cups suggests we need to look to family or community to band together through adversity. Total change will be necessary, and it will not necessarily be bad (Death). Most important perhaps is that Justice will prevail so that no matter what we go through we're assured a fair outcome in the end.

Our VIP Readings

We decided to give you not one, but two, VIP readings. That's because when Arlene went back and looked at the reading her students had done for Bill Clinton in October 1992, she was amazed by what she saw. You'll have to see for yourself if you agree.

Then, our book producer tried and tried everything she could think of (Actually, when we asked her, she said, "Ha!") to get Oprah to ask the cards a question, but, well, Oprah's pretty busy. We decided to ask the question we know Oprah would ask if she had the time. It's a question you'll want to know the answer to also!

A Look into Bill Clinton's Future—from October 1992

President Clinton's reading was done in October 1992 as a group reading with the students studying the Tarot at the University of Washington Experimental College. One person shuffled the deck as all present concentrated on this question: "Will Bill Clinton become our next President, and if so, how will he do?"

Remember, in the election of 1992, three candidates were running for the office: then-President Bush, Ross Perot, and Bill Clinton.

The Celtic Cross, October 1992:
"Will Bill Clinton become our next President, and if so, how will he do?"

> ### In the Cards
>
> It's easy to look at a reading with hindsight, so we present our reading for Bill Clinton in two sections: one, the initial interpretation of the reading; and two, how the cards go with what we know now. See what the two mean to you. We think they serve as a lesson not to rush into absolute interpretation!

In the Cards for Bill Clinton?

Everyone agreed that the Tower was a surprise about who would become President. Most of the students thought President Bush would stay in office when this reading was done, so they saw the 2 of Cups in opposition to represent a positive condition that would re-elect the incumbent President (Bush).

At the foundation of the question was the 3 of Wands. This represented that whoever became president would focus on business, enterprise, the economy, and working together with the public.

The Magician in the past seemed to be saying that the public would pick someone creative and powerful, with fresh ideas and lots of charisma. The King of Wands upright in the fifth position, which represents what may or may not happen, was a light-haired man of power, but as all three candidates had light hair and light eyes, the students disagreed about which candidate this represented! The King of Wands has the potential to be a good leader and has been a good father already. So the question still remained, "Who will it be?" Naturally, the students didn't want to venture a guess based on the cards so far!

Strength R showed up in the sixth position, what will happen. In its reversed position, Strength is preoccupied with power, or a loss of strength, stamina, and perseverance. Whoever became president would have to deal with loss of power or control of his position, this card seemed to be saying. Plus, since this is a fate card, difficult karmic conditions lay ahead for whomever would become president. Maybe, like the students said, the president really wouldn't have control over the country and would only be able to recommend what he wanted.

In the seventh position, fears or attitude, was the Queen of Cups. Who was this? Barbara Bush? Hillary Clinton? Mrs. Perot? All three women would of course have fears about the presidency, and all also have the power to overcome fear. Each in her own way is clearly a strong supporter of her husband and might actually be the powerful person behind the man, if we looked more closely. This Queen was upright, so whoever this lady was, she'd be able to handle her job very well as first lady, no matter what the adversity, and she'd continue to support her husband, too.

In the eighth position of outside influence was the 5 of Swords. Whoever became president would face a lot of adversity, legal problems, a scandal, or losses that require legal advice…

The ninth card, what the new president would go through to get to the outcome, was the 9 of Wands. Whoever won would be strong, well prepared to handle any adversity and/or legal problems, and would remain strong throughout whatever difficulty came his way.

The final outcome was the Wheel of Fortune R. The Wheel upright would have been as great and fortunate as any presidency could be, said the students. But, Arlene reminded the class, the card's reversed. What's up with this Wheel upside down? Whoever becomes president will have his work cut out for him in many ways he doesn't even know about yet.

First, the Wheel of Fortune R represents a presidency without control. It's a fated position, true, but this president wouldn't be able to get things accomplished as easily as he might have thought or hoped. Much opposition and blockage showed themselves surrounding this next President, and the next four years wouldn't be easy, or as fulfilling as he thought. The Wheel R indicates that luck wouldn't be with him either.

After this reading, the people who wanted President Bush to win said maybe he'd better not, the ones who wanted Bill Clinton to win were hoping the cards were wrong about all the adversity, and the ones who wanted Perot to win said he could handle anything!

The majority of the class felt sorry for whomever would be elected, though. All knew the job wasn't easy, but this reading showed great obstacles to overcome and almost overwhelming burdens before the next president could accomplish any of the things he'd like to. All in all, it didn't look like a good four years ahead for the next president .

Fools Rush In

Part of the reason this reading didn't answer the question asked was because the answer was fated. There are four Major Arcana here grounding the reading: card 1, the Tower; card 4, the Magician; card 6, Strength; and card 10, the Wheel of Fortune R. If this were a table, it would have four sturdy legs, but in a Tarot reading, it's not so fortunate.

Hindsight Is 20/20

So what do we make of this reading now? Well, Bill Clinton's been full of surprises (the Tower), with part of his problem being an attraction to the opposite sex (2 of Cups) that began long before he took office. His programs and ideas have actually been well received (3 of Wands), but his Magician's skill hasn't kept him out of hot water this time around.

Strength R clearly heralded the many problems Clinton would be facing, even though his strong-willed wife (Queen of Cups) remains steadfastly by his side. Or is that another woman (or women) there in the 7th position?

Ultimately, both Clintons seem surrounded by others' negative energy (5 of Swords), and even though they're ready to stand up for themselves, the Wheel of Fortune is upside down, already fated to turn their luck against them.

But what do you think?

We Imagine What Oprah Would Ask Us...

There's something about Oprah that makes each of us feel as if we know her personally, like a good friend. And Oprah *is* a good friend, not just on a personal level but on a universal one. As all her various efforts have made clear, Oprah really cares about the general public knowing more in order to better understand and improve society. With that in mind, we imagine that Oprah would ask a question like this of the Tarot: "What does the Tarot have to tell me about the role of women in the United States in the 21st century?" We don't know whether Oprah's used the Tarot in her own life, or how she feels about Tarot, but we *do* know that Oprah is passionately interested in helping people improve their lives. We'll ask the question on her, and our own, behalf.

As we began in this book, so shall we end—with a Celtic Cross, the basic ten-card spread that's been tried and true over the centuries. After all, as the Tarot illustrates, every journey eventually returns to its beginning.

"What does the Tarot have to tell us about the role of women in the United States in the 21st century?"

What the Cards Tell Us!

Arlene shuffled the cards while contemplating Oprah and thinking about our question. We think you'll find that what the cards have to tell Oprah applies to all of us—which, because they're Oprah's cards, should come as no surprise.

Card 1: The Star. This card represents the conditions surrounding women in the 21st century. The Star here indicates that women will bring hope, inspiration, and guidance toward optimism in the years to come.

Card 2: The Emperor. The second card is the opposition or conditions that could prove to be difficult for women in the next century. The Emperor here clearly represents male authority. It may indicate that power through men could be a struggle or a point of contention, but as it's upright, we think it represents that women and men will work together far better in the 21st century as they learn to understand and appreciate each other's differences.

Card 3: 4 of Swords R. Here we find the foundation—why we asked the question to begin with, and the 4 of Swords R indicates renewed activity as women become more involved in society and politics, and government and labor issues. Women will connect to society in a more intellectual, or logical, way, this card may be saying. By working in labor, politics, communications, and literature, women will make more real progress than in the past.

Card 4: The Moon R. Here we find the past, in this case, the years preceding the 21st century. This is where women collectively have been—or what past experiences women have collectively learned up to this point in time. The Moon R here shows that women have already learned about using their intuition, feelings, sensitivities, and their nurturing energy for society's good. They've enjoyed taking care of people, attuning themselves to family, personal issues, and emotions. But, as we know, that's their past role!

Card 5: 3 of Pentacles. The fifth card represents a condition that might occur or might be avoided, and the 3 of Pentacles here is a good card. We think this card could inspire women to take the opportunity it suggests: The 3 of Pentacles upright is recognition of women's skills and abilities, an understanding that everyone has gifts, abilities, and talents. The role of women in the 21st century could well be one of equal partnership with men, for being widely appreciated for having skills other than those of homemaking. Look at this card: On it you can see a man *and* a woman looking approvingly at a young artist's recent work. Men and women may very well work better together in the future than in the past!

Card 6: Ace of Pentacles. This card represents what will happen or conditions that will manifest themselves. The Ace of Pentacles is all about new beginnings connected to money, resources, or investments. This indicates new work for women on the horizon, perhaps more job opportunities—or new types of employment for which women weren't usually considered in the past. Clearly, the picture on this card illustrates new work to do, new soil to till, and new seeds to plant.

Card 7: 4 of Pentacles. In the seventh position we find fears or negative thoughts about the role of women in the future, and the 4 of Pentacles upright represents the fear that women might remain where they've been in the past, keeping the status quo. Holding on to old ideas, concepts, or values associated with roles for women would certainly inhibit forward movement.

Card 8: 10 of Wands. The card in this position shows how others may see women in the 21st century. The 10 of Wands indicates that women will still have to struggle and carry extra burdens or responsibilities in the future, or that women's roles of handling added responsibility of family or community may still be a big issue in our society. This could indicate that things may not change that dramatically for women.

Card 9: 2 of Pentacles R. The ninth card represents what women will have to process before getting to the outcome. The 2 of Pentacles R represents a need to handle many situations at once, juggling so many balls that personal plans can be interrupted. It looks like women will have their work cut out for them: not only bringing home the bread but baking it, too. Sound familiar?

Card 10: The Lovers! Here's the final outcome as we look ahead to women's roles in the century to come, what all our present work is leading to. The Lovers card here shows women becoming conduits for all relationships, with women's roles possibly being both unconditional love and helping others choose the direction of their lives.

This card could represent that women will become the connection between the material and spiritual worlds. Of course, women have always had this role, but because this card is upright, in the 21st century they'll be strongly supported in their efforts to help others who need material and spiritual help.

As you look at the Lovers card, you can see that the woman looks up directly to the angel while the man looks toward the woman to make that connection with above. We could say that the message of the card is that the male self—in both men and women—looks toward the female self in each in order to connect to the higher, spiritual self. Women's roles in the 21st century, then, will be one of love, says this card, with the heart and understanding, but also teaching others to connect to their spiritual natures.

In the next century, women will be put in positions that help to open up the spirit of humankind, making it easier for us all to look at what's truly important. Women's roles will be ones of individual spiritual awakening and of enabling society to look at the heart and soul of our collective lives, helping all to discover what really makes us work as human beings.

The World at Your Fingertips

If we could, we'd have a full rhythm section playing here. You know—drums, cymbals, maybe even some fireworks. That's because we really believe that the Tarot can bring the world to your fingertips.

The more you use Tarot cards to explore yourself and the world around you, the more attuned you become to the world's—and your own—rhythms. The Tarot is more than a metaphor for a journey; it's a tool to take on the journey that is your own life.

May all your readings be Stars!

The Least You Need to Know

➤ You can find your life's mission and purpose by doing a Mission Spread.

➤ The year 2000 won't be easy, but in the end, Justice will prevail.

➤ Did the cards tell Bill Clinton's future? You be the judge.

➤ We imagine what Oprah would ask about the role of women in the 21st century.

➤ With the Tarot, the world's at your fingertips.

Part 6
More Ways to Tell the Future

Beyond Tarot, you'll find everything from crystal balls to mah-jongg, and a spiritual tradition reaching back thousands of years. Tarot readers often have psychic ability, and you do too, if you know how to tap into it. Your dreams are connected to Tarot symbolism as well, and Tarot shares basic principles with both astrology and numerology. So join us for a tour along other fascinating paths to self-discovery.

Chapter 22

"Look into My Crystal Ball..."

In This Chapter

➤ Crystal balls, tea leaves, and Ouija boards

➤ Is your future in your hands?

➤ Magic crystals, the *I Ching*, and mah-jongg

➤ So what *do* you believe?

Beyond the imagery of Tarot lies a long history of fortune-telling methods from cultures the world over. Remember when Dorothy saw Aunt Em (and the Wicked Witch) in the crystal ball? Have you ever had a close encounter with a Ouija board? What about those magic crystals, the *I Ching*, and mah-jongg? And is your future really written in (or by) your own hand? It's time to embark on a quick tour of some of the other tried-and-true methods of looking at your future—and to discover secrets about yourself even you may not know.

Taking a Closer Look

Way back in Chapter 1 we talked about synchronicity, the principle of meaningful coincidence, studied in depth by psychoanalysis pioneer Carl Jung. It's our belief (and that means that you can take it or leave it) that all methods of fortune-telling are based on synchronicity.

The meaning of this is that you choose a particular fortune cookie because its message is the right one for you right now. It means that what the tea leaves or the crystal ball tell you is what you need to hear at the moment. It means that the "voice" of the Ouija board is coming from deep inside you. "How?" you ask. "And why?"

Physicists, including the esteemed David Bohm, assert that "the inner reflects the outer" and vice versa. This means that there are no coincidences, and that all matter is connected in ways that we mere humans can't even imagine. Does that mean there's no free will? Of course not. But it does mean that, like the proverbial stone in the pond, everything you do creates a ripple effect that extends far beyond itself.

David Bohm is very much alive, one of many contemporary physicists who are looking to the esoteric sciences as they explore the world's interconnectedness. Bohm's "claim to fame" is his willingness to look at the world from many angles, and he is not alone in this. A recent issue of "Mountain Astrologer" contains articles by numerous physicists exploring these connections more fully.

Whether you choose to believe the messages of the media (and here, unlike on today's news, the medium is *not* the message) or fortune-telling is up to you. But we think when you look into your heart of hearts, you'll find the same messages it's sending.

Crystal Balls: Going Deeper, Deeper...

Crystal balls are one of the media used by *scrying*, which involves using a reflective surface to see images of divination. Some of the surfaces used are mirrors (remember the queen in *Snow White*?), flames, liquids such as water, and crystal balls. Crystal balls are pretty expensive these days, so you might want to try something a little cheaper before you go out and invest in one.

As with the Tarot, the imagery you see in crystal balls is highly subjective. In fact, the imagery recorded during various historic times and places has been found to be quite specific to where and when it is seen. In medieval times, for example, images were largely Church-based, while these days, they're far more down to earth.

As you do before a Tarot reading, you'll want to prepare yourself before you leap into a session with the crystal ball or liquid of your choice. Spend some time unwinding and clearing your mind of the day's clutter. Concentrate your energy on focusing on your reflective surface, and after a little while, you may begin to see a mist forming.

Card Catalog

Scrying is the ancient art of using a reflective surface, such as a crystal ball, mirror, or liquid, to see images of divination.

It's possible a mist is all you'll ever see, but—good news!—even the mist has a meaning. White mists foretell good times ahead, while darker mists can mean things may not be so rosy. Green is about money, while blue is about work. Red can mean anger, yellow's your love life, and orange relates to your health.

If you discern more distinct images as you look into your liquid or crystal ball, look ahead to Chapter 24 where we discuss the stuff of dream imagery. Imagery and symbolism have both universal and highly subjective meanings, but both of these meanings are valid.

Tea Leaves: Welcome to the Tea Party

Compared to looking into crystal balls, reading *tea leaves* is a relatively "new" way of looking into the future, having begun in Europe in the mid-1600s, though the ancient Greeks were doing something similar with wine dregs long before. When you read tea leaves you're reading the pattern left by loose tea (no, you can't read a tea bag!) in the bottom of the cup. Here's how to read your own tea leaves.

Drink your tea until there's just about a half-teaspoonful left. Now, hold the cup by its handle *in your left hand* and swirl it quickly, counterclockwise, three times. Then turn the cup upside down on the saucer and leave it to drain while you concentrate on your question.

After a few minutes, pick the cup up. If there's any moisture left in it, turn it back over, as this may alter the pattern remaining. When the moisture is gone and the cup is settled, the reading begins.

The handle of the cup represents the questioner (in this case, you). So what's closest to the handle is most directly related to you, while what's across from it represents the unexpected, or things more distant from you.

The closer a symbol is to the rim or handle of the cup, the sooner it will happen. If a symbol's on the side, it's about two weeks away; on the bottom, about a month. Symbols to the left of the handle have already occurred, while those on the right connect the present and the future.

At first you may simply see mere bits of tea, but with a little concentration, you can't help but see images in the remaining blobs. It's like watching clouds float by—soon you'll be seeing flying horses and giraffes! We've included a few symbols in the following table, but you can go back to Chapter 4 for more details about the meanings of basic symbols.

Spinning the Wheel of Fortune

If you've come this far with us, you know that every picture means something special to you alone. If you're allergic to flowers or afraid of flying, those images may have very different meanings than the ones we've suggested. Remember, the best interpreter of any fortune-telling imagery is you.

Good Luck in the Leaves

Symbol	Meaning
Star	Good luck!
Ship	Success in business
Flowers	Good friends
Moon	Romance
Airplane	Travel

Ouija Boards: Letters from Another Dimension?

The *Ouija board* is called the "mystifying oracle" by Parker Brothers, Inc., which holds its U.S. patents, and most who've had a session with the board agree with this label. Those who've spent any amount of time with a Ouija board find that each presence has a different "voice" and "personality." Some of these presences can't spell to save themselves, and some move the pointer around the board at speeds we couldn't possibly achieve on our own.

In a previous life (well, okay, it was a previous marriage), Lisa had a way with a Ouija board. She'd put her hand anywhere near the pointer and that sucker would fly all over the place. Her ex-husband had fellow students in his dream class come over to check it out, and she had every one of them in touch with their dead relatives. And this was hands off!

In the Cards

The late American poet James Merrill wrote a series of poems that eventually encompassed three volumes, involving years of Ouija-board sessions with his partner David Jackson. Among the first to "talk" to them through the board was the poet W.H. Auden, and later sessions included the archangels, and even a god-like presence, called GODB (for biology).

The board itself is deceptively simple. It includes the letters of the alphabet, the numbers 1–0, a "Yes," a "No," and the words "Good Bye." The latter signifies that the spirits are signing off, and if you've spent any time with them, there's no mistaking when they've had enough—even if you haven't.

Two or more people can use a Ouija board together. The message pointer is placed on the board, and then the people hold their hands just above the pointer. Don't touch it—the pointer works from your energy, not your touch.

It may take a few minutes, but soon the pointer will begin to move. If you're new to the Ouija board, you may find nonsense messages at first. Someone should be assigned to be the scribe, though, to write down every letter, word, and number the pointer moves to. You'll know what the pointer is pointing to; there's a slight hesitation before it moves on.

If you can read the messages as you go along, you'll soon have a conversation going with whomever's there on "the other side." You're just as likely to encounter intermediaries as you are those you know or knew; it seems the spirit world is full of busybodies just dying to grab someone's pointer and chat (strange they haven't discovered chat rooms on the Internet yet—or have they?).

If you're like the poet James Merrill (see the previous "In the Cards"), you may soon be learning matters of global importance from your encounters with the Ouija board. So sit back, relax—and have fun!

It's All in Your Hands

Not only can you find the story of your life written in the lines of your hands (palmistry), your handwriting can tell your secrets to others, and automatic writing can let you know these secrets yourself. Before we start looking at what the hands and handwriting can tell us, though, let's limber up those fingers: one, two, one, two, and up, two, and down, two...

Will Your Handwriting Give You Away?

It would take a book (at best, an *Idiot's Guide*) to explore all the angles of *graphology*, or handwriting analysis, and here we've got only a page or two. So here's the quickie version:

➤ *Large handwriting* indicates an extrovert.

➤ *Small handwriting* indicates an introvert.

➤ *Narrowly spaced letters* indicate caution.

➤ *Widely spaced letters* indicate throwing caution to the winds.

Remember that lined paper from grade school, when you had to write all your letters between the lines, just so? Somehow we all learned the same way—and then we all developed our personal styles. In graphology, the areas between those lines are called the three zones.

The *middle zone* is where every letter makes some sort of an appearance, but all the vowels, plus "c," "m," "n," "r," "s," "v," "w," and "x," fit into this zone entirely. This zone is the everyday world and how you fit into it. If your middle zone is where the majority of the letter falls, you're a practical person, good at the day-to-day details.

The *lower zone* is where we find the bottoms of the letters "g," "j," "p," "q," and "y," as well as sometimes "f" and "z." This is the zone of your sexuality and physical energy, and people with this zone dominant in their handwriting are materialistic and sensual. They enjoy the creature comforts and are often active in sports.

In the *upper zone* are the tops of the letters "b," "d," "f," "h," "k," "l," and "t," as well as the dots of "j" and "i." This is the where you'll find your imagination and emotions. A dominant upper zone indicates a thinker, someone who's concerned about the larger world.

Card Catalog

Graphology is the study and analysis of handwriting to find clues to a person's character and personality.

329

Of course, there's far more to graphology than this quick overview. If you'd like to know more, check Appendix A, where we list some sources.

Palmistry: The Geography of Your Hand

Palmistry looks at more than just the palm of your hand. It also looks at your hand's shape and size, as well as your fingers. What can your hand tell you about you? To find out, let's take a brief look at its geography.

Most palmists look first at your fingers—their shapes and relative size, and the size of each of the finger's three sections. Each of your four fingers (the thumb's not included in this, poor guy) represents an area of your life, and their names are associated with the Roman gods who ruled those areas.

Palmistry's Who's Who of Your Fingers

Finger	Ruler	Tarot Connection
Little	Mercury	Communication (Wands)
Ring	Apollo	Music and the Arts (Cups)
Middle	Saturn	Security and Wealth (Pentacles)
Index	Jupiter	Worldly Matters (Swords)

Your hand's shape is equally important in revealing your character. Short, square hands belong to patient, hardworking folks, while conic hands with tapering fingers, belong to the charming or artistic. There are other hand shapes that palmists look at as well (if you'd like to explore them, we suggest a few books in Appendix A).

Even if you're not familiar with these two aspects of palmistry, you probably do know about the lines on your hand. The three most closely looked at are the life line, which runs up from the base of your thumb; the head line, which runs across the center of your palm; and the heart line, which runs above the head line near the base of your fingers. The career line is also an important line on your palm.

These lines are often connected by smaller lines, and they have other lines running to and from them in all directions. When you think about it, they really *are* a whole lot like life—sometimes it's about your heart, and sometimes you've got to use your head. Again, if you'd like to know more, please check Appendix A for further reading.

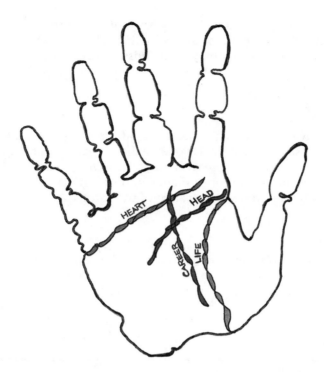

The head, heart, life, and career lines on your palm. Drawing by Elizabeth Toth.

Automatic Writing: Your Inner Voice

Those of us who make a career of writing will tell you that *automatic writing* happens any time you're on a roll. The characters take over and your book, paper, or whatever seems to write itself while you just take it down. Unfortunately, those rolls don't happen all that often; most of the time writing requires a lot of hard work.

Automatic writing is similar to what happens to a writer on a roll, we suspect. Lisa's even assigned writing exercises to her students that don't allow them to stop writing. If they can't think of anything, 'they're to just keep on going. This forces the subconscious to take over, and that's when a writer gets on a roll.

If you'd like to try your hand at automatic writing, you don't need a writing class. Just try this exercise:

Set a timer for ten minutes and have a pen and enough paper to fill that time without stopping. When the timer starts, so do you. Write whatever's in your head. Don't worry about spelling or grammar, don't worry about sentences, and don't worry about making any sense. Don't stop. Don't even pause. If you feel yourself hesitating, write the same word over and over again until you're going again. Lisa assigns a word, such as "potatobug," to her students to write over and over again when they stall. You can do this too if you want. Soon you'll be writing "potatobug, potatobug squash crunch ugh" or whatever—but you'll be rolling again.

Automatic writing exercises can help you get in touch with your subconscious thoughts. It's especially handy when you're trying to work through a problem (such as writing a novel...): Your subconscious may hand you the missing key to work your way through to the other side. Try it and see for yourself!

Fortunate Mysteries

There are more ways people have tried to divine the future—-from fortune-telling aids to more everyday methods. Those healing crystals you may have heard about began as fortune-telling devices, and the ancient Chinese wisdom of the *I Ching* is also used to see into the future. And your mother's mah-jongg tiles are more than numbered flowers, bams, and dots—they're the Chinese equivalent of the Tarot!

Those Divine Crystals

Crystals have always been ascribed special properties (see the following table), and the twelve semi-precious stones we'll talk about here are no exception. When used in a reading, these stones can help you uncover the answers to some of your more pressing questions.

Crystal Symbolism

Stone	Symbolism
Agate	Good energy, a pleasant surprise
Amethyst	Spiritual enlightenment
Bloodstone	Health problems
Diamond	Strength, courage
Emerald	Good memory, a possible secret admirer
Garnet	Cheerfulness
Opal	Daydreaming, moodiness
Ruby	Friendship
Sapphire	Peace and harmony, lucky in love
Sardonyx	Happy marriage, a wedding
Topaz	Caution in love
Turquoise	Protective amulet

While there's no set method for how to set and read crystals, one that we like involves the twelve astrological houses. Have the questioner place the stones in a diagram of the houses, such as the one in the following figure. When she's finished, you can interpret each stone's meaning based on the house in which she's placed it.

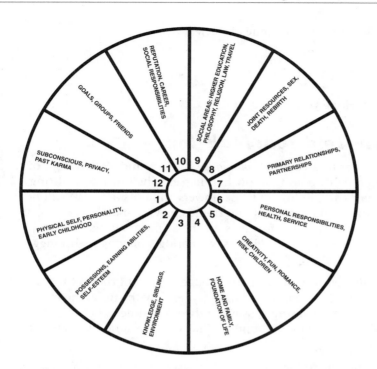

The astrological houses.

In addition to telling fortunes, crystals are also believed to have healing powers, which connect with the body's energy centers to produce wellness. If you come across a crystal that feels right to you, by all means, get it. For a crystal to work, after all, both your energy and the crystal's energy are required.

Wisdom in the Wings: The I Ching

The *I Ching* is divided into 64 sections, each of which is a six-lined hexagram. Depending on how you choose to consult the *I Ching*, you can cast sticks or even coins to arrive at patterns within the hexagrams. These patterns in turn lead to numbers, and each number has an assigned meaning.

While the *I Ching* is far too complicated to tackle here, we thought we'd give you a taste by providing a few examples of number interpretation directly from the original book:

➤ 1 Time to take action

➤ 2 Time for reaction

➤ 8 Help will bring success

Fools Rush In

We hate to mention this, but even crystal healing has its charlatans. Before you buy a crystal to cure your ills, make sure it feels right to *you*. Don't let anyone else try to convince you that you must have a certain crystal. Two energies must be present for a crystal to do its work: the crystal's and yours.

➤ 1 Being forceful will help you overcome obstacles

➤ 24 A good, profitable journey

➤ 37 Let the woman of the family decide!

Hey—we like this reading! Hope you do, too.

What Mother Never Told You: Mah-Jongg

Your mother may have never told you that *mah-jongg* is the Chinese equivalent of Tarot cards because she probably doesn't know that herself! She's just been sitting there with her yearly "maj" card, lining up those flowers and dots. Lisa can still hear those childhood echoes of her grandmother and friends playing maj downstairs, and you can bet those "girls" weren't telling fortunes. In the 50s, women played "maj" as many play bridge today, with weekly clubs. As with bridge, playing mah-jongg involves skill and strategy.

Not only is mah-jongg filled with symbolism and imagery, each of the 144 tiles has its own oracle name. This is similar to Tarot card imagery, and, with study, the imagery of mah-jongg tiles can reveal itself in a similar way. At the same time, a tile's exact message is quite dependent on the tiles around it. That should sound like Tarot to you as well!

While we haven't got room here to look at all 144 tiles, we can at least look at a few, which you'll notice sound a lot like some cards we know.

Mah-Jongg and the Tarot

Tile	Meaning	Tarot Equivalent
1 Bamboo	Peacock: Ambition	Ace of Wands
6 Bamboos	Water: Travel	Eight of Wands
1 Circle	Pearl: Wealth	Ace of Pentacles
7 Circles	Insect: Industry	Seven of Pentacles
2 Number	Sword: Dilemma	Pick a Sword, any Sword...

There are also seven tiles called the Honors, which represent the four directions and three colors (red, green, and white); and eight tiles called the Guardians, which represent special assistance.

If you're fortunate enough to have access to a mah-jongg set, we encourage you to lay out the tiles in some of the spreads we suggested in Part 5 of this book. And in Appendix A, we tell you where you can get more information on just what the tiles mean.

How Do I Know What—or Whom—to Believe?

By now, you probably know the answer to this question. You know instinctively what method of looking into the future is right for you. If the ancient beauty of the mah-jongg tiles is appealing, by all means, try your hand at using them to answer your questions. Or if the Ouija board pointer whizzes all over the board for you, as it does for Lisa, it may be the way for you to go.

Like the Tarot, each of these ways of divining the future—crystal balls, tea leaves, palmistry, automatic handwriting, crystals, *I Ching*, and mah-jongg—is also a way of looking inside yourself to find what you really desire. When you discover that, you'll know just what to believe.

The Least You Need to Know

➤ Crystal balls are one method of "scrying"—looking into mists to find answers.

➤ The patterns that tea leaves leave in cups can reveal what's going to happen.

➤ Messages about the future may be in your hands—and in your handwriting.

➤ Ouija boards can help you get in touch with your subconscious.

➤ Crystals, the *I Ching,* and mah-jongg are all ancient methods of divining the future.

➤ What you believe is up to you!

Chapter 23

Tarot and Your Psychic Powers

In This Chapter

➤ Are you psychic?

➤ Who were you before?: Reincarnation

➤ Knock, knock. Who's there?: Channeling spirits

➤ Using Tarot to tap your psychic powers

So what's the big deal about *The X-Files* anyway? Why do millions and millions of people tune in to this television show every Sunday night to see if Scully and Mulder will finally uncover the extraterrestrial plot?

UFOs are just one aspect of the psychic universe, which also includes phenomena like ESP, out-of-body experiences, psychic healing, psychokinesis, and channeling, to name but a few. Because Tarot naturally taps into your psychic abilities, let's explore these abilities a little more closely in this chapter.

Are You Psychic?

Have you ever known something was going to happen before it actually did? Have you ever picked up the phone and known who it was before the person said a word? Or have you ever known what someone was going to say before he said it? If so, you've had a *psychic experience*.

Card Catalog

Psychic experiences (or post-conscious cognitive experiences, in psychological jargon) are experiences that we perceive in ways other than our usual waking consciousness. These include everything from ESP to UFOs—anything, in fact, that modern science is at a loss to explain.

Spinning the Wheel of Fortune

Here's a simple psychic test for you to try: Next time you lose something, quit looking for it, and go do something else instead. We'll bet that once you've totally shifted your consciousness to a different task, the lost thing will "show" you exactly where it is. Go on, now. Don't laugh until you try it.

The concepts of psychic experience exist in a difficult-to-research borderland beyond waking consciousness. Everything from ESP to UFOs falls under the psychic blanket, because modern science can't explain how psychic experiences work.

Easterners (we mean those from India and China, not New Yorkers and Bostonians) take such experiences for granted, but more "rational" Westerners find them strange and unsettling. The more rational someone considers himself, in fact, the more likely he is to scoff at such experiences.

But the fact remains that most people have had some sort of psychic experience. Even Lisa's highly rational husband admits to having seen a ghost as a child (and he'll be furious to find that fact printed here), and the frontiers of theoretical physics are quickly approaching the borders of psychic theory. But are *you* psychic? Let's find out.

Are You in Tune with the "Vibes"?

Whether it's Puccini or Garth Brooks, everyone has a favorite kind of music that can "transport" them to another world. When we have such a feeling from music, we're personally experiencing it, and this is a good analogy for what occurs when we have psychic experiences, too.

Being "in tune with the vibes" simply means having all your channels open. As we mentioned in Part 1 of this book, to prevent overload we all have our sensory blockers on much of the time. But those who turn those blockers off sense far more than the distant train and the flash of sunlight off their car's front bumper.

Do You Believe in Psychic Abilities?

Psychic sensing is no more odd than sensing another's mood. After all, what sense do you use to "know" that your spouse had a bad day? How do you know that someone's "an accident waiting to happen"? Picking up another's unconscious signals is the first step toward becoming more aware of your psychic abilities. The truth is we all have them—we just haven't learned to fine-tune them yet.

Whether you "believe" in psychic abilities or insist they're a lot of bunk, they do exist. Westerners' main problem with the whole concept is that it can't be nailed down, it can't be reduced to a mathematical formula, and it can't be proven scientifically. "If I can't see it, it doesn't exist," says Rational Man.

So how does Rational Man explain that recurring nightmare that wakes him at least three nights a week? "It's just a dream," he says. *"Just a dream?"* we echo. More of our thoughts on *that* in the next chapter.

ESP: Knowing What's Going to Happen

In the early 60s, Lisa stood on a corner, chatting with a man in her neighborhood about her dog, whom she was walking. Suddenly, she "knew" the man was going to die. She didn't say anything, of course, and the "knowledge" wasn't exactly in words anyway. She thought it was weird, but then forgot all about it.

That is, until the next day, when she was watching the news with her father. A roofer had fallen off a roof and died, said the newscaster, and then he announced the man's name and showed his picture. Lisa gasped audibly. It was the man she'd been talking to the day before. She told her father what she'd "known," and to his credit he didn't laugh at her. But he couldn't explain what she'd "known" either.

What Lisa had all those years ago was an experience of precognition, an important aspect of *extrasensory perception*, or *ESP*. Thousands of studies have been done to examine this phenomenon, but while many have yielded extraordinary results, none have conclusively "proven" that ESP exists.

No less eminent a scientist than Einstein suggested that time is more fluid than we linear humans perceive it. Fans of *Star Trek* are well aware that we're more than capable of moving back and forth in time, for the theories of *Star Trek* are firmly rooted in quantum mechanics theory.

According to quantum mechanics theory, time moves more slowly, relative to the rest of the universe, as you approach the speed of light. If you were going the speed of light, in other words, a minute would take years.

It follows then, that if time is more fluid than we perceive it, we can sometimes catch a glimpse of the past or future through a window of time. Do you ever recall experiencing a smell and feeling yourself transported back to an earlier place and time when you experienced that same smell? Most of us have, and when we have we've traveled through a sensory window. What we're saying here is that those sensory windows open in two directions, creating extrasensory experiences.

Card Catalog

Extrasensory perception, or *ESP*, is the experience of knowing that something's going to happen before it does. It also includes the ability to see auras and other subtle energy fields, as well as past lives.

Exercises to Increase Your Own Psychic Powers

Chances are you use your psychic powers all the time but call them by different names. Does "luck" or "accident" ring a bell? How about "intuition"? Just as some of us are better at volleyball and others are mechanical whizzes, it seems that there are those whose psychic ability is more developed than others. But there are ways you can increase yours:

➤ *Meditation.* Those who meditate regularly have learned to "turn off" their left brain, the analytical side, and let the right brain, the "dreamy" side, take over. The left brain gets so busy processing information that it doesn't allow the right brain time to muse about any of it. When you meditate, though, sensory impressions, including extrasensory ones that the left brain blocks, can get in.

➤ *Exercise.* If you've ever experienced an "endorphin high" while running, you know that when real exercise kicks in, your mind seems to kick off. That's because at those moments you're in tune with your body in the way that yogis (those who practice yoga) are, and hence more open to sensory input.

➤ *Being open.* The next time you "know" something, don't dismiss it. Examine the feeling of the knowledge: Does it have a texture? A voice? A color? Write down any impressions you have. Knowing how your own ESP works can help you fine-tune and enhance it.

Researchers doggedly continue to try to prove the existence of ESP, while modern science just as doggedly continues to scoff. We predict that someday soon, it will be the ESP researchers' turn to laugh at the scientists—and we'll be there to laugh along with them.

In the Cards

Say you're driving from Denver to Omaha, when with a start you realize you've entirely spaced out from North Platte to Kearney. Having lived in Nebraska, Lisa realizes that it's not difficult to space out there occasionally, but what you've experienced if this has happened to you is your right brain taking over. For more on psychic intuition, read *The Complete Idiot's Guide to Being Psychic* (Alpha Books, 1999).

Back to the Future, Again

Not even Shirley MacLaine is certain how many past lives she can remember, but one of the more interesting aspects of her memories is the fact that the same people appear again and again throughout her various lives—in different guises, of course. She herself has been male as often as not.

Reincarnation is one of the more ancient ways of exploring the concept of life after death. According to Hindu tradition, you're moving up the ladder of reincarnation when you come back as a cow or water buffalo. And in Buddhist tradition, the Dalai Lama is the same spirit, reincarnated over and over again in different men throughout the generations.

Reincarnation: It Happened in Another Life

Reincarnation is the belief that the spirit or soul never dies, but rather after your death, moves to inhabit another physical entity. Both Hinduism and Buddhism accept reincarnation as a fact of life—and death—and Shiite Moslems and many native tribes in Africa and North and South America include reincarnation among their beliefs as well.

Those who can recall their previous lives often remember them in striking detail. Some documented cases in India have been able to be verified because a few of the past-life family members were still alive during the new incarnation. As with ESP, the big question about reincarnation seems to be why some people can recall past lives while most cannot, and the answer is probably a similar one: Some of us just have better memories.

Card Catalog

Reincarnation is the belief that the spirit or soul, upon the bodily death of one person, moves on to another body or form.

The Dalai Lama: Our Lives Are Like Beads on a String

According to Tibetan Buddhist tradition, the current Dalai Lama is the 14th incarnation of Buddha. The Dalai Lama is the spiritual leader of Tibetan Buddhism, and when one leader dies, his soul moves to a newborn boy. The search for that newborn is conducted through a series of traditional tests, and when he's found, he's then groomed for his holy position.

Circumstances with China have sent the current Dalai Lama into exile, where he's earned a Nobel Peace Prize for his efforts to return to his homeland. Those who've met this man and have been expecting an intimidating religious presence have been disarmed by his charm and sense of humor. After 14 lifetimes, though, he can probably afford to laugh at some of our human foibles—like Western skepticism about reincarnation.

Card Catalog

Past-life regression employs hypnotherapy to find out about the lives one lived before the present one. *Hypnotherapy* is a therapy that begins with information uncovered during hypnosis.

Exploring Hypnotherapy

One way that you can attempt *past-life regression* is through *hypnotherapy*. Some believe that by remembering your past lives in this way, you can find the key to your present-day problems—your karmic lessons, in other words. One way to think of this is as Freudian theory once removed—it's rooted in your childhood, but not necessarily the childhood of your present life.

Fools Rush In

Because there are charlatans who claim to channel spirits but who are in reality just making a quick buck, more skepticism surrounds this concept than any other psychic phenomena. That's unfortunate, but also a warning that you should take care with whom you trust to channel your spirits.

One of the problems with hypnotherapy is that, under hypnosis, people seem particularly susceptible to suggestion. So if past-life memories don't exist, the person may create them at the hypnotist's most subtle suggestion.

Still, if you sometimes have "flashes" of a place you've never been, perhaps a little hypnotherapy might help you determine if you're experiencing a past-life regression. A little more knowledge never hurt any of us, did it?

Heaven Knows

While some spirits prefer the Ouija board, others want a real voice, and find it when they "channel" their energies through people currently living. We'll be discussing two kinds of channeling—the single spirit/single human type, and the séance type—where you can talk with loved ones who've gone on to the other side.

Channeling Spirits

Those who have been in the presence of a person who becomes a channel or *medium* for a spirit have been struck by the change in not just the personality, but the actual physical appearance of the medium. One of the best-known contemporary channelers, James Van Praagh has written a recent best-seller called *Talking to Heaven: A Medium's Message of Life After Death.*

No one knows why a certain spirit picks a particular person to be its voice, although once again, it seems that those who can channel spirits seem to have a natural ability for it. So if you've been hearing one particular voice in your head, maybe you should see if it wants to get out—it could be a spirit using *you* as a channel.

Talking with Loved Ones Who've Passed On

Another type of channeling enables you to talk to your loved ones (or your hated ones—it's up to you) who've left this world. The mediums who practice this type of channeling don't channel for any one spirit but rather have trained themselves to sort of "scan the airwaves" to find the spirit you want to talk to. Because those who loved you are probably hanging around nearby you anyway (unless they've been reincarnated), mediums don't have to adjust their frequency much to find whom you're looking for.

If you're interested in finding a medium to channel the spirit of someone you loved, you need go no further than your local Yellow Pages. Just look under "Psychics." Of course, your local metaphysical bookstore can be an even better place to find reputable psychics.

Using Tarot Cards to Tap into Psychic Energy

The Tarot is a marvelous tool to open up your "third eye," the one that can see even more than your seeing eyes. The pictures and symbols on the cards, as well as all the colors, are thrown toward you in an instant. Sometimes, when that instant flash of the card happens, the right side of the brain says, "Wait a minute. I see more than just what the book says about this card. I see, or rather, I *feel* a journey coming."

The book may say a big change is ahead, but the reader picks up more than is obvious because her or his third eye is operating. It's as if the Tarot cards act like an electrical charge that stimulates the mind and spirit of the reader to pick up more than what's on the page.

We as readers are always challenged by our own clients to pick up more. They're always asking, "Do you see more?" "Did you tell me *everything*?" The more you read for others, the better you get at picking up these unseen (by the physical eyes, anyway) conditions or events. So we'll tell our Querent, "I may be going out on a limb, but here's what *I* see." We haven't broken any of our limbs this way—and we're often right on target.

Is Your Tarot Reader Psychic?

Most Tarot readers we know and like are intuitive about all the readings they do; they just can't help it! They keep improving their intuitive connection with the cards with every reading they do. (And you will, too.)

In addition, most readers consider themselves either intuitive or psychic. In other words, they see and feel more than the technical description of the card. The best reader seems to be one who can be technically accurate while at the same time have great sensitivity for the Querent across the table.

Psychic insight helps enhance the reader's ability to do his or her best work for the client. After all, if we as readers can help with the most information and most accurate insight (and that is our job, after all), we've helped empower the Querent in the process.

Tarot, as well as all other forms of metaphysics, actually allows the reader to become more psychic the more he or she reads for others. What a win/win situation!

Tarot's High Priestess (key 2) is a card of psychic intuition.

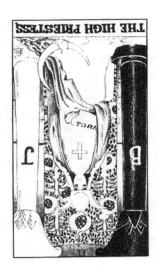

Intuiting the Cards

Here's an exercise to intuit the cards. Hold a card, any card, in front of you, before you read a book on the Tarot (well, okay, so maybe it's too late for that). What do you see and what feeling do you get from the picture on that Tarot card? Write it down or just remember it. Then go to the book and see how close your feelings were to the picture and its symbolism.

Take a second card and do the same: Look at the card and see and feel what's there for *you*. Arlene does this exercise every week, and sometimes every other day, using three different Tarot cards, one at a time, to test her intuitive side. She doesn't let the "book" meanings of the cards interfere with how she herself feels about them—and neither should you. The next best exercise for intuiting the Tarot is to pick a card out of the deck face down—don't look at it—and then write on a piece of paper what you think or feel is on the face side of the card. No cheating! Don't peek at the card or turn it over before you've written what you feel you see there.

After you've written down what you're feeling, turn the card over and see how close you came to its meanings. You will begin *feeling* each card the more you do this exercise (we suggest you do it every day for seven days in a row). Working in this manner over a period of time will open you up to your own intuitive powers.

The Least You Need to Know

➤ Everyone has some psychic ability, but most people haven't developed it to its full potential.

➤ ESP is a way of knowing things that can't possibly be known in conventional ways, such as what's going to happen before it does.

➤ Reincarnation is the belief that the soul doesn't die with the body but instead returns again and again in different physical forms.

➤ Some spirits like to have physical incarnations channel their energies.

➤ You can use the Tarot to tap into your psychic powers.

Tarot and Your Dreams

What *are* dreams, anyway? Native American tribes believed that dreams were visits from ancestors to help the dreamer, Sigmund Freud said they mirrored our repressed desires, and Carl Jung called them a gateway to our collective unconscious.

In more recent years, dream research has isolated a sleep period called *REM (rapid eye movement) sleep*, during which we do most of our dreaming. Discovered in 1953, REM is the time during our sleep that our most vivid dreams occur. This dreaming is accompanied by rapid eye movement beneath the lid, hence its name. Researchers today continue to study the connection between our waking and dream worlds to try to discover just what dreams are for. In this chapter we'll look at the connection between the Tarot and dreams.

You're So Dreamy!

People have been trying to unravel the meaning of dreams since history began. Loaded with imagery, symbolism, and *day residue*, they're a natural territory for any journey of self-discovery.

The first book of short stories ever written, *The Epic of Gilgamesh*, relates the adventures of the Mesopotamian prince, Gilgamesh, and is filled with dreams, dream imagery, and dream symbolism. Sometime after that book was written, ancient Hebrews became renowned as dream interpreters, and it was Joseph's talent at this that took him from slavery in Egypt to become counselor to the Pharaoh.

Those same ancient Egyptians believed that happy dreams foretold problems, while a nightmare meant good times were coming. The ancient Greeks enhanced this theory, and also built temples to their dream oracles, including the most famous, the Delphic Oracle.

One of the continuing draws of Shakespearean drama is its use of dreams to reveal character. And some Oriental traditions believe that we have separate or different consciousnesses, one of which leaves us during sleep.

Whatever the tradition, it's clear that what happens while we're sleeping will always be a source of fascination to us. Because dreams are just that: fascinating.

Card Catalog

Day residue is any dream image that derives from the day's events. You may, for example, repeat a conversation you had, only in a dreamlike way, or you may be sitting at the same traffic light you did that day as your otherwise different dream images unfold.

Do You Remember Your Dreams?

Everybody dreams. There are those who insist they don't, but that's simply because they don't remember theirs. And while the debate about whether or not animals dream continues, we animal co-habitors are here to tell you that we *know* ours do: Lisa's dog Mr. Too, in particular (don't ask what kind of dog he is—he's got more varieties than Heinz) appears to have the same dream every night, always involving some yelping and rapid paw movement.

Chances are, the dreams you remember best are those you have just before waking. That's one of the reasons we tend to remember our nightmares: They usually wake us up. One branch of dream research involves waking up the subject after each episode of REM sleep so that each dream can be recorded. And those who wish to remember more of their dreams actually set alarms to wake them periodically so that they can write their dreams down before they "lose" them. We'll talk more about this later in the chapter.

Dreams Speak in Images and Metaphors

Like the Tarot, dreams speak in images and metaphors. It's one of the things that makes them so interesting. Is your father really your father? Does a lion represent danger or protection? Does repeatedly stabbing your boss mean you want to kill her or have sex with her? (Or both?)

In the Cards

One school of dream theory insists that dreams are nothing more than random electrical impulses that the mind insists on ordering into something more meaningful. We think that seems to be putting the cart ahead of the horse, don't you?

The imagery of your dreams is highly personal. Nineteenth-century dream books, and in fact many dream books today, try to tie specific meanings to specific images. So did Freud for that matter. If you dreamed of a lake, you were back in the womb, according to Freud. End of story.

It's worth noting that one current school holds that every person in your dreams is actually an aspect of yourself. So if you dream of your sister, she's the part of you that reminds you of her. It's probable that this is one aspect of dreams—but it's not the only one.

Writing It Down: Your Dream Journal

A dream journal is a wonderful way to get in touch with yourself. Here are some of the reasons:

➤ Recording your dreams helps you remember them.

➤ Noting a dream's details on waking preserves things you would otherwise lose as the day progresses.

➤ Dream imagery has levels of meaning, from the obvious to the metaphoric, and writing down a dream helps you to see these levels.

➤ The more you record, the more patterns will begin to emerge in your dreams, unlocking keys to your unconscious and your creativity.

Some people keep dream sketchbooks in addition to written notes. Pictures are uniquely suited to the often other-worldly imagery of dreams, after all. In a few pages, we'll talk about using the imagery of Tarot to get in touch with your dreams, too.

In Your Book of Dreams

When you first start recording your dreams, it's hard to know just what to include. The answer? Everything. The smallest detail may be key to unraveling your dream. Colors, street signs, even furniture, shouldn't be ignored. In your Book of Dreams, each is a metaphor.

Here's a sample dream entry. Note how the dreamer includes details such as the shape of the attic entrance and some of the emotions she felt. Her interpretation follows.

Dream:

I was climbing a tall ladder into an attic, which was accessed through a square hole in the ceiling, carrying box after box of things up to store (hide?) there. My brothers (their young selves, though I was my current self) kept shaking the ladder and I kept telling them to stop. I wasn't really angry with them, though. Suddenly, I realized that I didn't need to "hide" things in the attic anymore; I could keep them out and use them. This was a tremendous relief to me.

Interpretation:

Now that I'm writing again, I dream of my family when I was a girl more and more. In this dream, my brothers are shaking the ladder, much the way we used to do things to each other as siblings do. But suddenly, I realize that I don't need to be climbing up to the attic over and over again anyway, because I can "use" these things here. This is my writing. I'm not hiding things "in the attic" anymore. Of course it's a relief.

Recognizing Your Personal Dream Symbols

As you record more and more dreams in your dream journal, your personal dream symbols will begin to emerge. Perhaps you often seem unable to move your foot from the gas pedal to the brake in your dream car, or whenever you look at a watch its face is cracked.

Your personal dream symbols are like a letter to yourself from your unconscious. There are no definitive meanings for any symbol, any more than there are definitive meanings for any Tarot card.

If you regularly dream of a room with a locked door, for example, it doesn't mean that you feel trapped. Maybe you wish you could lock the door, or maybe you want to open the door but are afraid. The color of the door is important as well. Only you can ultimately unlock your personal dream symbols, and when you do you will grow in the process.

Ways to Boost Dream Recall

Keeping a dream journal will boost your dream recall before you know it, but it takes practice and a positive attitude in addition to pencil and paper.

➤ First, you have to *want* to remember your dreams. As you fall asleep, tell yourself: Tonight I will remember my dreams.

➤ Don't just write down your dreams and forget about them. Think about them during the day. Are there details you didn't write down? Are there emotions that remain with you throughout the day? Maybe a nagging sense of something you've forgotten? All of these may be important; note them whenever they occur to you.

➤ Look over the journal entries you've already made. They'll inspire you to dream further.

➤ Set an alarm clock to wake you every two hours after you fall asleep. You'll wake up after each REM sleep period and be able to remember your dreams quite clearly. We don't recommend this the night before the big exam, though!

➤ Relax. This isn't the big exam!

The Tarot/Dreams Synergy

If you're of two minds about this, you're already on the road to connecting your conscious and unconscious minds. That's what letting dreams into your waking life is all about, and the Tarot is closely connected with the imagery of dreams.

Let's use a Tarot card as an example to explain what we mean.

2 of Wands.

Look at this picture as if it were something you'd dreamed. In fact, *record* this picture as if it were something you'd dreamed. Write down your Tarot card dream here. Don't go on to the next section until you do.

My 2 of Wands Dream

_____

_____

_____

_____

_____

Letting the Image Sink In

What was *your* 2 of Wands dream? Was the world your oyster? Were you about to set off on a voyage? Or were you waiting for someone to arrive, trying to peer into your globe to see when—or who—that would be? Maybe the man in the picture didn't represent you but was instead someone you dreamed of; maybe *he* was waiting for *you* to arrive.

Using the Tarot cards this way will help you work with your dream imagery. When you allow your imagination to create a story for a card, you're letting the image sink in.

You're *not* demanding that the image be something or someone specific. You're *not* interpreting the image or assigning it meaning. What you're doing is allowing the image to speak for itself. And that's what dream images do: Each has a voice all its own, just waiting to tell you what it's saying.

Connecting the Conscious and Subconscious Minds

Over, under, sideways, down.

What goes up must come down.

Opposites attract.

There's two sides to everything.

Sayings like these exist for a reason. There *are* two sides to everything, but sometimes we forget just how interdependent those two sides are.

The ancient Chinese concept of *Yin* and *Yang* explains this idea more beautifully than any other analogy we've encountered. *Yin*, the female energy, and *yang*, the male energy, co-exist. Neither is dominant, and neither is complete without the other.

In the same way that yin and yang complement each other, your unconscious mind can complement your conscious mind. Because your conscious mind tends to be logical and straightforward, it can literally miss the forest for the trees. Learning to use your unconscious mind is like putting on glasses for the first time: "Wow! I didn't realize trees have individual leaves!"

Yin and yang.

Using Tarot Cards to Help Understand Your Dreams

If, like us, your talent with a pen doesn't go beyond words, the imagery of Tarot cards can help you understand your dreams without drawing pictures. Seventy-eight pre-drawn images are just waiting there to depict every possible human situation, and all you have to do is find the right card!

Reach for It!

Let's go back to the dream recorded earlier in this chapter—the woman climbing the ladder to the attic to hide her boxes of stuff. Take out your Tarot deck and see if you can find any cards that you think approach the imagery of this dream.

The dreamer herself pulled out the Ace of Wands almost immediately. But she didn't stop there. She also pulled out the Hanged Man, the Tower, the Star, and the Fool. And wait, here's the Ace of Cups! And the 10 of Cups! All these cards seem to have been pictures of her dream.

For the next step, the dreamer arranges the cards into a "story" of her dream. Here's her arrangement:

One dream's "journey."

Spinning the Wheel of Fortune

Dreams aren't linear. That means they don't follow the past/present/future timeline that we're accustomed to in our conscious life. When you use Tarot cards to tell your dream "story," you shouldn't try to place them in the order of "this happened, then this happened." Instead, place them in an order of emotional importance and see what happens.

Card Catalog

Creative visualization is the process of using pictures to achieve one's goals. One example of this is a long-distance runner picturing herself pushing through the winner's tape.

The dreamer began with the Tower, an analogy for climbing the ladder, which her brothers were shaking. Then there's the Hanged Man, hanging from the ladder by one foot. All at once, the Ace of Wands appears: her revelation that she doesn't need to climb the ladder. And the Ace of Cups represents everything she'd been keeping inside, now spilling out of the Cup.

The 10 of Cups is her "happily ever after" card, but she moves beyond that to the Star, pouring water in and out of the river of consciousness, and to the Fool, who represents herself, the writer, every time she begins a new book.

Making Your Dreams Come True

Making your dreams come true is not as impossible as you think. If you're dreaming something, in fact, you're halfway to making it real. After that, the most important step in making your dreams come true is *creative visualization*.

In the often–reprinted book, *Wishcraft*, Barbara Sher and co-author Anne Gottlieb suggest writing down a story of your perfect day. Don't let anything stand in your way, Sher says. Not your job, not your kids, not anything.

Begin where you wake up. What's your bed like? Are you in it alone? What time is it? What does your room look like? Did you wake to an alarm clock? Are you in the country or the city? What city?

Continue through the rest of your day in this fashion. Do you work at home or go to an office? What do you do for lunch? What do you do in the evening? What time do you go to bed?

After you've written your account of your ideal day, examine a real day, and then list what's standing between the two. Ah, the two top "obstacles" seem to be jobs and kids.

But are they really obstacles? Who's really standing between you and your perfect day?

Once you realize you're your own worst enemy, you can begin to turn your dreams into reality. We're not kidding. We both did this ourselves.

More on the Road to Self-Actualization

Tarot and dreams are only the beginning when it comes to self-actualization. In the next two chapters, you'll explore the connection between Tarot and astrology—the study of your own unique place in the world—and Tarot and numerology—how your personal numbers can help you achieve your dreams.

Fools Rush In

How do you separate the wheat from the chaff in the self-improvement section of your bookstore? How do you keep from being misled by a charlatan? The answer is to trust yourself. Trust your instincts—and your friends—to steer you to the best way, and to the best book, to help you be all you can be.

The Least You Need to Know

➤ Everybody dreams, but not all of us remember our dreams.

➤ Keeping a dream journal can boost your dream recall.

➤ Remembering your dreams can help you make a connection between your conscious and unconscious minds.

➤ The Tarot can help you unlock your dream secrets.

Chapter 25

Tarot and Astrology

In This Chapter

➤ Astrology and the Tarot deck

➤ The energy of the Major Arcana

➤ The elements and the Minor Arcana

➤ What astrology can reveal about you

Like the symbols of the Tarot, the symbols of *astrology* represent the total energies of the universe. The main difference is that, where the Tarot uses pictures, colors, and numbers to help you better understand yourself, astrology uses the planetary positions at the date, time, and place of your birth to create a unique picture of you. It's important to remember that astrology and Tarot are two very different disciplines; but, that said, there are connections between them.

Seeing Stars: The Ancient Science of Astrology

People have always been interested in the sky and constellations, and the study of the heavens is as ancient as humanity itself. From generation to generation, astrological knowledge has been passed down along with astronomical knowledge—the two weren't separated until the late 1600s, in fact.

But while both astronomers and astrologers study the movements and history of heavenly bodies, the basic concept behind astrology is that the heavenly bodies above us reflect what's happening below, on earth.

The ancients navigated by the stars and planets. Without maps or computers, tribal groups decided when they should migrate to another territory by watching the sky and the planetary movements. Signs in the sky, such as where the sun set or where a particular star or planet was positioned, signaled when tribes should move from their winter grounds to their summer grounds, or back again.

Planetary movements also helped our ancestors get a fix on where they were going. Not only did they use the stars to decide how to get there, they also used them to chart changes they needed to make to keep everyone safe in their tribal community. The planets were like a language to the ancients, symbolic of cycles they'd been following for hundreds of years.

The lights in the sky, they knew, came and went in patterns, both at every seasonal change and monthly, as the moon went through its phases. The tribal groups knew how to read those planetary cycles, just as readers of the Tarot know how to interpret the pictures on the cards, which come up over and over again to tell a particular story and reveal a pattern. You can read these planetary cycles as well. You start with your birth sign.

Card Catalog

Your *birth sign*, or *Sun sign*, is the astrological sign the Sun was in when you were born. There are twelve of these signs in the *zodiac*, the pattern that the Earth follows on its elliptical journey around the Sun every year.

What's Your Sign?

Elementary astrology begins with your *birth sign*, or *Sun sign*, which is the astrological sign the Sun was in at the time you were born. Your birth sign correlates to the position of the Sun in the sky at that moment. There are twelve signs in the *zodiac*, the pattern the Earth follows on its elliptical journey around the Sun every year.

In the Cards

Astrology has long been one of this country's favorite pastimes. When Arlene was growing up in California in the 60s and 70s, the famous one-liner was, "Hey, what's your sign?" Everyone knew what sign they were, of course, and people actually tried to "read" each other to see if the sign's meaning was true or not. They also had fun guessing what someone's sign was—something you can still do today.

So how do you find *your* sign? It's easy! Just use your birth date to find your sign on the following chart.

The zodiac: Find your birth date and you'll find your astrological sign.

The Astrological Energies of Tarot's Major Arcana

Like your birth sign, each of the 22 Major Arcana has an astrological sign attached to it. These signs can help those of us who already know astrology to get better acquainted with the Tarot. Astrological signs represent the energies of Tarot's Major Arcana.

The Fool, for example, is of course the first sign of the zodiac, Aries. Freedom-loving Aries goes well with the new beginnings represented by the Fool. The Magician corresponds to the sign Aries as well, as this card's message is to initiate and create.

You'll note that many cards have more than one sign, and that most signs appear for more than one card. That's because, like you, signs are far from simple. They represent the many different facets that make you unique.

The Major Arcana and Their Signs

The Fool is Aries. Aries, the first sign, is the sign of new beginnings, and, like the Fool, people with Aries figuring prominently in their birth charts can sometimes rush into things before thinking them through. Aries likes to lead and has the confidence and enthusiasm we'd expect of someone with the Fool's high hopes. Aries is the sign of the ram, another good metaphor for the Fool.

The Magician is also Aries. The Magician is Aries for very different reasons. Aries represents the birth of ideas—creativity, in other words—and that's exactly what the Magician's holding in his bag of tricks. Because Aries people are idea generators, it's important that someone else be there to pick up an Aries' project once it gets going. Like the Magician, Aries will work the magic—but will then move on to something else.

The High Priestess represents both Pisces and Virgo. Pisces is the sign of dreams and intuition, and Virgo is the sign of serving humanity. All of these wonderfully female traits are embodied in the High Priestess as well. Pisces is the most compassionate of the signs, and its natives are naturally intuitive. Virgo is the sign of bettering the world, and among its archetypes is the Virgin Mary, who is in turn *the* archetype for the High Priestess. The High Priestess card, in fact, is about intuitive service, and that equals Pisces + Virgo.

The Empress is connected to Taurus and Libra. Taurus energy is sensual and down-to-earth, and more than content to keep the home fires burning. The Empress certainly embodies these Earth Mother characteristics. Libra is the sign of beauty, balance, and social grace, also clearly qualities of the Empress. In fact, Libra is the most charming sign of the zodiac, and the Empress makes no secret of her ability to charm, either.

The Emperor's signs are Aries and Scorpio. Aries, as you've probably figured out, is full of male energy, and the Emperor is a clear representation of that. A born leader, Aries can't help but embody the Emperor's kingly qualities. Similarly, Scorpio is the sign of deep-seated power. With its connection to sexuality, Scorpio is also the sign of the parent, so its association with the Emperor should come as no surprise. Put Aries and Scorpio together and you've got the Emperor in one tidy Tarot card!

The Hierophant is Taurus. In addition to being down to earth, Taurus is a very conventional sign. Like the Hierophant, those with Taurus prominent in their birth charts like things just as they are. Taureans are the ones who will go fish their ratty favorite chair from the trash, and honestly won't understand your desire to throw it out in the first place. They feel the same way about changing the status quo; like the Hierophant, they prefer things to remain the same.

The Lovers are Gemini. Gemini is the sign of dualities—after all, its symbol is a pair of twins. Like Gemini, the Lovers card is about partnership and the two sides of every issue. This is a sign of mental abilities, of thinking on your feet and landing on them, too, and the Lovers card, representing the choices we all must make, represents the same abilities.

The Chariot represents Sagittarius. Sagittarius is all about motion, and it's always forward motion. People with Sagittarius prominent in their charts never stay in one place for long, as if they had a Chariot with fresh horses every moment of every day. And, just as the Chariot can help you get where you want to go, Sagittarians are eager to get there—and then move on to the next place!

Strength is the card of Leo. In Leo, we find pride, courage, and the self-confidence to overcome any obstacle. Leos, in fact, may not even notice they've got obstacles, so strong is their faith in themselves. Like the woman in the Strength card, Leos are determined not to let a little thing like fear stand in their way. Besides, Leo's a lion—and appears as such on this card!

The Hermit is connected to Virgo. One of the characteristics of Virgo is a dedication to finding the sacred patterns in everything, and the Hermit card, with its focus on introspection, represents this aspect of Virgo perfectly. (Of course, Virgo loves perfection, too.) At the same time, those with prominent Virgo can be highly critical of themselves, but self-analysis is what the Hermit is all about.

The Wheel of Fortune has four signs: Aquarius, Taurus, Leo, and Scorpio. Each of these cards represents a season: Aquarius is winter, Taurus is spring, Leo is summer, and Scorpio is autumn. If you think of each season as an archetype for a certain way of life and then remember that the Wheel of Fortune is all about luck and chance, you realize that which season the Wheel stops at can determine how something will go. Winter (Aquarius), for example, is a time of gestation, when seeds lie dark before little seedlings pop up in the spring (Taurus). Summer (Leo) is a time of growth and sunshine, and autumn (Scorpio) a time of reaping the harvest. Everything that happens must go through each of these cycles, and so everything that happens is represented here in this card, the Wheel of Fortune.

Justice is the card of Libra. Libra is the sign of harmony and balance, and people with this sign prominent in their charts have the uncanny ability to see *everything* from both sides. If there's a compromiser in the group, you can bet it's Libra, and with their dedication to finding the perfect balance, Justice could be their middle name.

The Hanged Man's sign is Pisces. Pisces is the sign of Jesus, and the Hanged Man, hanging on a cross of his own making, is often associated with Jesus as well. Pisces is the sign of spirituality as well as faith and intuition, and, like Pisces, the Hanged Man seems to be caught between two worlds, the spiritual and the material. Pisces without spiritualism can descend into addiction, and the Hanged Man too must weigh his choices carefully before he comes down from his branch.

Death is one of the cards of Scorpio. Scorpio is the sign of transformation, of leaving one thing behind in order to start another. A metaphor for the Death card might be how the autumn's leaves on the ground provide protection for the spring's unborn plants—the leaves must die to bring forth the new life. This idea is what both Scorpio and Death represent—rejuvenation, rebirth, renewal, and transformation.

Temperance represents Cancer. Cancer is above all a moody sign—though we could also interpret it as changeability. The moods and changes of the sign happen because Cancer doesn't like change, which is exactly what Temperance is all about. Temperance represents the need to balance everything around you, as well as cooperating with existing conditions. Cancer constantly seeks emotional balance and nurturing, and the two cups between which the archangel Michael is pouring water signify that emotions can change rather quickly and that patience is required to see things through.

The Devil's sign is Capricorn. Capricorn is the sign of ambition and practicality, and, with their goals firmly in mind, Capricorns will plot a steady course to see that they're achieved. Like the people in the Devil card, those with prominent Capricorn can become slaves to their ambitions, but remember—the chains around those peoples' necks aren't locked. Capricorns may look at people who stand in their way as stepping stones rather than hurdles, because, like the Devil, they've got a specific end in mind. And that specific goal can become an obsession with Capricorn!

The Tower is connected to Aquarius. Aquarius is the sign of inventiveness and the unconventional or even eccentric. Like the Tower card, people with prominent Aquarius will come up with a response out of left field, one that occurred to no one else—and it will be just the response the question or problem needed. You never know what to expect with either Aquarius or the Tower. But at least you know life will never be dull!

The Star is also connected to Aquarius. Another aspect of Aquarius is its humanism; this is the universal sign of hope and a better tomorrow. Like the Star, people with Aquarius prominent in their chart are the seemingly impossible dreamers who go their own way—only to have everyone else fall in behind later on, when their way has proven to be the better one. Some examples of people in this category include Charles Darwin, Susan B. Anthony, Thomas Edison, and Wolfgang Amadeus Mozart. See what we mean?

The Moon represents both Cancer and Pisces. Sensitive, moody Cancer and intuitive, dreamy Pisces are both water signs, and the Moon, ruler of the tides, is closely tied to both. Both the Moon card and these two signs are associated with the unconscious and the night, both aspects of the feminine archetype. You may not know what you know, but the Moon knows.

The Sun is the card of Leo. Self-confident, proud, unafraid—these are the qualities of the Sun card and of Leo. Leo expects everyone to naturally adore him, and the child of the Sun card is equally self-assured. With their sunny optimism and outlook, both the card and the sign seem to assure success, and in this case, they reap what they've sown.

Judgement is another Scorpio card. Like Death, Judgement is about transformation, in this case rising to a new level of understanding. Judgement represents a total change of awareness, that big "Ah-ha! Now I know what that means" feeling. When Judgement appears, the light bulb has just gone on. Scorpio's known for its quiet, secretive, or passive side, and even though we know these people as pretty intense, they have that too-quiet side. Judgement is the type of Major Arcana that arrives to enlighten you to a truth you just discovered, and Scorpio loves to reveal the mystery and discover the truth. So Judgement and Scorpio open the same door.

The World belongs to Capricorn. The World is the highest level of success and attainment, the Major Arcana teaches us. Capricorns, like the World, will focus on their goals no matter how long it takes them to satisfy that Capricorn thirst for attainment. The World shows us attaining all our goals—personally, spiritually, and materially—and understanding our ability to continue to attain those goals. "Ain't no mountain high enough" for Capricorn to conquer or climb to the top of. Just ask them!

Don't Forget the Minor Arcana

When we get to the Minor Arcana, we find each suit correlated with an astrological *element*. The elements, remember, are fire, earth, air, and water, and represent the basic qualities of the signs.

Three astrological signs can be found in each of the four elements, and once you know what sign you are, you'll also know which element is your life's focal point. Then, when you add in the associated Minor Arcana suit, the picture becomes even clearer.

> **Card Catalog**
>
> The astrological *elements*—fire, earth, air, and water—represent the basic qualities of the signs and of life.

Element	Astrological Signs	Minor Arcana Suit
Fire	Aries, Leo, Sagittarius	Wands
Earth	Taurus, Virgo, Capricorn	Pentacles
Air	Gemini, Libra, Aquarius	Swords
Water	Cancer, Scorpio, Pisces	Cups

Wands and the Fire Signs

If you're a fire sign—Aries, Leo, or Sagittarius—the suit of Wands will be your focus. You'll be learning to develop power and personal drive and work on your ambition and growth.

Fire signs are energetic, idealistic, self-assertive, courageous, and often visionary. These are active, "fiery" people who express themselves creatively and are passionate about everything they do.

Pentacles and the Earth Signs

If you're an earth sign—Taurus, Virgo, or Capricorn—the suit of Pentacles will be the focus of your life's experiences or your life's work. Money, financial issues, and lessons about prosperity will be an important part of your growth.

Earth signs are practical and skillful, good at managing physical assets and financial matters—or any form of matter. People with earth signs are down to earth and strong authority figures.

Swords and the Air Signs

If you're an air sign—Gemini, Libra, or Aquarius—the suit of Swords is an important part of your life's experiences. You'll be working with the mind and logic, and developing courage and mental strength.

Air signs represent social and intellectual capabilities—ideas, communications, thinking, and social interrelationships. These are people who exist in a mental plane, in the "air," in other words.

Cups and the Water Signs

If you're a water sign—Cancer, Scorpio, or Pisces—the suit of Cups will be your focus. This includes family, emotional ties, relationships, and joy and emotions.

Water signs are sensitive and romantic; they think with their feelings, are intuitive, and can be emotional. People with water signs put their hearts ahead of their heads—but they won't always let you know it.

What Astrology Can Reveal About You

Card Catalog

Your *astrological chart*, also called a *birth chart*, is a representation of the position of each of the planets at the time you were born.

There's more to you than just your Sun sign. In fact, all twelve signs appear in your *astrological chart*, or *birth chart*, in twelve segments called houses. Each house is an area of your life, from the first house—your self and your self-image—to the twelfth—your hidden side.

Astrology uses the date, time, and place of your birth to create an astrological chart that's unique to you. All of the planets, which for astrological purposes also include the Sun and the Moon, reside somewhere in your astrological chart. The planets are placed in your chart according to what sign each planet was in at the moment you were born.

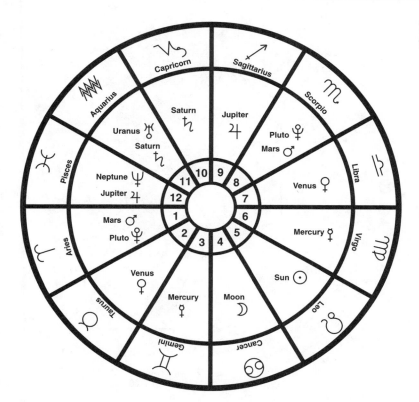

The astrological houses with their natural signs.

Your Astrological Chart: The Heavens at Your Birth

When you put this all together, your entire life is represented in your birth chart, from your birth (and who your parents are) to your school years, to your marriage(s), to your career and later years.

We like to think of an astrological chart as a metaphor for a person. For example, we know that a person with a twelfth house Moon in Cancer is going to be someone who hides her emotions (Cancer Moon = emotional nature; twelfth house = hidden aspects). And we can tell that someone with a fourth house Mars in Scorpio may have had some authority issues with his father when he was growing up (Mars = male figure; Scorpio = power; fourth house = childhood).

A (Very) Quick Look at Oprah's Birth Chart

Just to give you a peek at what an astrological chart looks like, we've included Oprah's here for you to see. You might want to compare what Oprah's chart reveals about her with the question we asked for her in Chapter 21. Note that the symbols in each house represent the planets and the signs.

Oprah Winfrey
Natal Chart
Jan 29 1954
7:51 PM CST +6:00
Kosciusko Miss USA
33N03 05 089W35
Geocentric
Tropical Zodiac
Placidus Houses
True Node

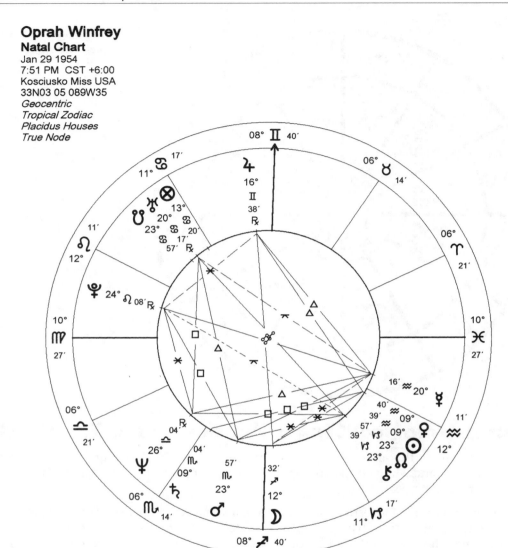

Oprah's birth chart.

The first important thing to notice in Oprah's birth chart is that her Sun is in Aquarius in the fifth house. This is the house of creativity, and Oprah's Sun is *conjunct* Venus here as well.

Aquarius is an air sign, so the intellect is emphasized. Sun sign Aquarians like Oprah are imaginative and inventive, often taking unusual but successful approaches to matters. In addition, Oprah's Aquarian objectivity makes her a good communicator with the public.

Oprah's Moon is in Sagittarius in the fourth house. This indicates that she enjoys literary issues, books, philosophy, educational studies, and has a genuine interest in humanity from all its many angles. Different cultures, foreign philosophies, and religious and spiritual subjects probably interest her as well.

Oprah's Moon *opposes* her natal Jupiter in Gemini near the midheaven in the 10th house of the public, so people naturally are attracted to her because her Moon (her feelings) is connected to Jupiter in Gemini (the communicator)—in the house of her career!

Speaking of careers, possible ones for Oprah include acting (the Sun in the 5th house enhances this), teaching, being a spokesperson, advertising, journalism, or in some way focusing on opinions of the day. Oprah's chart shows an open-minded person who's very curious about peoples' habits and lives and just what makes them tick. She's especially interested in people who do amazing things. Above all, Oprah's chart assures her of being a good and inspirational teacher.

Card Catalog

A *conjunction* is when two planets are aligned in the sky. You can tell this by the notations next to the planets in Oprah's fifth house: The Sun's position and Venus are only 1′ apart.

Card Catalog

An *opposition* is just what it sounds like: Opposing planets are exactly opposite each other in the heavens.

In the Cards

Do you remember Oprah early in her career in the movie *The Color Purple?* She played Sophia, the woman who refused to be pigeonholed into a traditional female role. Even in her acting career, Oprah was being Aquarian and resisting tradition!

That's just the beginning of what we see in Oprah's chart. Does it make you just a little curious about your own? If so, you can take your birth date, time, and place to your local metaphysical bookstore and get your birth chart done. It's a great metaphor for you—just like the Tarot.

The Benefits of Heavenly Navigation

Beyond your planets in their signs and houses are more advanced astrological techniques that chart the movement of the planets in relation to your birth chart. When astrologers look at these movements, called *transits* and *progressions*, they can look at things that have happened in your life and that may happen in the future.

But even if you don't have an astrologer analyze your transits and progressions, the benefits of heavenly navigation are many. You may know, for example, that you're quick to start something new and then soon lose interest but not know why. Your astrological chart may show that your Sun or Mercury is in Aries, so while you're naturally always rarin' to go at the start, it's hard for you to stay excited about something that's no longer new.

Card Catalog

Transits show where a planet's current position is affecting your birth chart. *Progressions* show how you and your chart evolve throughout your life.

That quick trip to your New Age bookstore armed with the date, time, and place of your birth can get you a birth chart in less than five minutes (it's all done by computers these days). Or you can pick up *The Complete Idiot's Guide to Astrology*, by Madeline Gerwick-Brodeur, and someone we know rather well, Lisa Lenard (Macmillan, 1998). If you'd like some psychological insight into why you do the things you do, astrology may be just the ticket.

The Least You Need to Know

➤ Tarot and astrology use symbolic language to paint a picture of you.

➤ The Major Arcana are associated with the twelve astrological signs.

➤ The Minor Arcana suits are associated with the four elements: fire, earth, air, and water.

➤ Astrology can help you make psychological insights about why you do the things you do.

Chapter 26

Tarot and Numerology

In This Chapter

➤ Numbers in the Tarot

➤ The numbers of the Major Arcana show you the steps

➤ The numbers of the Minor Arcana show you the way

➤ Find the timing in the numbers

➤ Your personal year

What's with the numbers on the cards, anyway? Are these numbers important? Do the numbers influence the cards? Yes and yes. The numbers on the cards add meaning to your interpretation of the cards. The numbers tell more of the story. In metaphysics, there are no accidents, so the card you draw and the number on that card has a message for you.

To look more closely at what numbers do mean, let's investigate a science devoted to just that: numerology.

Numerology Is the Language of Numbers

Numerology is the ancient science of names and numbers. One of the oldest sciences, it's a companion to both astrology and the Tarot. Numerology puts meaning to the numbers. Understanding the meaning of the numbers allows us to do many things, including:

Card Catalog

Simply stated, *numerology* is the language of numbers. Numerologists study the meanings of numbers and their connection to everything in the universe.

Card Catalog

The *master numbers*, which include 11 and 22 (along with 33, 44, 55, and so on), are numbers with special properties. Master numbers teach self-mastery. They indicate great power but carry great responsibility.

➤ Understand relationships

➤ Analyze human qualities

➤ Awaken spiritual awareness

➤ Predict the timing of events

➤ Have universal understanding

The ancient science of numerology is used in the Tarot deck in a number of ways (pun intended, of course). How? Here's the scoop.

The Numbers and the Tarot Deck

As you already know, the Tarot deck is divided into two sections: the Major Arcana and the Minor Arcana (Note that the "2" is for balance...). Each card bears a number, but precisely applying the meaning of a particular number to the corresponding meaning of a particular card doesn't always hold consistently throughout the 78-card deck.

While there's no question that numerology and Tarot are connected, exactly what the numbers on the cards mean is open to debate. In fact, the first recorded Tarot decks from the 16th century didn't contain any numbers at all. The numbers came later. Still, there are two significant facts about the Tarot deck and its numbers: There are 22 Major Arcana and 56 Minor Arcana. The numerological significance of this: 56 adds up to 11 (5 + 6), a *master number*, and 22 is also a master number. This can't be a coincidence, so we begin our discussion of the cards and numbers from this premise. The numbers on the cards are important symbols to be used for understanding your destiny.

The master number 11 is the number of self-illumination through spiritual inspiration appropriate for the Minor Arcana. The number 22 is the number bringing cosmic law into the material and physical world to build a new world of highest principles (the essence of the Major Arcana).

There are 22 Major Arcana—A Master Number

The Major Arcana has 22 cards (0–21 to be exact) and, as we've already explained , the number 22 is a master number. In fact, 22 is considered the most powerful of all the numbers. It's called the master builder number, because it symbolizes the potential for bringing spiritual understanding into physical form. The 22 symbolizes mastery and inspiration, and utilizes intuitive insights, coupled with practical methodology. The 22 is meant to serve the world in its mastery.

In *Choice Centered Tarot* (Ramp Creek Publishing, 1984), Gail Fairfield calls the Major Arcana "the twenty-two steps of the spiritual path from the material world…back to oneness with 'God.'" So we might say that the Major Arcana cards serve to bring spiritual knowledge to our earthly life—not bad for a pack of cards, eh?

The Minor Arcana Adds Up to 11: This Master Number Points the Way to Heaven!

The Minor Arcana has 56 cards. If we add 5 + 6 (this is called reducing the number), we get the master number 11. The 11 is the most intuitive of all the numbers. It symbolizes illumination and intuitive understanding, especially of spiritual truths or principles. The 11 focuses energy on "other world" consciousness, but we can use that same energy to turn inward to create fears and intense conflict in our lives. The 11 symbolizes truth found in faith, not in logic and the Minor Arcana is all about how to do life.

Because the Minor Arcana are ruled by the 11, these cards hold intuitive understanding for how to live in the everyday world. Where illuminated truth is lacking in the events of our lives, we can either meet the challenge with fear or with faith: The cards will point the way.

Spinning the Wheel of Fortune

We want to remind you that, like every meaning of the Tarot, its numerological representations are a starting point rather than an end point. As we've said all along, what the cards mean is up to you!

What's Behind Those Numbers?

Now that we know that the Major Arcana will show us the steps and the Minor Arcana will point the way, let's see about the numbers themselves. We'll start at the very beginning with the basic meaning of numbers. Take a look at the following "cheat sheet":

Number	Meaning
0	Unformed, empty and full, free will, no karmic debt
1	New beginnings, courage, originality, the self
2	Balancing, relationship, duality
3	Creative and emotional expression, synthesis, celebration (party time!), joy, happiness
4	Stability, foundation, form
5	Change, instability, adaptation
6	Idealism, assistance, advice, problem-solving, matters of the heart, committed responsibility

continues

continued

Number	Meaning
7	Perception, insight, inner work, reflection, wisdom
8	Power, control, organization, mastery
9	Endings, loss, grief, completion, fulfillment, vision, wisdom
10	Renewal, karmic completion, mastery

The Meanings of the Numbers in the Major Arcana

Before we go into the numbers individually, we'd like to look at them in groups. That's because single-digit numbers have straightforward meanings, but the double-digit numbers are a little more complicated.

➤ **Cards 0–9.** These numbers' meanings are fairly straightforward, with the exception of the Hierophant card, which we'll discuss shortly.

➤ **Cards 11–21.** These numbers are double digit and therefore have double meanings as well: one for the double-digit number (i.e., 12), and one for the reduced number (for 12, 1 + 2 = 3). For the Major Arcana, it's important to consider both numbers, but the double-digit one is the most significant.

In addition, from 11 to 19 is where you'll find the karmic numbers. As you'll recall, karmic refers to a law or universal principle of individual responsibility and signifies some kind of past lesson or debt that hasn't yet been resolved. The karmic numbers are 13, 14, 16, and 19; the karmic cards are 11, 12, 13, 14, 15, and 16.

➤ **Cards 20 and 21.** The number 20 is the beginning of a second cycle of 10 (which is itself the number of rebirth that begins the new cycle that closes at 19). The number 20 trumpets another new time, only now it's with even greater awareness. The 20 signifies a breakthrough into a new cycle (just like the year 2000, only with more zeroes!). The number 21 belongs to this 2nd cycle of 10 as well, so it signifies a newness, one of greater importance than in the first cycle of 10 (Wheel of Fortune).

Spinning the Wheel of Fortune

Numerology Rule #1: Reduce numbers by adding its digits together until only one digit remains. Numerology Rule #2: Don't reduce master numbers like 11 and 22.

The Beginning of the Journey: Numbers 0–9

0 The Fool. The zero is the number of the unformed, or unmanifest. Zero is empty and full at the same time, an open channel to the spirit world. It stands for free will (that's to say, no karmic debt!).

1 The Magician. The 1 is the symbol of individuality. It stands for the inventive, courageous, independent, and strong-willed—all in keeping with the qualities of the Magician.

2 The High Priestess. The 2 deals with intuition and psychic awareness; the number 2 signifies the balancing of opposites (good/evil, honesty/deceit, male/female, etc.). This is the essence of the High Priestess card.

3 The Empress. The 3 symbolizes a trinity—the union of the 1 and the 2 to make a 3rd. The 3 is the number of luxury and extravagance in its negative form. At its best, 3 is the number of creativity: creative expression, and the ultimate creative force—motherhood.

4 The Emperor. The number 4 rules establishments, foundations, and stability. The Emperor is an appropriate card for the 4, which is about establishing a foundation for the self by setting boundaries, rules, and order.

5 The Hierophant. Here the number doesn't seem to fit the card, except in situations where one's opposing convention, seeking freedom from rigidity of the Emperor, or rebelling against the status quo. The 5 is about adaptation and change, while the Hierophant is decidedly the status quo.

6 The Lovers. The 6 rules love, commitment, and responsibility, and the Lovers card is about making choices in these matters.

7 The Chariot. Here the number 7 relates to perfection, the sacred, and inner wisdom that must be sought. The Chariot is a victory card over imbalances of the human soul and life, and it's the inner strength of Charioteer that allows him (or her) to conquer the foe.

8 Strength. The 8 is the number of achieved power and success. The number here seems to suggest that your power comes from the strength to control the beast within (your "lower passion" or lust). Success is possible here.

9 The Hermit. The 9 is the number of the cosmic teacher, one with wisdom and healing power. It's the number of the visionary, too. The number 9 is about completion, closure, and endings, and seeks wisdom through spiritual insight and inspiration. The Hermit card, bearing the number 9, speaks to an inner journey, a time of silence where wisdom might be revealed. It also indicates that a wise teacher is present to help you in your search. The 9 completes the first circuit of your journey.

The Middle of the Journey: Numbers 10–19

10 Wheel of Fortune. The 10 is the number of completion and rebirth. It's a karmic number (but good karma). The 1 stands beside the 0 of unmanifested energy, and the 1 has moved through an entire cycle of 9. Now, at the 10, the 1 energy is ready to begin anew. Some experts believe the Wheel of Fortune itself is represented by the 0 of the 10, and that the post holding the wheel is the 1. So, for the Wheel to be balanced, all must be completed, and only then is the Wheel ready to spin a new cycle.

11 Justice. Two 1's side by side stand ready to begin a new cycle, but the warning is that it must be a new beginning in a balanced manner. Careful thought must be given to individual thoughts, words, and deeds. Like the justice scales, each thought and deed must be weighed carefully. After all, we're dealing with karmic justice and fairness here. An individual (the 1) can no longer hold out for personal gain; it's time to move into a higher awareness. The union of the 10 (rebirth) + the 1 (self) becomes the 2—a new sense of balance and blending.

12 The Hanged Man. This card's numbers are 10 and 2, which added together bring in the force of the 3. Here's a card that can signify a need to surrender, a stuck place, and a guy who's definitely "hung up." He has to maintain balance even though he's hanging upside down (his bent knee provides the balance). Let's face it, though, this guy needs help. Note, however, that his halo's still on straight (that's his spiritual aura, remember). Because this is the second part of the journey, and the card is grouped in with the karmic cards, maybe the number reflects the struggle between his inner and outer selves: he has to find the balance between them. His spiritual power is available to him. The conflict between the 1 (independence) and the 2 (joining forces with others, in this case with a higher power) keeps him hanging until he realizes a balance is necessary. Enlightenment is possible by accepting appropriate limitations between self (1) and others (2). Then he moves to a happier state (the 3) as indicated by the glow on his face and his karmic debt is lifted.

13 Death/Rebirth. The numbers on this card are 10 + 3, which add up to 4. The 3 in this karmic number suggests the creation of something new. A rebirth is at hand, for a death has occurred at this part of the journey. An individual (the 1) will engage in the hard work (the reduced number 4) of death and rebirth. As a karmic number, the 13 reveals that in the past, there was frivolity (God forbid), excess, and disregard for the creation of life. Superficiality dies at this point, and it's now time to cut yourself free so the new can be born. It's not easy (the 4); it takes transformation of your energy from one form to another to give birth to the new.

14 Temperance. In Temperance, we have the number 14 (10 + 4), with the 4 demanding self-control, discipline, organization, and planning. Its reduced number 5 (10 + 4 = 5) suggests adaptation, change, speaking out, communication, and resourcefulness—all qualities of the number 5. This makes a successful combination, which is the essence of the Temperance card. The 14 is a karmic number and implies that past abuses existed around a lack of discipline, hard work, frugality, and practicality. It's time to temper this karma with moderation, adaptability, and change. This card also suggests that it's time for an integration of self-control (4) and change (5).

15 The Devil. In the Devil card, the 5 reflects the negative aspects of its number: addictions, abuse of sensual pleasures, failure to make changes. Because 15 is also in the second part of the journey, where the 10 is joined with the 5, it's a time to complete these "devilish" habits and rise up into the energy of the 6 (10 + 5). The 6 leads you back to making the choice again, with the reward of getting to live with love. Back to the Garden of Eden and the Lovers (card number 6), in other words!

16 The Tower. This nasty little karmic number is about house-cleaning. The 6 here demands balance at the domestic level and is the number of duty and responsibility, family, and love. The 6 is about commitment and the truth that lives in the heart, as well as balancing work and home life. The karmic number 16 tells of abuses from the past around commitment and responsibility, usually involving poor choices (echoes of the Lovers card). The reduced number 7 (10 + 6) symbolizes purification, a time for self-improvement; the number 7 brings insight into murky things hidden from view.

It's important to remember, though, that this card is part of the middle journey, and so you have the force of the 10 with the 6—a time of renewal. This is all part of your climb upward in the evolutionary awakening of yourself.

17 The Star. The number 7 is the key number in the Star. The seven stars represent the seven *chakras,* or energy centers, of the body, and the number 7 symbolizes purification, inner reflection, and spiritual awareness. The reduced number 8 (10 + 7) is about the power you have achieved to make your wishes manifest. The combined influence of the numbers on this card brings inspiration, leadership, and confidence. An inner power has awakened!

Card Catalog

According to Hindu tradition, there are seven *chakras,* or energy centers, of the body. Each corresponds to places in our body or emotions. The seventh chakra is the center spirituality.

18 The Moon. The number 18 of the Moon card implies an exploration of the secret realms, the inner path of wisdom. The Moon card numbers are 10 + 8, which suggest a degree of mastery is present to examine the illusive (as in illusions) forces of one's psyche: the unconscious, dreams, illusions, and deceit. This karmic card means you have the power (the 8) now available to travel the inner chambers of the psyche. The reduced number 9 (10 + 8) is strongly present in this Moon card, too. It's reminiscent of the first 9 of the Major Arcana, the Hermit. The number 9 tells us this is a card of intuition, unfolding of psychic abilities, and a time to look within for wisdom.

19 The Sun. The number 9 in this card is paired with the 10 and brings us to the completion of the second part of the journey. The 9 here represents all the positive aspects of the number: rewards, completion, and fulfillment. The karmic number 19 symbolizes past abuse of spiritual and psychic wisdom, but the 19 of the Sun card, the last card of this karmic cycle, means that these past transgressions are completed. Spiritual and material success are now yours. Joy and happiness shine on you. The cycle of karma is over!

The Completion of the Journey: Numbers 20–21

20 Judgement. The Judgement card belongs to a new cycle. It's a rite of passage and so calls for a paradigm shift. The number 2 stands for cooperation and sensitivity to others—connecting the dots, so to speak. The 2 coupled with the 0 brings all the power of the spirit world to bear upon the union of people, things, attitudes, and your psychological process. There's an awakening here, and "the power belongs to he or she who knows." You've journeyed through the evolution of the 2 energy from the High Priestess (2) to the Hanged Man (12) to Judgement (20).

The 20 here suggests that the highest qualities of the 2 and the 0 are present and potent at this juncture: psychic awareness, intuitive knowing, a balance of opposites, resolution of duality, sensitivity to the forces of nature and man, and of heaven and earth. The number 20 on the Judgement card signals that you are now on the verge of blending it all together: The Fool has successfully completed his journey and has found what he needed along the way. Now he's ready to merge with the universal.

21 The World. It's been said that the number 21 is the most joyful of all the numbers. It blends the 2 and the 1 into a third energy, the 3. With the 21, the second cycle in the numbers is complete and you stand at the threshold of a new cycle, which has been called the "cycle of angelhood." The issues of duality (the 2) are no longer separating you from yourself (1), and your higher consciousness has merged with your independent earthly self. The number 3 (2 + 1) is strongly present with this card as well, bringing a profound feeling of being glad to be alive and a sense of "dancing with joy." As Eden Gray says, "It is a life well lived and a job well done." The power of spirit-inspired creativity (3) seeds your next cycle.

The Numbers and the Minor Arcana

The Minor Arcana is made up of 4 suits; each suit has four court cards and all the rest of the cards are numbered Ace through 10. The significance of these numbers is that 4 represents order and 1 through 10 represents a cycle completed. That's a lot of cards (56 to be exact) to remember, so a quick way to learn the cards is to pay attention to the numbers. A basic understanding of the numbers helps, too.

Do the Numbers Really Matter?

With no historic evidence to say what the meanings of the cards' numbers are, we'd nonetheless like to offer a few pointers. First, the numbers give order to the deck. It's a neat system for knowing which cards belong where.

Second, the numbers on the cards usually symbolize the timing for the question asked. The number on the card will indicate how many days, weeks, or months are involved. This applies only to the Minor Arcana, which are about the daily life events over which we have direct control. For example, if you draw the 4 of Swords, it would indicate that your need for recuperation from stress or illness will take four weeks or four months. The numbers relate a time span. For more information, see the later section "Timing and Numbers."

Third, what we can trust about these numbers is that they provide a method of sequencing the cards, hence the journey one is making through the cards. For example, if our life finds us working our way through the journey of the Cups (emotions), we can see our progress from the 7 of Cups (where we're fantasizing and deluding ourselves) to the 8 of Cups (a time to withdraw oneself or leave a situation), to the 9 of Cups (the perfect dream come true). Without the numbers to indicate the sequence, we might fail to note that there is in fact progress, and that we're at some specific point in this process!

Spinning the Wheel of Fortune

On any specific card, count the number of Pentacles, Swords, Cups, or Wands for a clue as to how many people might be involved, how much time a situation might take to be resolved, or how much money is involved. The numbers count!

Here the Numbers Count

Right side up or upside down, the numbers' meanings don't change. Regardless of the suit, the numbers reveal a theme for each card.

Numbers—No Matter What Suit They Wear

Aces. Aces are the number 1, and all Aces deal with the potential for beginnings, a new time, initiating a new start, or a birthing.

Twos. The number 2 deals with duality, balance, and relationships. In the Tarot, the 2 deals with choosing or comparing two people, options, viewpoints, or situations.

Threes. The 3 symbolizes fun, joy, playfulness, celebration, creative expression, and emotional expression. The number 3 is also about triangles, or threesomes. Hmmm…

Fours. The number 4 represents foundations, stability, and the status quo. It also deals with health and hard work.

Fives. The 5 is the number of change and adaptation and in the Tarot it usually means conflict and strife. The change that's required is what causes the conflict, and the Minor Arcana 5's tell us that there's a need to adapt to unpleasant changes.

Sixes. The number 6 represents the benefit of giving to others, problem-solving, and assistance. The 6 is the number of service and responsibility.

Sevens. The number 7 deals with awareness and wisdom. It's the number of inner work, self-reflection, research or study, and rejuvenation. In the Tarot, it signals changes brought about by wisdom and insight into a situation.

Eights. The 8 is the number of money, power, success, control, authority, and expansion. In the Tarot, the 8 shows control, mastery over a situation or lack of it, where self-reliance and autonomy may be required (your power!).

Nines. The number 9 is about endings, loss, completion, and fulfillment, and the wisdom and understanding that come from the completion of the cycle. It's an intense number, filled with the energy of all the numbers (and all the cards in each suit—Ace through 9).

Tens. The number 10 means rebirth and renewal at the end of the cycle of Ace through 10. The 10 is a karmic number and means renewal is earned through work from the past. In the Tarot, the 10 indicates that lessons have been learned and mastery achieved, so a rebirth is at hand or is necessary. When one sword will do the job, who needs 10?

Timing and Numbers

The numbers on the cards in the Minor Arcana (but *not* the Major Arcana) can indicate the time interval covered for a question. The suit tells whether it will be a matter of days, weeks, or months, and the number tells how many!

The Cards	The Timing
Ace through 10	1 to 10 days, weeks, or months (depending on card, of course)
Page	11 days, weeks, or months
Knight	12 days, weeks, or months
Queen and King	Unknown time—it's up to you!

The Suit	Period of Time
Cups	Days
Wands	Weeks
Pentacles	Months
Swords	Undetermined—it's up to you (because you're working it out in your mind)

Combining the numbers and the suits tells the story. For example, the 8 of Wands means it will be eight weeks until the new project will start. The 2 of Pentacles indicates two months until the money comes in. The 4 of Cups shows it will take four days until you get his letter. And the 9 of Swords indicates an undetermined amount of time until your mind is made up.

In cases where the timing can't be determined, it's because too many factors are present to indicate accurate timing. The message when this happens: It will take more time for the angels to get things lined up.

The Personal Year and the Tarot

While the Major Arcana numbers aren't used to find the timing of an event, they *can* be used to tell us the theme for a given year. In numerology, we have a way of discovering what a current calendar year's theme is for each individual. Called your "personal year," this method was pioneered by Angeles Arrien in *The Tarot Handbook* (Arcus Publishing Co., 1987). If you want to know what 1999 (or 2010) will mean for you personally, here's how to do it.

Fools Rush In

Don't use the numbers of the Major Arcana to tell time! The Major Arcana are about the here and now because they're governed by forces outside you and indicate the ongoing process you're involved in psychologically.

number, you'll add —in a very specific your birthday only, ndar year.

oked like for Bill s + calendar year

which was his ear number

h/Lust) is the number 8 personal year. We think 's Strength/Lust year, he was trying to tame the **tant note**: If the final total is a double-digit 10 and 21. Your personal year equivalent is a

number, the next step is to find the Major Note that you can't have a 0 year (even if it h to the personal year system. Sorry, Fools.

Card

stess (once in a lifetime)
The Empress
The Emperor
5   The Hierophant

continues

continued

Personal Year	Major Arcana Card
6	The Lovers
7	The Chariot
8	Strength
9	The Hermit
10	Wheel of Fortune
11	Justice
12	The Hanged Man
13	Death
14	Temperance
15	The Devil
16	The Tower
17	The Star
18	The Moon
19	The Sun
20	Judgement
21	The World

In the Cards

Here's an example of what this looks like for the United States' birthday, July 4th:

$7 + 4 + 1998 = 2009 = 2 + 0 + 0 + 9 = 11$

This equals the Justice card. So 1998 was a Justice personal year for the United States. Hmmm, a little karma for the old U.S. of A.?

Another note: Your personal year begins in January of each year, but the full impact of a year's theme will be felt from birthday to birthday.

So You Say You're Having a Devil of a Year?

If you've got an attitude this year, maybe it's in the cards. Here are the meanings for each personal year number and its corresponding Major Arcana card. All the Major Arcana cards (1–21) are used for this part except the Fool (0). Once you've located the number and card for your personal year, you can read the corresponding description for insight into the theme and direction for your year.

1 The Magician. A year of independence, strong will, enterprise, and new beginnings.

2 The High Priestess. A year to develop intuition, with an emphasis on the need for harmony and balance. Not recommended for marriage, although relationships may be prominent this year.

In the Cards

Interestingly, we only have one High Priestess year in a lifetime. Maybe that's why we haven't developed much intuition—we only get one chance to learn!

3 The Empress. A year for emotional clarity, a time for creative expression—even the creation of new life.

4 The Emperor. A year to establish foundations and build something. This year finds you having to set boundaries, claim your own authority, and order your world. Stability is the goal.

5 The Hierophant. A desire to be free and unrestricted runs through this year, even though you'll be dealing with conventional laws. Rebellion and restlessness could be present if you got into a rut in your Emperor year. Change is predominant this year, as well as an intense need to "get out there" to explore beyond your own world. Note again that this doesn't jive with what we know of the Hierophant card.

6 The Lovers. A year of making a choice, usually about love or relationships. It's a time of commitment, responsibility, and family obligations. There's some kind of choice between risk and security. It's a time of combining the head with the heart, a time of integration.

7 The Chariot. A year of purification in health. A time of gaining wisdom through change, even possible transformation. Spiritual questing and rejuvenation through nature are hallmarks of this 7 year.

8 Strength. A personal year where you'll find the strength to endure and to come into your own power. A time to wrestle with control issues, this 8 year is about manifesting and learning the laws of abundance.

9 The Hermit. A year of major completions, endings, and closure, the 9 year brings wisdom and connection to higher forces. It's also a time of great reward and mastery. You may be called upon to hold the lantern for others on the path.

10 Wheel of Fortune. A karmic year of rewards from past efforts. This is a time of breakthroughs and self-realization. This can be a time of initiation and rebirth. You're moving in a positive direction!

11 Justice. The 11 year's theme is about fairness and balance, as well as karmic justice and the resolution of legal issues. The search for truth about yourself and finding balance both demand your attention now, and cooperation and negotiation are major components of this year.

12 The Hanged Man. A year to listen to your inner self. It's a time of waiting and patience—suspended action, in other words, and you'll find the emphasis to be on receptivity. This year you may find yourself feeling a bit like a victim—definitely an old pattern to break. This is another karmic year where patterns from the past are dissolved.

13 Death (Rebirth). A year where new growth is possible (the 3) through elimination and severance. Since the karmic number 13 reduces to 4, this year can be hard work. It's a time to transform the old and to release old karmic situations.

14 Temperance. A time to be open-minded, free and expansive, adapting, and resourceful (all the reduced number 5 qualities). It's also a time to adopt a conservative attitude, use moderation, and to be self-disciplined (the 4). This karmic number 14 year suggests a past influence of irresponsible ways that need to be tempered.

15 The Devil. A personal year where you deal with things you're attached to or that are addictions in your life (like the opposite sex, work, substances, sugar, the Internet...). There's negative 5 energy present in this karmic card. It's a time to look at possible co-dependency (the reduced influence of the 6), and all those things that "bedevil" you.

16 The Tower. This is a year for spiritual awakening—a bolt of insight, a time for self-analysis and purification—all influences of the reduced number 7. You may have unexpected karmic awareness this year because there's some kind of a wake-up call. The path changes. This karmic number suggests a past abuse of commitment and love (the karmic quality of the 6 in the 16), and now's the time to wake up.

17 The Star. This is not a karmic year! It's the emergence from the karmic influences of the past, a personal year for meditation, inspiration, and spiritual regeneration. Inner wisdom brings power this year (the essence of the 7). This 17 personal year is one for manifesting our wishes and analyzing your hopes for the future, and using systems of insight such as astrology, the Tarot and numerology will be helpful this year. There's an opportunity to be a leader—or a "Star."

18 The Moon. This year brings psychic power, or illumination about areas where you may be living in denial. This is a time for manifestation (the 8 influence) but it's not about money. It's a potent time for psychic manifestation, a time to get something from the "other side."

19 The Sun. The 9 heavily influences your Sun year. It's a time of clarity and wisdom. The self comes full circle in this year of creativity, recognition, and high hopes. You have the potential to be intensely happy this year. You draw to you what you need, for you're energized, vital, and magnetic this year. This is the last of the karmic numbers, as it suggests past abuses of power and wisdom have resolved as the Sun shines on you this year.

20 Judgement. In this rite of passage year, you'll have a strong desire to merge (the 2). This year is a "call" to the spiritual (the 0) and a time of breaking through old self-judgments and moving toward cooperation with others. The emphasis is on integration of the past and present. Integration is good; it sure beats isolation or endings!

21 The World. A year of joy and rapture, creativity, and vision. The energy of the 3 is fully present this year but you may be called to expand to high ground (it's the world, after all!). It's a time of living from a spiritual knowing, a time of universal service, and seeing with global awareness. You've arrived!

Your personal year is a 52-week journey of learning the lessons and evolving in an upward spiral of self-mastery. Knowing your personal year number and personal year card will help you target these lessons and chart a course through the murky waters of life.

It's clear that the teaming up of numerology and Tarot is very powerful. So use and master these tools to wend your way through the mystery of life. May all your karmic lessons be in the cards!

The Least You Need to Know

➤ The numbers on the Tarot cards have specific meanings.

➤ The Major Arcana numbers represent your life's journey.

➤ The Minor Arcana numbers show the timing of an event.

➤ The Major Arcana numbers tell the theme for each personal year.

➤ Your personal year can help you understand the theme for each year and your karmic lessons.

Further Reading

Arrien, Angeles. *The Tarot Handbook*. Sonoma, CA: Arcus Publishing Co., 1987.

Carlson, Laura. *Tarot Unveiled: The Method to Its Magic*. Stamford, CT: U.S. Games Systems, Inc., 1988.

Celestine. *The Mammoth Book of Fortune Telling*. New York, NY: Carroll & Graf, 1997.

Cheiro. *Cheiro's Book of Numbers*. New York, NY: Arco Publishing Co., 1977.

Connolly, Eileen. Tarot: *A New Handbook for the Apprentice*. N. Hollywood, CA: Newcastle Publishing Co., 1979.

Fairfield, Gail. *Choice Centered Tarot*. Smithville, IN: Ramp Creek Publishing, 1984.

Garen, Nancy. *Tarot Made Easy*. New York, NY: Fireside (Simon & Schuster), 1989.

Gerwick-Brodeur, Madeline and Lisa Lenard. *The Complete Idiot's Guide to Astrology*. New York, NY: Alpha/Macmillan, 1997.

Gray, Eden. *The Complete Guide to the Tarot*. New York, NY: Bantam, 1972.

———. *Mastering the Tarot*. New York, NY: Penguin, 1988.

Greer, Mary. *Tarot for Your Self*. North Hollywood, CA: Newcastle Publishing, 1984.

Louis, Anthony. *Tarot, Plain and Simple*. St. Paul, MN: Llewellyn, 1997.

Martello, Leo Louis. *Reading the Tarot*. Garden City Park, NY: Avery Publishing Group, 1990.

Pond, David and Lucy Pond. *The Metaphysical Handbook*. Port Angeles, WA: Reflecting Pond Publications, 1984.

Wanless, James and Angeles Arrien, eds. *Wheel of Tarot* (anthology). Carmel, CA: Merrill-West Publishing, 1992.

Wilson, Joyce. *The Complete Book of Palmistry*. New York, NY: Bantam Books, 1980.

More Tarot Decks

U.S. Games, Inc., publisher of the Universal Waite Deck we've used in this book, also publishes literally hundreds of other Tarot decks. Their terrific catalog of Tarot decks and books is available by calling them at 800-544-2637. U.S. Games also has a Web site at **http://www.USGAMESINC.com**. The site includes links to other Tarot web sites and we did find a number of other interesting Tarot sites, many of them interactive.

As you work with the Tarot, you'll want to try different decks. You'll also prefer different decks at different times and for different moods: This is all quite natural, so go with it!

Which decks you ultimately choose to own and work with is a highly personal matter. We've included but a few of the many possibilities here to whet your appetite. Ultimately, you'll find there's a deck (or more) to suit every one of your moods. Happy shuffling!

Traditional Decks

The Universal Waite Deck is available from U.S. Games. There's also the Albano-Waite deck, and a Tiny Universal Waite Tarot, which is great for carrying with you (and is a real bargain as well). We like the deck we've used, the Universal Waite, for its colors and accessibility, but any of these decks would be good basic ones.

A Beginner Deck

One of the more interesting decks U.S. Games offers is the Starter Tarot deck. Specifically designed for beginners, this deck has several upright and reversed meanings printed right on the cards. Our reservation with this is that you might be tempted to think these are the only meanings each card could have, but, as you've learned, that's not the case at all. If you want to do readings for others without carting this book everywhere you go, the Starter Tarot might be a good investment.

Symbolic Decks

Among the many choices in this category are the Morgan-Greer deck, the Unicorn deck, the Witches Tarot, the Gendron Tarot, the Goddess Tarot, the Fairy Tarot, the Dragon deck, the Haindl Rune Oracle deck, and many, many more. There's a symbol for everyone among these decks!

Native American Decks

Quite a few decks in recent years have applied Native American symbolism to the Tarot. Among the decks that use this motif are the Santa Fe Tarot, the Native American deck, the Tarot of the Southwest Sacred Tribes deck, and the Medicine Woman Tarot.

Unusual and Collector Decks

So many decks fall into this category that the few we've selected only begin to give you a taste. The Motherpeace Round Tarot deck "celebrates women's culture throughout the world," and, with its lack of squared-off edges, reminds us that all the world's a circle.

The Tarot of Baseball deck is divided into the suits of Balls, Bats, Gloves, and Caps, and is illustrated with players such as "The Rookie" and "The Pitcher of Balls." It's very clever—and definitely worth a look if you're a baseball fan.

The Dali Universal Tarot deck was designed by the great surrealist, Salvador Dalí, himself. Each card has a copy of the artist's signature (not an original one!), and the deck comes in special packaging. If you're interested in what a master artist made of Tarot's symbolism, this is a deck worth exploring.

More Gorgeous Decks

The Chinese Tarot deck, with its lovely brush paintings, is a fine deck for meditation, as is the Ukiyoe Tarot, which uses Japanese imagery. The Tarot of the Cloisters uses stained glass windows from the 13th century; the Kazanlar Tarot explores the connection between the Tarot and Christianity, Judaism, and Islam—in living color.

The Halloween Tarot translates Halloween images into Tarot symbolism. The Experimental Tarot features astrological and cosmological symbols. The Ibis deck uses Egyptian figures and symbols. The Art Nouveau deck is, well, Art Nouveau; it's lovely.

A Deck of Your Own

Browsing through U.S. Games' catalog will make you want to explore more decks in person. Most bookstores, including the big chains, have good selections of Tarot decks. Many keep the decks behind their counters, and, if you ask, some will let you take out the individual cards and look at them before you buy a deck.

We like to explore the used decks at our local New Age bookshops. It's fun to feel the previous owner's energy coming from a deck, and, as these decks have already been opened, it's much more likely you'll be allowed to look at every single card before you decide to buy a deck. And they're cheaper, too!

You don't have to have a deck of your own to read this book, but we bet you'll want one by the time you've finished. May all your readings be adventures.

Glossary

air signs People with these signs are great thinkers, always applying their mental capacities to any problem they encounter. The air signs of the zodiac are Gemini, Libra, and Aquarius.

allegory A symbolic system in which words or images represent a much larger story than is shown. The allegory of the Prodigal Son, for example, represents a parent's love for his child.

ankh The Egyptian ankh is an ancient symbol of the cross of life.

archetypes The various types common to all our stories. Jung called archetypes "mythological motifs."

astrological chart Also called a birth chart, this is a representation of the position of each of the planets at the time you were born.

astrology A discipline that uses the cycles of the universe and the position of the planets at the time you were born to draw a unique picture of who you are and who you can be.

birth sign Also called sun sign, this is the astrological sign the sun was in when you were born. There are 12 of these signs in the zodiac, the pattern the earth follows on its elliptical journey around the sun every year.

Celtic Cross Also called the Keltic Cross, this Tarot spread represents everything there is to know about a question. While it uses the Christian symbol of the cross as its basis, it uses this form to show how a question (and Querent) move through time.

chakra According to Hindu tradition, there are seven chakras, or energy centers of the body.

creative visualization   The process of using pictures to achieve one's goals. One example of this is a long-distance runner, picturing herself pushing through the winner's tape.

Cups   The cards of emotion and sensitivity.

day residue   Any dream image that derives from the day's events. You may, for example, repeat a conversation you had, only in a dreamlike way, or you may dream you're sitting at a traffic light as you did that day.

earth signs   As their name implies, people with these signs are down to earth, content with the status quo. They're not, as a rule, big adventurers. The earth signs of the zodiac are Taurus, Virgo, and Capricorn.

elements   Fire, earth, air, and water represent the basic qualities of the signs and of life. The four elements are the four basic materials that make up everything. In the Tarot and in astrology, these are also used as types by which to classify the nature of things.

extrasensory perception (ESP)   The experience of knowing that something's going to happen before it does. It also includes the ability to see auras and other subtle energy fields, as well as past lives.

fire signs   People with these signs are always the first in line, ready to try everything from bungee jumping to signing on for the next space shuttle. The fire signs of the zodiac are Aries, Leo, and Sagittarius.

Gabriel   See *Raphael*.

graphology   The study and analysis of handwriting to find clues to a person's character and personality.

hieroglyphs and **petroglyphs**   Two forms of ancient carving on stone. Hieroglyphs are a more symbolic system, while petroglyphs use representative pictures to tell their stories.

horoscope   Also called a birth or astrological chart, this is an astrological map for the moment of your birth. It's divided into 12 pie sections called houses, each representing a specific area of your life.

Horoscope Spread   A twelve-card spread that looks at your year in cards.

hypnotherapy   A therapy that begins with information uncovered during hypnosis.

karmic lessons   Also called life lessons, these are lessons that are necessary for you to learn in this life because of past errors. You may have resisted them, but karma will always find a way to make certain you learn what you need so that you can proceed to the next level of awareness.

key numbers   The key numbers of the Major Arcana cards can be thought of literally as keys to opening up a card's meanings and possibilities.

life lessons   See *karmic lessons*.

Major Arcana   Also called the fate cards, these 22 cards represent your life's journey toward enlightenment. These cards depict situations of major, archetypal significance in your life. You could think of these cards as the many forks along your own particular road.

master numbers   The numbers 11, 22, 33, 44, and so on are numbers with special properties. They indicate giftedness and leadership qualities for people, and master qualities for the numbers themselves. For example, the number 11 is the number of inspiration, and the number 22 is the number of the master builder.

meditation exercises   Ways of helping us to use more than our logical, analytical left brains to look at things. Looking at Tarot cards in this way, without preconceived ideas and allowing the images to "tell" us what they mean, is one such exercise.

metaphors   Tarot readers consider Tarot cards metaphors, rich images that hold meanings which can be transferred or carried over to the querent's particular situation or question.

Michael   See *Raphael*.

Minor Arcana   Also called the free will cards, these 56 cards concern your daily life, including everyday events, your beliefs and behavior, and how you relate to others.

Mission Spread   A 21-card spread that enables you to look at your past, present, and future life's mission and purpose.

myths   The stories we tell ourselves to explain the unexplainable.

nimbus   Represented by a halo or bright disk around someone's head (this is often seen around the heads of saints in religious paintings from the Middle Ages), a nimbus stands for someone's spiritual aura. People who have such an aura are blessed and protected by a higher power.

numerology   The language of numbers. Numerologists study the meanings of numbers and their connection to everything in the universe.

oracles   Sacred objects or altars used by many cultures throughout history for the reception of divine guiding messages and holy truths. The site of the oracle is considered a holy place and traditionally often only priests or shamans could visit it.

Palmistry   The study of the lines and mounds in the hand, and what your hand has to say about who you are.

past-life regression   This technique employs hypnotherapy to find out about the lives one lived before the present one.

Pentacles   The cards of the material world, of money and possessions.

petroglyphs   See *hieroglyphs*.

progressions   These movements show how you and your birth chart evolve throughout your life.

psychic experiences   Also called post-conscious cognitive experiences in psychological jargon, these are experiences that we perceive in ways other than our usual waking consciousness. They can include everything from ESP to UFOs; anything, in fact, that modern science is at a loss to explain.

Raphael   The angel of air and one of three archangels who appear in Tarot imagery. The others are Michael, the angel of fire and the sun; and Gabriel, the angel of water.

reincarnation   The belief that the spirit or soul moves from one physical entity to another after the death of the first one.

REM (rapid eye movement) sleep   Discovered in 1953, this is the time when we're sleeping that our most vivid dreams occur. This dreaming is accompanied by rapid eye movement beneath the lid, hence its name.

reversed cards   These occur when the lessons of a particular card are more challenging for a Querent, or when a Querent is fighting him or herself on an issue.

Querent   From the Latin word *quaero*, meaning "to inquire or seek" or to embark on a quest, the Querent is a person who asks questions of the Tarot.

royal Minor Arcana cards   Also called court cards, these cards can stand for various aspects of your self or for those around you. Sometimes they stand for certain times or seasons as well.

scrying   The ancient art of using a reflective surface, such as a crystal ball, mirror, or liquid, to see images of divination.

shadow side   Our archetypal hidden self, our secret nature.

sun sign   See *birth sign*.

Swords   The cards of mental activity and action.

synchronicity   The principle of meaningful coincidence, studied in depth by psychoanalysis pioneer Carl Jung. Jung also postulated that human experience could be categorized into common archetypes, typical patterns, situations, images, or metaphors that recur among all humankind.

Tarot   The word Tarot has several meanings, each based on several different possible sources of the words. In Egyptian, *tar + ro* means "A path royal"; in Hungarian Gypsy, *tar* means "a pack of cards"; in Hindustani, *taru* also means "a pack of cards."

Tarot readings   These occur when the cards are laid out to reveal a particular story. A Tarot reading brings together a Tarot reader and a Querent with a question. The reader uses a Tarot spread, or card layout, to explore the Querent's question.

Tarot spreads   Different methods of laying out the cards during a Tarot reading.

transits   The current movement of the planets through your birth chart.

Wands   The cards of enterprise, growth, and development.

water signs   People with this sign are the intuitive among us, ruled by their emotions, changing with the tides. The water signs of the zodiac are Cancer, Scorpio, and Pisces.

yods   Representations of the Hebrew letter yod. Not only is this letter used to represent the name of God, it is also symbolic of the life force, or the light from heaven that protects us all.

Index